Christ Our Rest;
The Doubts and Fears of the Believer Practically Considered

Christ Our Rest;
The Doubts and Fears of the Believer Practically Considered

By

David Pitcairn

REFORMATION HERITAGE BOOKS
Grand Rapids, Michigan
2006

Reformation Heritage Books
2965 Leonard St. NE
Grand Rapids, Michigan 49525
616-977-0599 / Fax 616-285-3246
e-mail: orders@heritagebooks.org
website: www.heritagebooks.org

10 digit ISBN 1-892777-73-8
13 digit ISBN 978-1-892777-73-7

Taken from second edition
London: J. H. Jackson, 1845

All rights reserved.

For additional Reformed literature, both new and used, request a free book list from the above address.

TO

THE MANY DEAR CHILDREN OF GOD,

WHOSE CHRISTIAN CHARACTER IS INJURED, AND
WHOSE CHRISTIAN COMFORT IS IMPAIRED,
THROUGH THE PERNICIOUS INFLUENCE OF

DOUBTS AND FEARS,

THIS VOLUME

Is specially and affectionately dedicated.

PREFACE

TO THE SECOND EDITION.

This is a work on personal and experimental religion. It treats largely of the Doubts with which so many pious people are harassed; and it is hoped that those who are distressed in their minds from the weakness of their faith, may here find some relief and encouragement. To this interesting class of Christians the volume is particularly addressed. With a special view to their case it has been composed; and to their serious and prayerful consideration it is now commended.

But it were quite a mistake to imagine that the volume is wholly occupied with discussions on the subject of Doubts; or that it is designed for the exclusive benefit of Doubters. Its contents will be found to correspond with the twofold character of its title. The author has intermixed copious expositions of Scripture with his remarks on the different topics which he deemed it of importance to illustrate; and in many parts he has intentionally introduced what critical readers may call digressions. But from first to last it has been his object, if possible, to excite the interest, and promote the spiritual edification, of all classes of Christians. On this account, in exposing the sad prevalence and the pernicious influence of Doubts, and in tracing them to their manifold causes, he has studied so to exhibit the gospel of our salvation, both in its doctrines and in its privileges, that the faith of the doubtful may find food for its strengthening; and that believers in general, whether weak or strong in the faith, may have their attention continually directed to the Saviour. It is only in the Lord Jesus Christ himself, and in the freeness and fulness of his finished work, that a true and abiding and satisfying rest for the soul can ever be attained. And, therefore, a clear knowledge and a firm faith of the Saviour will always prove the best preventive of doubts, as well as their most effectual remedy.

The sale of a large edition within little more than half a year, is a gratifying proof that the work has been favourably received by the Christian community. And in issuing a new edition, without abridgment, or any material alteration, the Author trusts that God may accept of this endeavour to advance his glory in the spiritual welfare of his people; and that, with an increasing circulation of the volume, there may also be an enlarged blessing accompanying its perusal.

Aug, 1845.

CONTENTS

LETTER 1
THE EXISTENCE OF DOUBTS IS NOT INCOMPATIBLE WITH A STATE OF GRACE.

LETTER 2
THE EXISTENCE OF DOUBTS IS NOT INCOMPATIBLE WITH A STATE OF GRACE—*Concluded*.

LETTER 3
THE VARIOUS KINDS OF DOUBTS THAT ARE PREVALENT AMONG PROFESSING CHRISTIANS.

LETTER 4
THE PERNICIOUS INFLUENCE OF DOUBTS.

I. THEY DISHONOUR GOD.

LETTER 5
THE PERNICIOUS INFLUENCE OF DOUBTS.

II. THEY ARE PREJUDICIAL TO THE CHRISTIAN CHARACTER AND COMFORT OF THE DOUBTER.

LETTER 6
DOUBTS ARE INJURIOUS TO THE CHRISTIAN CHARACTER AND COMFORT OF THE DOUBTER.

IV. THEY COOL THE ARDOUR OF HIS LOVE TO GOD AND MAN

LETTER 7

DOUBTS ARE INJURIOUS TO THE CHRISTIAN CHARACTER AND COMFORT OF THE DOUBTER.—*Continued.*

V. THEY CHECK HIS SPIRITUALITY AND HEAVENLY-MINDEDNESS.

LETTER 8

DOUBTS ARE INJURIOUS TO THE CHRISTIAN CHARACTER AND COMFORT OF THE DOUBTER.—*Concluded.*

VI. THEY DAMP AND DARKEN HIS HOPES FOR ETERNITY

LETTER 9

THE PERNICIOUS INFLUENCE OF DOUBTS.

III. THEY EXHIBIT THE RELIGION OF CHRIST TO THE WORLD IN A FALSE AND FORBIDDING POINT OF VIEW.

LETTER 10

THE CAUSES AND THE CURES OF DOUBTS.

I. PHYSICAL OR NATURAL CAUSES.

LETTER 11

II. SPIRITUAL CAUSES OF DOUBTS, AND THEIR CURES. FIRST, THE HIDINGS OF GOD'S FACE.

LETTER 12

SPIRITUAL CAUSES OF DOUBTS.—*Concluded*

II. THE TEMPTATIONS OF THE DEVIL

LETTER 13
MORAL CAUSES OF DOUBTS, AND THEIR CURES.

LETTER 14
RELIGIOUS CAUSES OF DOUBTS, AND THEIR CURES.
I. IMPERFECT AND INACCURATE VIEWS OF THE PERSON OF CHRIST.

LETTER 15
RELIGIOUS CAUSES OF DOUBTS. —*Continued.*
II. IMPERFECT AND INACCURATE VIEWS OF THE WORK OF CHRIST, AND OF HIS QUALIFICATIONS FOR THE WORK.

LETTER 16
RELIGIOUS CAUSES OF DOUBTS.—*Concluded.*
III. IMPERFECT AND INACCURATE VIEWS OF THE SINNER'S WARRANT TO BELIEVE IN THE SAVIOUR.

LETTER 1

THE EXISTENCE OF DOUBTS IS NOT INCOMPATIBLE WITH A STATE OF GRACE

On the nature of *faith* much has been written; but *doubts* are not specifically treated in popular Theology.—Importance of the subject.—Topics discussed in the following Letters: the existence and prevalence of Doubts;—their varieties;—their pernicious influences;—their different causes;—and their appropriate cures.—Doubts not to be confounded with unbelief.—Though inconsistent, yet not incompatible, with a state of grace.—Illustrations from the Old Testament: Jacob—Abraham—Job—Moses—the Psalmist.—Their occasional failures, and subsequent restoration, afford encouragement to weak believers.—Yet this must be taken cautiously.—We should seek to imitate their Faith, not their Doubts.—Faith was the rule, Doubts the exception, amongst the Old Testament saints.

My dear Friend,

Much has been written with a view to explain the nature of *faith* in its connection with the salvation which the gospel of our Lord Jesus Christ reveals; but, so far as I know, the subject of *doubts* in connection with Gospel Faith, has not yet received that measure of attention which it merits. In many books of popular and practical theology we do meet with incidental allusions to the prevalence, or to the influence, or to the causes of doubt; but where shall we find the subject systematically and largely treated? And yet it must be acknowledged to have strong claims on a specific, and careful, and patient investigation; as it cannot be denied, that, in a greater or less degree, and with more or less frequency, all the people of God have their minds tossed and agitated by the intrusion of anxious or unwelcome doubts.

This subject, which is so closely interwoven with the religious experience of religious people, must, on that very account, be felt to possess no ordinary share of interest. It directly involves questions of the highest practical importance. And thus, whatever are his peculiar opinions as to the sinfulness, or the danger, or the discomfort of doubts, I should imagine every doubting Christian will be ready to admit that their continuance or removal imparts a favourable or unfavourable character to personal religion. The clouds and sunshine of his Christian life—his seasons of painful depression or of holy cheerfulness—of spiritual retrogression or advancement, are chiefly dependent on the presence or the absence of doubts. In all this the glory of God's sure word of promise, and the honour of Christ's blessed Gospel in the world, as well as the Christian's individual welfare, are most deeply concerned. Truly, it is an interesting, an instructive, a practical, and a most important subject, on which I have undertaken to address you. It has occupied a large portion of my thoughts for several years past; and now, I propose, in a succession of Letters, to place before you its various aspects and bearings, in the light in which they have been presented to my own mind.

In Letters 1-2 I shall confine my remarks to an illustration of the very pleasing fact, that however much *doubts* are to be deprecated and deplored, *their existence is not incompatible with a state of grace.* In subsequent letters it will be my object to explain—the various kinds of doubts that are prevalent among professedly Christian people; the pernicious influence which they exercise, in dishonouring the God of truth, in injuring the believer's own character and comfort, and in exhibiting Christianity to the world in a false and forbidding point of view; the many different causes, physical, spiritual, moral, and religious, to which they may be attributed; and what is the scriptural method, either of preventing their existence, or of removing them where they already exist.

Such is a brief but comprehensive outline of the topics which are to be submitted to your candid consideration. And I do trust it may be in my power to offer at least some hints and suggestions which, by the blessing of God, may prove useful in fortifying you against that continual tendency to the indulgence of doubts, which arises from the weakness of our faith.

It is a cheering circumstance, and strikingly displays the wisdom and lovingkindness of our God, that, at the very outset of this subject, we are permitted, on scriptural grounds, to meet all doubters with a friendly salutation, and to offer them a word of consolation before subjecting them to warning or reproof. It would, indeed, be anything rather than real friendliness to approve of their doubts, or to encourage their contentedly remaining in a state of mind which is never desirable—which is often dangerous—which is always distressing. But, with a view to the removal or mitigation of their distress, it is a blessed thing to be able to say to them in the name of the Lord, "Peace be to you: your *doubts* are very different from *unbelief*. Be not afraid: the *weakness* of your faith must not be confounded with the *want* of faith. Be of good cheer: there is nought in your case to stamp you as outcasts from the society of true believers. Do not despond: for all the saints whose experiences appear on the pages of Scripture—and appear there, let it be remembered, expressly for our admonition and instruction, were, in some way or other, or at some period or other of their lives, afflicted just as you are."

Such is the language of encouragement in which we are permitted to counsel the doubting Christian. For certainly if we give heed to the faithful records of Scripture concerning the most eminent and excellent of the human race, we shall be constrained to acknowledge, that, however inconsistent, it is by no means incompatible, with a state of gracious acceptance with God, to doubt whether we really are accepted of him: yea, even to doubt whether he has so clearly revealed his forgiving grace, as to warrant any assurance of pardon and acceptance. In making this acknowledgment—in discovering this truth, no one can fail to participate in the consolation which it brings along with it. But still the timorous and dejected believer may say, "Whether I am in a state of grace—whether I am born again of the Spirit—whether I am a new creature in Christ Jesus—whether I am a child of God—whether I have any true faith at all, is the very thing about which I stand in doubt." To such an objection all that need be answered in the meantime is simply this: "Take encouragement from the case of holy men of old, who had their doubts of their own safety and acceptance with God, as you have now. You are satisfied that *their* doubts were groundless. You are satisfied that *they* were good men who found favour with God, notwithstanding the sins and imperfections which caused them to doubt. Surely, then, you should at least, with all thankfulness, entertain *the hope* of a coming day, when your own doubts will appear to yourself to be equally groundless." And now let us consult "what is written," in order to ascertain whether a hope so cheering is based on a foundation of sufficient solidity and strength.

In reading the Bible, you must have often observed, that, in its historical as well as preceptive portions, *faith* stands forth in bold relief, not only as a powerful and purifying principle of action, but as that one thing which, above all others, is indispensable to the safety and blessedness of a rational creature. God enjoins and encourages men to believe what he says to them, and to put unwavering trust in himself as their Friend, their Guide, their Portion, their Saviour, their All. And it is highly instructive to mark with what a childlike simplicity and sincerity those who truly feared God acted up to his injunctions. They did believe and obey his word. They firmly rested on the faithfulness of the unerring and omnipotent Jehovah. But on the subject of *doubts* the Scriptures of the Old and New Testaments supply very scanty information. We do, indeed, glean here and there, at distant intervals, some incidental statements which lead to the conclusion, that certain individuals whose temper and conduct generally indicated a stedfast trust in the perfections of God's character, or on his sure word of promise, or on the rectitude of his providential arrangements, were sometimes so far unhinged by transient causes as to indulge sinful suspicions of the Divine revelations made to them, or of their own relationship to God as his chosen and redeemed people. And every Scripture example of the failure of Faith in ancient times speaks to the doubting Christians of our own times in a voice of comfort as well as of warning.

Patriarchs and prophets, whose names have been transmitted to posterity as men of God,—as men who were distinguished in the ages in which they lived, and who still command admiration, as displaying the power of faith in an eminent degree, were nevertheless far from being exempt from the pernicious intrusion of occasional doubts and fears. But it may not be unnecessary to remind you that the doubts to which these patriarchal saints gave way, assumed less of a spiritual complexion than is now usual among professing Christians. And the cause of this is readily discovered in the less spiritual character of the earlier dispensations. The revelations which it pleased God to make to these ancient worthies chiefly concerned things that might be called temporal, inasmuch as they had reference to duties to be performed, and blessings to be enjoyed, during their earthly existence. On this account it is reasonable to expect that the nature of their doubtings should harmonize with the objects of their faith. The principle, however, which is involved, and the evil consequences which result, are very similar, whether the declarations and promises of God that are doubted have respect to things temporal or to things spiritual.

Passages in the histories of Abraham, and Isaac, and Jacob, will at once occur to your recollection, which teach us the humiliating lesson that men, who, by the grace of God, had attained to strong faith, and had thereby often ascended high on the mount of heavenly communion, sometimes by the weakness or the waverings of their faith, disgraced themselves, and dishonoured God; and under such circumstances we need not be surprised to find them sinking into the depths of spiritual anxiety and discomfort. Jacob, for instance, gave indulgence to faithless misgivings, when the many-coloured coat of his beloved son Joseph was brought to him covered with blood. He hastily concluded, "an evil beast hath devoured him: Joseph is without doubt rent in pieces." Thus the patriarch mourned. He rent his clothes, and put sackcloth on his loins. His family rose up to comfort him; but it is painful to read that "he refused to be comforted; and he said, I will go down into the grave unto my son, mourning," Gen 37:33-35. In like manner, at a future stage of Jacob's history, when Simeon was detained in Egypt as a hostage, and a demand was made for the appearance of Benjamin also, the parental feelings of the venerable patriarch acquired an uncontrollable ascendancy over his faith. He seems, at that moment, to have forgotten the great God who had manifested himself so graciously at Bethel, and on many subsequent occasions. Like a man altogether destitute of a Divine Refuge to which he might flee, and ignorant of a Divine Arm on which he might lean, he faithlessly says to his sons, "Me ye have bereaved of my children: Joseph is not; and Simeon is not; and ye will take Benjamin away: all these things are against me." "My son (Benjamin) shall not go down with you, for his brother is dead, and he is left alone: if mischief befall him by the way in which ye go, then shall ye bring down my grey hairs with sorrow to the grave," Gen 42:36,38. All this is exceedingly pathetic and affecting. But if such bursts of agonized feeling prove the passionate fondness of Jacob for his children, and endear him to our hearts as a most affectionate parent, we must not allow ourselves to palliate, far less to justify, his want of trust in God amidst his domestic afflictions. This was a culpable imperfection;—a stain in his character which is recorded not for our imitation, but for our warning. And truly, when it is remembered that Jacob had twelve sons, the bitterness of soul in which he mourned over his ideal bereavements, and the desponding doubts of divine support or deliverance which he evidently harboured, form a very unfavourable contrast with the confiding conduct of Abraham, when "he that had received the promises offered up his only begotten son; of whom it was said, that in Isaac shall thy seed be called; accounting that God was able to raise him up even from the dead; from whence also he received him in a figure," Heb 11:17-19.

The unflinching obedience of Abraham in offering up Isaac "his son, his only son," at the command of God, fills us with amazement. It is, indeed, an illustrious and impressive example of the power of faith to carry us triumphantly through trials of the severest description. But even Abraham, so honourably known to all succeeding generations as "the friend of God," and "the father of the faithful," did not always "hope against hope," nor was he always "strong in faith, giving glory to God." He, too, had his seasons of declension. Thus, when it is recorded, "The word of the Lord came unto Abram in a vision, saying, Fear not, Abram: I am thy shield, and thy exceeding great reward," Gen 15:1, the preceding context teaches us to interpret this as a voice of rebuke as much as of encouragement. It appears that the patriarch had been giving way to unbecoming fears. He had feared man; and his timidity had drawn him into prevarication and deceit. His dread of suffering injury at the hands of his fellow-creatures had overcome his trust in the protection of Almighty God. And hearing these words from heaven, "Fear not, Abram," it is easy to imagine how his conscience would smite him for the fears which he had already entertained, and for the sin into which his fears had betrayed him. The conscious failure of his faith, when only slightly tried, would awaken feelings of shame and self-reproach; and increase his astonishment that the God whom he had so basely dishonoured should nevertheless promise to be his "shield and exceeding great reward." It is thus that the very goodness of God leads us to repentance. But neither the gentleness of the reproof, nor the greatness of the promise given by God himself to the patriarch, secured him against another fall. The Bible, in its biographical details, conceals neither faults nor imperfections. And it grieves us to read that Abraham repeated at Gerar the sin of which he had been previously guilty in Egypt. He denied that Sarah was his wife. He affirmed that she was his sister; and he did so, because in faithlessness he yielded to the thought, "Surely the fear of God is not in this place; and they will slay me for my wife's sake," Gen 20:2 and 4.

Of Job, likewise, to whose general character as a righteous man, such noble testimonies are given in different parts of holy Scripture, it is recorded that sad seasons of darkness and of doubt agitated and overwhelmed him. His usual confidence in God was shaken. Under heavy and complicated bereavements he could neither realize the favourable light of God's countenance to cheer him, nor could he betake himself for safety to the divine promises, and there rest as on an immovable rock, when all other refuges had been swept away. The man whose name has become proverbial for patience under suffering, had not always a sufficiency of faith to uphold him in the happy assurance of God's favour, and to preserve his peace unimpaired amidst the trials to which he was subjected. There was at least one period in his life when Job doubted the wisdom and goodness of God. He complains of being weary of his existence. He even desires that God might destroy him. And it is both humbling and affecting to learn, that the same individual who, at one time, could exclaim in the triumph of faith, "Though he slay me, yet will I trust him," Job 13:15, at another time, with many execrations, cursed the very day in which he was born. Job 3 *passim*.

In this enumeration of doubters and defaulters, Moses ought not to be omitted,—even that Moses who "was very meek above all the men who were on the face of the earth." When the children of Israel became discontented in the wilderness with the manna which God rained from heaven every morning, "and wept again, and said, Who shall give us flesh to eat?" the spirit of Moses was overwhelmed, and in faithlessness he addresses his complaint to God, "Whence should I have flesh to give unto all this people?" He goes still farther. He yields to despondency, and thus pleads with God: "If thou deal thus with me, kill me, I pray thee, out of hand, if I have found favour in thy sight; and let me not see my wretchedness." And when God appoints seventy elders to bear the burden of government along with him, and also promises to furnish flesh in such abundance that the whole people should eat of it for a whole month, until they loathed it, Moses, for once at least, doubted the word of *him*, of whose omnipotence he had experienced the most signal displays on so many different occasions. "And Moses said, The people among whom I am are six hundred thousand footmen; and *thou* hast said, I will give them flesh, that they may eat a whole month. Shall the flocks and the herds be slain for them, to suffice them? Or, shall all the fish of the sea be gathered together for them, to suffice them?" Here is a most humiliating doubt, boldly avowed by an honoured servant of the Lord. Moses doubted either the sincerity of God in the promise which he had given, or his ability to accomplish that which he had promised. There was a provoking degree of distrust in the speech he ventures to address to God. But if we are constrained to blame Moses, how can we sufficiently admire the longsuffering and forbearance of God, in administering rebuke so mildly, and yet so effectually? "And the Lord said unto Moses, Is the Lord's hand waxed short?" Num 11:21-23. The Almighty is also the Unchangeable. And surely whenever we may feel ourselves to be oppressed with difficulties and doubts, and cannot draw consolation from the promises of God, because they are viewed either as too good to be enjoyed by us, or too great to be performed by Him, it will be wise in us to remember these reproving and encouraging words, "*Is the Lord's hand waxed short?*"

In the way of illustration, I shall only add at present, that, in the book of Psalms, which, of all the books of the Bible, is preeminently the book of religious experience, we learn how deeply the holy men "who spake as they were moved by the Holy Ghost," mourn over their want of spiritual light and enjoyment, whilst they also penitentially confess their failures and shortcomings. True it is, that the prevailing sentiment in the Psalms is that of trust—a firm and fixed, a humble and holy trust, in God. There is also, in abundance, the language of elevated and joyful praise. But the writers of these sacred songs were not uniformly of a cheerful spirit. The stedfastness of their faith was sometimes shaken by the outward calamities in which they felt themselves involved. They could not always sing the sweet songs of Zion. And we hear them complaining that God had withdrawn from them his gracious presence, which was the joy of their heart; and his loving favour, which they valued more than life itself. Thus in Ps 77, by whomsoever it was indited,—whether it was David, or Asaph, or some other prophet,—we know that he must have been a holy man of God; and yet in the day of his trouble he gave utterance to his thoughts within him, in very desponding language: he says, "My soul refused to be comforted. I remembered God, and was troubled: I complained, and my spirit was overwhelmed." He goes on to contrast his former light and gladness with his present darkness and sorrow. And amidst the anguish which a state of doubt respecting his acceptance with God had produced, he communes with his own heart, and with his spirit makes diligent search. "Will the Lord cast off for ever? And will he be favourable no more? Is his mercy clean gone for ever? Doth his promise fail for evermore? Hath God forgotten to be gracious? Hath he in anger shut up his tender mercies?" These are the mournful breathings of a soul which, in losing its hold of the divine promises, had also lost its enjoyment of spiritual happiness and safety. But the intense distress which this privation occasions, is the clearest possible proof, that God, and God alone, was the true restingplace of that soul, and its only satisfying portion. And this is a specific illustration of what I mean by the title prefixed to this letter. The religious experience of the most deeply exercised saints warrants the assertion, that *the existence of doubts is not incompatible with a state of grace.*

It is unnecessary to extend our references to all those Old Testament worthies, "who *through faith* subdued kingdoms, wrought righteousness, obtained promises," "out of weakness were made strong, waxed valiant in fight, turned to flight the armies of the aliens," "and others were tortured, not accepting deliverance; that they might obtain a better resurrection," Heb 11:33-35. Mankind are very much alike in every age of the world, and under every variety of external circumstances. Considering, then, that these ancient and eminent individuals, to whose personal histories I have alluded, were men of like passions with ourselves, it ought not to appear anywise marvellous that they were subject to such alternations of strength and weakness, of confidence and doubt, as are recorded concerning them. We ourselves have painful experience of our own liability to similar alternations. And therefore we may reasonably draw encouragement and consolation from the recorded fact, that the very men on whom God himself has stamped the character of "righteous," did, on some occasions, swerve from the fixedness of their trust in God, and were consequently deprived of that peace and of those hopes, which an assured faith alone can impart and preserve. Thus it is that we still claim kindred and connection with them. Had their characters exhibited *perfection* of practice as well as of principle, our own defective practice might have led us, with propriety, to question whether we possessed the right principle at all. But perceiving how these best of men have failed in the exercise of their faith, and the preservation of their holiness, we feel permitted and disposed to cleave to them, in sympathy, as partakers with ourselves of the same frail and fallen humanity, as having lived in the same evil world, as having drunk of the same mixed cup, and as having experienced the vicissitudes of clouds and sunshine, during the period of their pilgrimage to "the better country."

But, my dear friend, if at any time we are distressed by doubts, and attempt to take consolation and encouragement from those doubts by which even Scripture saints were sometimes overtaken and overcome, it behoves us to act with caution. The consolation which their religious history administers to us, does not lie in their having ever been in spiritual distress; nor must encouragement to us be drawn from their failures and imperfections. I do conceive, however, that it is hardly possible for a conscientious Christian, when he happens to lie under the depressing influence of doubts and darkness, to discover any points of resemblance between his own experience and that of the devoted servants of God, to whose cases we have referred, without feeling himself to be both encouraged and comforted. That their faith now and then did fail need not in the least surprise us, when we recollect how dim were the revelations made to them; how scanty were the rays of divine light that shone around them; and how comparatively dark and obscure was the dispensation under which they lived. On the other hand, it may indeed surprise us, and also put us to shame, to observe how strong and how stedfast was the faith which in general they maintained and manifested. Such simple trust in God is most admirable. And in this respect, the example of these men teaches us, who enjoy the fulness of gospel light and of gospel privileges, how much greater should be our anxiety to imitate, and if possible to surpass, their faith, than, behind their misgivings and failures, attempt to screen and to excuse our own. For them a better excuse can be made than for us. To palliate their conduct is far easier than to palliate ours. Jesus Christ, whose day they only saw dimly and at a distance, but who in these latter days has himself spoken unto us, lays down this equitable principle of judgment, "that to whomsoever much is given, of them shall the more be required." In proportion to our advantages must be our responsibilities. Highly favoured, then, as *we* are, we have much to answer for. The feebleness of our faith, the frequency of our doubts, the inconsistencies of our conduct, and the deficiency of our fruitfulness in every good word and work, are things for which these men of darker and less privileged ages do certainly condemn us. Nevertheless it is true, and oh! what a blessed truth it is, that, to all his people, under every variety of external condition and of inward conflict, our gracious Lord and Saviour dispenses mercy, and forbearance, and forgiveness. He knows the temptations to which they are exposed. He sympathises with the infirmities under which they labour. He compassionates the spiritually weak, the sick, the deaf, the blind, the lame; and amidst the imperfections which more or less belong to the whole members of "the household of faith," *he* still regards them as his own chosen servants: yea, he loves them as his brethren. *He* stands in the presence of the *Father* as their Surety and their Friend,—as their righteous Advocate and all-prevailing Intercessor. And, as their best encouragement and consolation, *he* pledges his own omnipotence, that to whom he gives grace, he will also in due time give glory.

You will remember my remarking, at the commencement of this Letter, how wonderfully silent the Scriptures are on the subject of doubts. From this silence we may warrantably conclude that *doubts* are not designed by God to hold any place in *his* method of saving and sanctifying our sinful race. It teaches us, moreover, that doubts enter very sparingly into the experience of the people of God; so far at least as their experience has been recorded in the Bible. Thus it is obvious to every person of ordinary reflection, that *faith* is the rule, and *doubts* are only the exception. The scantiness of the illustrations we have gleaned from the Old Testament Scriptures cannot fail to impress this truth on our minds. It is an important truth; and many Christians of the present day, who are too indulgent of the doubts which disturb their heavenly tranquillity, and interrupt their cheerful activities in the service of God, would do well to give heed to it. And when we come to search the New Testament Scriptures, in the prosecution of the same subject, our gleanings from that field of inquiry will prove even more scanty than they have been from the Old. In the next Letter the nature and amount of these additional gleanings will be submitted to you. At present I shall merely mention, that, so far as my recollection serves me, *the Gospel history* furnishes only a few isolated instances of doubting, whilst the subject can scarcely be said to have a place at all in the *Apostolic Epistles*. And this may be adduced as a proof, with all fairness, that the Christianity of the primitive churches was as distinctively marked by a simple and sincere and stedfast faith, as modern Christianity is by the prevalence of doubts among those who call themselves believers.

Greatly desiring that both of us may be comfortably "built up in our most holy faith," and preserved from the snares of a doubtful and desponding state of mind,

I remain, yours, etc.

LETTER 2

THE EXISTENCE OF DOUBTS IS NOT INCOMPATIBLE WITH A STATE OF GRACE—*Concluded*

In the infancy of the Christian church there were few doubters.—Doubting Christians were not excluded from church fellowship.—Illustrations from the New Testament, that doubts are not incompatible with a state of grace.—In the Epistles, the allusions to doubts and doubters, are scanty: the case of the Romans;—St. Paul's exhortation to Timothy;—St. James's counsels to waverers, and the double-minded.—In the Gospels there is a singular silence on the subject of doubts:—the case of the man who said, "If thou canst," explained;—the case of St. Peter when walking on the water;—some of the eleven Apostles doubted, even when worshipping their Lord previous to his ascension.—The results of our scriptural researches.—The best of men have sometimes doubted.— The God who pardoned and strengthened them is also our God.—Doubting Christians should never despond.—They should judge charitably of others.—Extreme opinions are to be avoided.—No countenance should be given either to a doubting or to a dogmatic spirit.

My dear Friend,

In the infancy of the Christian church, when the canonical books of the New Testament were written, it appears that the number of doubters was so small, and the cases of doubting were of such rare occurrence, as not to require any special notice. It is indeed delightful to think of this. At the same time, from a few thinly scattered passages in the Gospels, and in some of the Epistles, it may be gathered, that, amongst the early Christians, there were certain individuals, whose faith in Christ Jesus was not sufficiently strong and stable to guard them against doubts and their accompanying dangers. But as it is nowhere mentioned that these doubters were, or ought to be, excluded from the fellowship of the gospel, or from the privileges of the church, we are reminded of the essential difference which subsists between doubt and unbelief. And as it is very desirable that this difference should be deeply impressed on the minds of all Christians who are afflicted with doubts, you will permit me to state, that the *unbelief* which the Bible condemns, is that total absence of faith in God and in Jesus Christ, his incarnate Son, which constitutes the Christian. *Doubt*, on the contrary, always implies the presence of faith in a certain, although it may be in a low, degree. Doubt stands opposed to assurance; just as unbelief is the opposite of faith. And, therefore, whilst the ascendancy of unbelief in any human heart indicates the entire destitution of that grace of God by which we are saved, through faith; we are confirmed in the correctness of our former assertion, that the existence of doubts, dishonouring though they be to God, and detrimental as they necessarily are to the Christian's own prosperity, must on no account be denounced as wholly incompatible with a state of grace.

Let us now calmly examine such cases as the New Testament Scriptures present to us; and I prefer beginning with the Epistles.

You will probably expect me in the first instance to quote Rom 14. The first and last verses seem to give us distinct intimation that there were doubters among the Christians at Rome. You must not allow yourself, however, to be misled merely by the introduction of certain words and phrases. The marginal readings of these two verses deserve your attention. The whole chapter indeed must be carefully perused, and then I think you will be satisfied that St. Paul has in his view a class of persons who were not doubters, either of the truth of the gospel, or of their own interest in it; but who had imbibed some peculiar and contracted notions about the food which it was lawful for them to eat. These notions were in themselves harmless. They did not affect the matter of salvation. But the persons who entertained them, according to the apostle's estimate, were "weak in the faith." And it is beautiful to observe how tenderly he desires that the other members of the church at Rome should receive them in love, and not for judgment. At the same time, we may rest assured that the apostle would exercise the same spirit of charity and forbearance towards all at Rome who laboured under doubts on points of greater importance, if there were any such doubters. But that there were none seems to be very manifest. For if St. Paul does particularly advert to the proper treatment of doubters on points of comparatively trivial moment, we may be sure he would not have omitted anything that essentially concerned the spiritual welfare of these Roman converts.

The same apostle, and with the authority belonging to his office, writes thus to Timothy, his "own son in the faith:"—"I will therefore that men pray everywhere, lifting up holy hands, without wrath and doubting," 1 Tim 2:8. Timothy was an evangelist, who was sent from place to place to preach the gospel, and plant churches, and ordain elders. At the commencement of the chapter from whence the above quotation is taken, St. Paul enjoins "that first of all, supplications, prayers, intercessions, and giving of thanks, be made for all men." How truly catholic is this! And the encouragement to embrace the universal family of man in our prayers to our common God and Father, lies in the cheering declaration, that "God will have all men to be saved, and come to the knowledge of the truth." But this catholic duty must be performed in a catholic spirit. The words to which I have directed your attention contain an authoritative command from the apostle, "I will, therefore, that men pray everywhere." Here he repeats his exhortation to the great duty of prayer. His principal object, however, is to enforce a peculiar mode of performing the duty, "lifting up holy hands, without wrath and doubting." It is obvious that "the lifting up of holy hands," is designed to express the outward manifestation of inward reverence for that great and holy God to whom our prayers are addressed: it is an act of solemn and devout adoration. Again, the praying "without wrath," has respect to the state of our feelings towards other men. It is the putting away of all anger, and bitterness, and malice, and envy, and evil-speaking. It is the cultivation of humbleness, and kindness, and forbearance, and forgiveness. Eph 4:31; Col 3:12-13; 1 Pet 2:1. And this is needful to enable us to bear the case of our fellow-creatures on our hearts before God. It is especially necessary before we can, in the spirit of true charity, love our enemies, and bless them that curse us, and pray even for those who despitefully use us and persecute us, Matt 5:44. But the apostle adds, that our prayers must be offered up "without *doubting*." This part of the injunction has respect to the state of our feelings towards God. It is the casting aside of every hesitation to approach his throne of grace, and of all suspicions of his open ear and loving heart, and of all doubts in regard to his readiness and delight to grant whatever we ask, agreeable to his will, in the name of Christ. And this, too, is needful to ensure sincerity and importunity when we pray, either for ourselves or for others. St. Paul, then, in exhorting "that men pray everywhere without doubting," must have known, or at least must have deemed it probable, that Timothy would meet in his travels with Christian converts who did not wholly neglect the duty of prayer, but whose state of mind hindered their offering up the prayer of faith which availeth much. Their doubts and suspicions would in a great measure deprive them of the benefits of prayer. And as the apostle ardently desires the progress and prosperity of the church, he therefore enjoins Timothy to warn "men everywhere" of the evil consequences to be expected, if doubts are allowed to counteract the legitimate and blissful influences of prayer.

It is rather singular that the exhortation which St. James addresses to doubters should also be in connection with the right discharge of the duty of prayer. He says, "If any of you lack wisdom, let him ask of God, who giveth to all men liberally, and upbraideth not, and it shall be given him. But let him ask in faith, *nothing wavering*; for he that wavereth is like a wave of the sea driven with the wind and tossed. Let not that man think that he shall receive anything of the Lord. A double-minded man is unstable in all his ways," James 1:5-8. In an after part of his epistle, when inculcating the duty of drawing nigh to God, he reiterates his word of advice and warning to the double-minded. "Draw nigh to God, and he will draw nigh to you. Cleanse your hands, ye sinners; and purify your hearts, ye double-minded," James 4:8.

The double-minded, with whom the apostle is here dealing, are not the treacherous and dishonest men of the world, but members of the church, who are of a vacillating and inconstant disposition. It is not of intentional deceitfulness and duplicity of conduct that he speaks, but of a constitutional fickleness and fluctuation in their religious opinions and services. Literally, they are men of two minds, (δίψυχοι). They shift from side to side of a subject; looking at it, first in one light, and then in another, without knowing which to approve. Thus are they tossed about by every wind of doctrine, and cannot find rest. They halt between two opinions; always doubting, and never decided. Emphatically they deserve the name of *waverers*: and the word (διακρινόμενος) which in this passage is translated "he that wavereth," is the same which in the epistle to the Romans is translated "he that doubteth." These doubters and waverers are compared by the apostle to the waves of the sea, "driven with the wind and tossed." This comparison, which so appropriately depicts their uncertainty and restlessness, conveys also a very sharp rebuke. And what he adds as to the reception and result of their prayers may well cause all such doubters to tremble; "let not that man think that he shall receive anything of the Lord." These are awful words; and they plainly teach us how indispensable is a stedfast faith, in order to the acceptable performance of the duty of prayer, and to the enjoyment of the blessings which we desire to obtain. But this one passage, more expressly than any other in the New Testament, informs us, that, among the members of the primitive Christian church, certain individuals were characterized,—I might almost say, were stigmatized, as doubters.

You will not fail to notice, as something which directly bears on the subject of our present consideration, that, whilst these wavering and doubting Christians exclude themselves from the benefits of one of the highest and most precious privileges belonging to true believers, the apostle James acts with the same charity towards them, as we have already seen the apostle Paul exercised towards the same description of people. He expresses no doubt of their Christianity; nor does he throw out the slightest hint respecting their exclusion from church fellowship. Notwithstanding their unhappy and pernicious doubts, he still ranks them in "the company of faithful men,"—he regards them as partakers of that grace of God which bringeth salvation. And it is further worthy of your notice, that the instructions which St. Paul delivered to Timothy were chiefly intended to guide his official intercourse with converts from heathenism; whereas the epistle of St. James is addressed "to the twelve tribes which are scattered abroad." Thus we learn that among both Jews and Gentiles, who had embraced Christianity, and who were considered members of the church of Christ, there were a few whose faith had not attained stability,—a few whose minds were distracted by doubts, and yet even divinely inspired apostles recognised them as being in a state of grace. It is, however, as remarkable as it is gratifying, that in only three out of twenty-one apostolical Epistles, can we find any allusion either to doubts or to doubters.

When we come to treat of the different kinds of doubts which perplex Christian minds, and of the different causes from whence they proceed, we may have occasion to revert to these passages in the Epistles of St. Paul and St. James, which I have just quoted. In the meantime, let us open the Gospel histories, with the view of ascertaining whether doubts did exist in the minds of any of those individuals, who are there represented as believers in the Lord Jesus Christ.

We often read that something said or done by our Lord made a strong impression, at one time on his opposers, at another time on his followers, in consequence of which "they reasoned with or among themselves." These reasonings resulted from perplexity of mind, or suspense, or doubt, in regard to the particular topic to which our Lord had directed attention. You will find an example of what I refer to in Matt 16:5-8: "And when his disciples were come to the other side, they had forgotten to take bread. Then Jesus said unto them, Take heed, and beware of the leaven of the Pharisees and of the Sadducees. And they reasoned among themselves, saying, It is because we have taken no bread. Which when Jesus perceived, he said unto them, O ye of little faith, why reason ye among yourselves?" etc. The same Greek word (διαλογίζομαι) to which the signification of "reasoning" is here given, has in other passages been translated "doubting" and "wavering." But although the persons who took part in these reasonings might, in a certain sense, be said to be in a state of doubt, yet their doubts were not of that kind of which we are in search. These reasonings were mere exercises of the intellect, in regard to the right interpretation of some speech delivered, or of some action performed, or of some benefit promised; and they must not be confounded with those painful stirrings of the heart and conscience which doubts respecting revealed or personal religion are so apt to engender.

And of such reasonings we need say no more at present. Let us look for examples of a more appropriate character.

We know that our Lord went about continually doing good, and healing all manner of diseases. This was his daily practice wherever he happened to sojourn during the brief but busy period of his public ministry. The number of his miraculous cures must have been immense, for we read that "there were brought unto him all who were diseased," but we never hear of anyone being sent back unhealed. Those cases of which a particular narrative has been judged deserving of a place in the sacred page, appear to be selected with the wise intention, not only of exhibiting the Saviour's power over death and the devil, as well as over every kind of malady to which sin has rendered mankind obnoxious, but of recording, as a profitable stimulus to others, that unhesitating faith in our Lord by which some individuals were distinguished. There is nothing in the Gospel history itself to warrant the hope that the multitudes who experienced the Saviour's almighty compassion had any belief in him as the Son of God, or the true Messiah. Had it been so, his faithful adherents would have formed a numerous company, instead of being limited to the hundred and twenty who met together with one accord, in one place, after his ascension; or, even to the five hundred brethren, of whom St. Paul says he was seen at once after his resurrection. And therefore I strongly incline to the opinion, that the special cases of cures which are fully detailed, and which invest the writings of the evangelists with so much interest, have been preferred to others, chiefly on account of the faith displayed by the persons on whom our Lord performed these miracles of mercy. I do not mean to deny that the primary and principal design of the Holy Spirit in the whole Gospel record, is to present to us a faithful outline of the sayings and doings of Jesus of Nazareth, "that we might believe that Jesus is the Christ, the Son of God; and that, believing, we might have life through his name," St. John 20:31. But, according to human judgment, any other of the mighty works which marked his progress through all the cities and villages of Palestine, might have answered this purpose equally well. And on reading the interesting accounts, for instance, of Jairus, the ruler of the synagogue, whose daughter was raised from death to life, Mark 5:21, etc.; or of the leper who was cleansed of his leprosy, Matt 8:1-4; or of the centurion, whose servant was healed, Matt 8:5-13; or of the Syrophenician woman, whose daughter was dispossessed of a devil, Mark 7:24-29: I say on perusing the accounts of these miraculous cures, and others of the same kind, it is difficult to resist the conviction, that they were selected to teach us how firmly certain individuals did believe in Christ, although the great majority of those who witnessed or even experienced his divine power, continued in unbelief, because of the blindness of their eyes and the hardness of their hearts. And it strikes me, besides, that this selection has been made to teach us another great lesson, which is exceedingly cheering, viz., that the few who did believe in our Lord, and who are commended for their faith, were not only of both sexes, and of different stations in society, but also of different nations and countries. "The Saviour of the world" welcomed all applicants. An afflicted female from the coasts of Tyre and Sidon, and a Roman soldier, shared his mercy along with young and old, rich and poor, of the chosen seed of Abraham.

Among those, then, whose faith in Christ has secured their honourable notice in the Gospel history, it will occur to you that there is one man whose case is an exception to the rest. He does not come, saying, "Lord, if thou wilt, thou canst make me clean;" neither does he say, "I am not worthy that thou shouldest come under my roof; but speak the word only;" nor, "If I may but touch his garment I shall be whole." And of him the Lord did not say, "I have not found so great faith, no, not in Israel;" neither did the Lord address him as he did some others, "Great is thy faith;"—"thy faith hath saved thee: go in peace." This is a particular case, and we find it recorded with different degrees of minuteness by Matt 17, Mark 9, and Luke 9, to which chapters you may refer at your leisure. The man had a son who was lunatic, whom he had taken to the disciples for cure; but they had not succeeded, although their divine Master had invested them with authority to cast out devils, and to heal all who were diseased. He afterwards brought his son to Jesus, saying, "If thou canst do anything, have compassion on us, and help us." Jesus replied, "If thou canst believe, all things are possible to him that believeth." And straightway the father of the child cried out, and said with tears, "Lord, I believe; help thou mine unbelief."

Now, it is to be observed, from these simple statements, that this affectionate parent was not wholly destitute of faith in Christ; and according to his faith it was done unto him, for we are informed that his child was restored both to health and to reason. But still his faith was faint and feeble. It had not strength to raise him out of doubts and fears. He had already applied to the disciples of our Lord, and they had failed to effect a cure. Now he applies to the Lord himself; but the application is couched in language which implies a want of confidence—almost a want of hope of success. He begins with an *if*; but it is not, if thou *wilt*: it is "*if thou canst* do anything." Clearly to understand his state of mind, we must keep in view the disappointment he had just experienced. He comes with a complaint as well as with a petition. "Your disciples cannot relieve my afflicted child: if *thou* canst do anything, help us." There is an evident distrust of Christ's ability to perform the cure,—a doubt whether the Master himself could do what his ordained servants could not. And although the Saviour did show his wonted compassion, and did not withhold the exercise of his Almighty power, yet ere he healed the son, he gently rebuked the father. Instead of answering his application with a distinct avowal of both his ability and his willingness, he, too, commences with an *if*; "If thou canst believe." And from what follows in the narrative, it is obvious that the man felt the reproof, and was conscious how justly he deserved it. But the words of our Lord were spirit and life to him. With shame, and penitence, and tears, he now addresses Christ as his Lord; and in the same breath in which he acknowledges his faith, he laments his unbelief, and prays for its removal. "Lord, I believe; help thou mine unbelief." There is a great deal of meaning in this short speech. The doubter is now assured. The Saviour has become the object of his worship, and of his confidence. There is a remarkable change in his feelings, and therefore also in his manner of expressing them. We should have expected him to say, "Lord, I do indeed believe; I have no longer any doubt of your divine power to destroy the works of the devil, and to heal all kinds of disease; do help us, and heal my son." But the impulse given to his faith constrains him to an entirely different mode of renewing his application. Jesus had said to the man, "If thou canst believe, all things are possible to him that believeth." To this he responds, "Lord, I do believe; and now my petition is, *help thou mine unbelief*—Put forth your merciful power for *my own* deliverance from this evil heart of unbelief, and then all shall be well with my son. Lord, I believe; help *thou* mine unbelief; for I desire henceforth to be freed from all doubt. I desire to be firmly established in the faith; and to *thee* I look for this great blessing."

This is surely the prayer of a man whose heart has been made to feel the quickening power of divine grace. Here there is exhibited in lovely combination, spiritual enlightenment and conviction of guilt, together with humility, and penitence, and faith. But with all these indications of a broken heart and a contrite spirit, his faith was mixed with unbelief; or rather, his faith was so weak that he could not rid himself from misgiving fears and doubts. And this man stands solitary in that interesting class of persons, whose faith is recorded in connection with our Lord's miracles of healing. Amongst all the men and women, distinguished for their faith in Christ, whilst experiencing his healing power, he is the only doubter of whom the Gospel history gives us any account.

The case of Peter, one of our Lord's chosen disciples, furnishes a still more striking illustration of the existence of doubt in a true believer.

In Matt 14:22-31, we read, "And straightway Jesus constrained his disciples to get into a ship, and to go before him unto the other side, while he sent the multitudes away. And when he had sent the multitudes away, he went up into a mountain apart to pray; and when the evening was come he was there alone. But the ship was now in the midst of the sea, tossed with waves, for the wind was contrary. And in the fourth watch of the night, Jesus went unto them walking on the sea. And when the disciples saw him walking on the sea, they were troubled, saying, It is a spirit; and they cried out for fear. But Jesus straightway spake unto them, saying, Be of good cheer, it is I, be not afraid. And Peter answered him and said, Lord, if it be thou, bid me come unto thee on the water. And he said, Come. And when Peter was come down out of the ship, he walked on the water to go unto Jesus. But when he saw the wind boisterous, he was afraid; and, beginning to sink, he cried, saying, Lord, save me. And immediately Jesus stretched forth his hand, and caught him, and said unto him, O thou of little faith, wherefore didst thou doubt?"

In this beautiful and instructive narrative, it is impossible to overlook how rapid were the alternations of faith and doubt in the heart of Peter, as exhibited in his conduct, in reference to one event, and within a few moments of time. It is not surprising that the unexpected appearance of some one "walking on the sea," dimly discovered amidst the haze of the early dawn, excited the fears of the disciples. A little reflection, however, should have calmed their agitated spirits. Their eyes were accustomed to the sight of all kinds of miracles; and therefore, before the sound of any voice was heard, they might have concluded that none save their own divine Master could plant his footsteps on the tempestuous billows, and safely tread as on the solid ground. But when Jesus did speak, and gave them so gracious and so soothing a salutation, O! then, it does surprise us that his well-known voice, and his equally well-known compassion, did not instantly banish all their fears, and awaken within their breasts a joyful recognition of their Lord.

Of the other disciples no particular mention is made; but Peter was by no means satisfied. To the announcement of Jesus, "It is I," he answers, "Lord, if it be thou, bid me come unto thee on the water." Here he intimates how painfully his mind was agitated between doubt and belief. He addresses Jesus by the usual title, "*Lord*!" and he believes that his Lord was able, not only himself to walk on the sea, but to cause his disciples to do the same. This was an expression of strong faith that with his Lord nothing was impossible. But, on the other hand, he doubted whether it really was Jesus, whose figure he imperfectly saw, but whose voice was distinctly heard. "Lord, *if it be thou*." And when he adds, "Bid me come unto thee on the water," this request, although evidently made with the honest desire to have his doubts removed, was in itself exceedingly presumptuous. Jesus stops not to reprove this rashness, knowing that its punishment was at hand; but, desiring to gain the confidence of his disciples, he said unto Peter, "Come." Bold invitation! which, being so promptly given in compliance with Peter's own request, must have carried conviction to his mind that it was none other than Jesus himself who approached the vessel. The doubting disciple was now assured of the presence of his Master. He believed that it really was Jesus who "said unto him, Come:" and he believed still further that Jesus was able to keep him from sinking. In the exercise of faith he accepted the invitation, and ventured out of the ship. Yea, more than this; he not only made the attempt, but he succeeded in going to meet his Lord *on the water*. It is recorded that he actually "walked on the water to go unto Jesus." How strong his faith must have been at that moment! We might well imagine that at last he had given all his doubts and fears to the winds. Never was any sinful man placed in such an extraordinary position. No better opportunity could possibly occur for rending in pieces and trampling under foot the suggestions of unbelief. Everything was done that could be done to satisfy Peter that he both saw and heard his Lord. His own heart's wish, unreasonable as it was, had been granted to him—"He walked on the water." The heaving billows did not open to swallow him up. The liquid sea supported him. How strange must have been his sensations! And we naturally conclude that at every step he advanced, fresh energy would be imparted to his faith, until in joyful triumph he clasped his Lord in his arms. But the sacred narrative informs us of a very different result. Peter's faith failed him. He seems to have forgotten the terms and the object of his own request. His eyes were withdrawn from Jesus still walking towards him. He gazed on the waves which dashed and foamed at his feet:—he listened to the howling winds; and, "he was afraid." Fear supplanted faith, and he began to sink. What a lesson to Peter, and to the other disciples who sat in the ship, anxiously watching how this experiment would end! and what a lesson to ourselves also! Its language is, "Be not high minded, but fear;"—"be not faithless, but believing." Peter was now in a very perilous situation; and his feelings of helplessness, and his sense of danger, were the means of reviving his faith. Beginning to sink, he cried, saying, "*Lord, save me.*" This was the cry of faith. It was a cry which reached the ears of Him who is able to deliver. Peter was heard, and he was saved. "Immediately Jesus stretched forth his hand, and caught him." O what an endearing proof of the patience, and forbearance, and lovingkindness of him who is the Friend and the Saviour of sinners! But, in this instance, he has likewise given proof of his faithfulness. No sooner had he caught the sinking disciple, and saved him from a watery grave, than he accosted him in the language of reproof: "He said unto him, O thou of little faith, *wherefore didst thou doubt?*"

The conduct of Peter was not blameless; but we must not call in question his sincerity. He was an honest man. In this affair he abounded in candour, however deficient he may have been in cautiousness. And if he doubted more than his companions, or confessed his doubts more frankly than they did, be it remembered that his faith was also greater than theirs. None other of the disciples dared to say to Jesus, "Bid me come unto thee on the water." He alone, of all who were in the ship, ventured to walk on the sea when Jesus said, "Come." But the greatness of his faith was of short duration; and the doubts which succeeded, and which exposed his life to imminent danger, are ascribed by our Lord to the littleness of his faith. "*O thou of little faith*! wherefore didst thou doubt?"

The Greek word (διστάζω) which is translated "doubt" in this place, is far more pointed and expressive than the various words to which the same translation has been given in other passages of Scripture. It expresses the idea of a man standing at the point where two roads meet, and not knowing whether to turn to the right hand or to the left. Nothing could be more significant of a state of doubt. And this same word occurs only in one other passage. After our Lord's resurrection, we read, "Then the eleven disciples went away into Galilee, into a mountain where Jesus had appointed them. And when they saw him, they worshipped him; *but some doubted*," Matt 28:16-17. Who were the doubters on this occasion, or how many of them there were, we cannot tell. This much we do know, that they were of the eleven disciples, for none else appear to have been present. And it is a solemn and humbling truth, that these men, even while worshipping Jesus, were troubled with real doubts. Highly favoured as they had previously been during upwards of three years with incontestable evidence of his Messiahship; and so singularly favoured as they were at this particular moment,—for the arisen Saviour stood before their eyes, and met them in the very place and manner specified by himself before his crucifixion; still it is true that some even of the disciples doubted. But instead of wondering at their doubts, and blaming their unreasonableness, let us weep and mourn over "the evil heart of unbelief" to which we are all so prone; and diligently watch and pray, lest we also fall into temptation.

I can find no additional illustrations. And surely you will agree with me in considering it a cause of thanksgiving, that the Gospel narrative furnishes so few cases of *doubt*, whereas it abounds with the most interesting examples of a simple and strong *faith* in Jesus.

The illustrations, however, which I have been able to adduce, first, from the Old Testament Scriptures, and now from the New, have extended considerably beyond what was expected. I hope you will not condemn their length. My own interest in the subject continued to increase as I advanced in the prosecution of it; and I shall be sorry if your interest in it also has not been sustained.

We have searched together through the Scriptures of the Old and New Testaments, with the desire of obtaining information: and the acquisition of useful knowledge is pleasant, from whatever source it is drawn. But to search the oracles of divine truth will never fail to prove edifying as well as interesting, if the work of searching be conducted with a humble and patient and teachable spirit. We always find it very interesting, whenever we can do it, to study human character and conduct. On this account books of biography are a favourite description of reading. But the biographies with which the Bible abounds, possess the unrivalled advantage of being compiled with heavenly wisdom and faithfulness. And thus, whilst occupied with these sacred studies, our attention is not confined merely to what relates to our fellow-creatures. The character and conduct of *God* is constantly presented to us in some particular aspect, and we feel ourselves as in his presence. We breathe a holy atmosphere, and tread on holy ground. We trace his footsteps everywhere; and it is only in this wondrous volume that his voice salutes our ears. This imparts a deeply solemn and peculiar charm to Scripture characters. And, in my opinion, the more we study them, and the better conversant we become with their principles and practices, we seem to grow in the better knowledge, not only of ourselves, but likewise of that great unseen though ever present *Being*, who was the God of Abraham, and of Isaac, and of Israel, whilst they sojourned on the earth, and who is the same God with whom we ourselves have to do.

The direct object of our researches at this time has been to ascertain whether the most godly of men—the men of whom the Lord himself speaks as his "chosen" and his "friends," and who, in the language of the Bible, are called "the righteous" and "saints," were so stedfast in their exercise of faith, as never to let go their hold of the promises of God, and never to have their confidence shaken, or their hopes obscured. And the result of our researches is in many respects painfully instructive—I had almost said, painfully comforting.

We have found that both in the patriarchal ages, and under the Law, and under the clear light of the Gospel also, doubts have darkened and distressed the minds even of the best of men. And this is instructive. It teaches ourselves not to despond when we unhappily sink into a state of doubt. Indeed we can scarcely expect that our faith is to surpass in strength and in stedfastness that of patriarchs and prophets and apostles. But when we see how *they* did sometimes fall away from their faith, and always in some way suffer for it, how jealous should we be of *ourselves*! And if it is painful to contemplate the falls of such eminently good men, how painful must it be to find ourselves falling after the same example of unbelief! But along with this pain there is a consolation too. God did forgive them, and he restored them, and he caused them yet again to enjoy the light of his countenance. And here is hope for us. Their God is our God, "the same yesterday, today, and for ever." When, therefore, our minds are at any time overcast with doubts and fears, it is our privilege to recollect what we have read of the experience of Scripture saints. For whilst it is a very miserable kind of consolation to know that others have been as doubting and as distressed as we are, there is a peace-giving consolation in the knowledge that God does not rank us amongst hypocrites and unbelievers because of our occasional doubts. And all doubters ought to enjoy a genuine and great consolation in knowing that the existence of doubts, however displeasing to God, and injurious to ourselves, is not incompatible with a state of grace.

But we must carefully watch against the abuse of this comforting fact, and never lose sight of the distinction which exists between the doubts themselves, and the distress of mind which they occasion. The comfort which the word of God provides must be applied to the distress, and not to the doubts. For of this we ought to be fully aware, that however patiently and compassionately God deals with his people amidst all their infirmities, he is as much displeased with their doubts, as he is grieved for their distress. All our researches have taught us that doubts are dangerous things. They dishonour the God of truth and faithfulness; and they injure our own souls; and they bring up an evil report against the religion of Jesus, as if it made men melancholy and miserable. We must, therefore, when we do suffer under the malignant influence of doubts, resort to all proper expedients for the strengthening of our faith as the surest method of deliverance from them. If we neglect this duty, the probability is that our doubts will cease to distress us; and we ourselves will cease to desire either the reviving grace, or the scriptural consolation, which we so greatly need. Alas! such a deplorable cessation is of too frequent occurrence. And, oh! what a fearful step a believer takes when he settles himself down in a state of permanent doubt! And what a melancholy spectacle it is to behold a Christian man relax in his Christian decision and devotedness, and gradually lapse into a state of dangerous apathy and indifference! And what shall we think of those who would be mightily offended were other people to doubt their Christianity, but who are themselves sinfully content to remain in a state of doubt, and even make a merit of their doubts, as if they were evidences of Christian humility?

I am willing to believe that you hold such opinions and practices in abhorrence. I trust we are agreed in condemning doubts as indications of "little faith," and as the forerunners of many evils, and as the causes of great discomfort to the Christian. And if, by the grace of God, we are for the present built up in an assured faith, let us cultivate an abiding spirit of humility and of thankfulness for the measure of grace already vouchsafed unto us, and earnestly implore that continuance of grace, by which alone we can "stand fast in the faith, and quit us like men." Such, however, is our frailty, and so far are we as yet removed from Christian perfection, that we may expect occasions of doubt to arise, and seasons of spiritual darkness or distress to overtake us. In these circumstances it is our privilege to do as others before us have done. It is our privilege meekly to receive our Lord's rebuke, and yet in fervent prayer to say, "Lord, I believe; help *thou* mine unbelief." It is our privilege never to despond; but even when we seem to be sinking, still to cry in faith, "Lord, save me." This is the Gospel method of deliverance. We must value our privileges: we must use them.

But it would be unpardonably selfish to confine the application of the subject under review to our own personal comfort and encouragement. We ought to think of our fellow-Christians, who are in a doubting state of mind, and learn to treat them with forbearance, compassion, and kindness.

Allow me to remind you that all our scriptural researches at this time will prove to be very unserviceable to us, unless they have impressed two great facts upon our minds. The one is, that the truest servants of God,—the dearest and most honoured of his children on this earth, are at times deprived of that glorious liberty that rightfully belongs to them as his children, and are subjected to the tormenting bondage of doubts. The other is, that a state of doubt leads to instant and mischievous results, both as it respects themselves, in their swerving from the direct path of holy obedience, and in their lamentable descent from that moral elevation of character to which a simple and unwavering trust in God had raised them; and also as it respect others, in the stumblingblock which such inconsistent conduct throws in their way. These two leading facts are well calculated to teach us two very important practical lessons. The one is, to beware of giving any sanction or indulgence to doubts in ourselves. The other is, to beware how we feel and act towards our doubting brethren. On the first of these I need not add to the remarks which have already occurred in the course of this Letter. The other is a lesson which requires to be plainly taught and often repeated, in order to guard us against the tendency to judge harshly of one another, to which all of us must plead guilty of being very prone.

Surely, my friend, you will readily acknowledge, that the patience, and forbearance, and forgiveness of God in his dealings with doubters, should make us emulous to imitate his example. A spirit of tenderness and charity is what we should constantly study to cherish and to manifest. A spirit of hasty and censorious judgment we must anxiously check and suppress. If others are enslaved by doubts, whilst we are enjoying exemption from their depressing and hurtful influence, we should gratefully and humbly remember who it is that makes us to differ. And as God has been pleased in his mercy to strengthen our faith, it becomes us, in all the meekness and dutifulness of Christian love, to express the sympathies of our hearts, and to extend a helping hand to them who as yet, or, who at present, are weak in the faith. We should take pleasure in offering them our counsel and advice, if they will listen to us; and, at all events, it is our duty to carry their cases to the throne of grace, in the confidence that the God of all grace will listen to our supplications, and in the hope of his granting a favourable answer in his own time and way. It is always good to pray for others. Should our prayers prove of no benefit to them, in whose behalf they have been presented, it is a vast benefit to ourselves to have the spirit of true catholicism,—the spirit of brotherly kindness and charity, called into active operation. Such prayers return into our own bosoms, richly laden with the blessings of heaven.

Let us, then, be always tender and charitable towards the doubters; whilst we never cease to wage a spiritual warfare against the doubts which they entertain. This is a distinction of which we ought not to lose sight. And it is too often lost sight of. I am sure, in your intercourse with mankind, you must have met with some pious and devoted people, who were themselves "strong in faith," and who strenuously advocated the mistaken notion, that assurance is so essential to the Christian character, and a state of doubt so utterly repugnant to it, that unless a man is assured of his own salvation, he is not at all entitled to the right hand of fellowship as a believer in the Lord Jesus Christ. And it is still more probable you may have met with good and holy men of the exactly opposite school, who decry the doctrine of assurance as a presumptuous and dangerous error, and who maintain that a state of doubt respecting his own spiritual condition and prospects, is the safest and the most desirable for the Christian. But it is evident that the ultra opinions which both of these adverse parties entertain, are directly at variance with those numerous portions of Scripture which have come under our notice in the preceding parts of this Letter. The one is sadly deficient in Christian indulgence towards the doubters; and the other grievously errs in overindulgence to the doubts. When we see how even good men make shipwreck of charity on the rocks and shoals of their own theories and fancies, it will be wise in us to avoid all extreme opinions, and never to permit them to influence our judgment of others. The exhortation of our blessed Lord and Saviour is too often forgotten:—"judge not, that ye be not judged. For with what judgment ye judge, ye shall be judged; and with what measure ye mete, it shall be measured to you again," Matt 7:1-2.

It is a cause of deep regret that men are always so apt to run into extremes on religious subjects. In this way the seeds of discord are sown among brethren. Those who are united in Christ Jesus, and who ought to be "endeavouring to keep the unity of the Spirit in the bond of peace," Eph 4:3, become alienated in affection, and separated in action and intercourse. This is a sore evil, because it furnishes the world with too good a reason for the reproachful sneer, "See how these Christians fight and quarrel," whereas it should be our holy ambition so to live, as still to extort from the world the honourable testimony of ancient times, "Behold how these Christians love one another!"

We may trace to a variety of sources those extreme opinions regarding assurance and doubts, to which I have had occasion to allude. Amongst Christians we should be prepared to expect important differences in their mental constitutions, as also in the measures of grace conferred upon each, and consequently in their religious experiences. Some men are favoured with peculiar advantages, and are more spiritually enlightened, and are of a larger spiritual growth, than others. Some men, likewise, are naturally of a keen and sanguine temperament, whilst others are phlegmatic. And these reasons sufficiently account for the want of uniformity in their sentiments, and feelings, and attainments. Perfect uniformity ought not to be looked for in the church, as it is not to be found in any of the departments of nature. All God's works are adorned by a profuse display of variety. But there are few men who escape the snare of erecting their own individual views and experiences into a general standard of truth, by which all other men must be tried. Oh! who can enumerate the many bitter controversies that have originated in this one mistake, or contemplate without sorrow the endless divisions which, by its instrumentality, have torn to pieces the Christian church, so much to the scandal of the Christian religion!

Constant watchfulness is required to guard us against the dangers of this insidious snare, and our prayers are wanted for renewed supplies of the Spirit of all grace, that we may ever follow after charity. Surely it behoves us to be very cautious in setting limits to the mercy of God, or in pronouncing harsh judgments on our brethren. Each of us, indeed, should look well to his own creed and conduct, that they correspond with each other, and with the word of God. And no true believer should give any encouragement or countenance either to a doubting or to a dogmatic temper, as both are condemned by the precepts of the Gospel, and by the example of Christ himself, our Lord and Master.

And now, my dear Friend, I commit this Letter to your careful perusal, and commend yourself to God and to the word of his grace, which is able to build you up, and to give you an inheritance among all them which are sanctified, Acts 20:32.

Believe me, yours, etc.

LETTER 3

THE VARIOUS KINDS OF DOUBTS THAT ARE PREVALENT AMONG PROFESSING CHRISTIANS

The Hebrew Christians who were tempted to apostasy must not be ranked amongst doubters.—Mere professors are in reality unbelievers.—The convictions and compunctions to which they are liable, differ essentially from the doubts and fears of true Christians.—Doubts may be thrown into two classes; 1, those which respect God himself and his revealed word; 2, those which respect our own belief and interest in what God has revealed and promised. These different kinds of doubts must again be subdivided into 1st. Such as are occasional and temporary; 2nd. Such as are systematical and permanent.—Doubts respecting God and his word are generally transient.—Doubts respecting our own spiritual condition, are sometimes systematical, which is wrong.—Sometimes they are allowed to become permanent, which is dangerous.—Sometimes they are professed when not really felt; and this is sinful.—Hypocritical professors of doubts foster spiritual pride under the semblance of humility. Concluding remarks.

My dear Friend,

You state it as your opinion that into the list of scriptural illustrations of the existence of doubts amongst persons who rank highest for devotedness to God, with which my two former Letters were occupied, I might have introduced, with advantage, the case of those primitive Hebrew converts to Christianity, to whom one of the most interesting and valuable

Epistles in the New Testament is addressed. I also, at one time, was of the same opinion; but more mature reflection brought me to the conviction that the *unbelief* against which these Jewish Christians are so faithfully warned, ought not to be confounded with the *doubts*, of which it is my object exclusively to treat.

The apostle, in writing to the Hebrews, was evidently impressed with the fact of their being beset with strong temptations to abandon the profession of their faith in the Gospel of Christ, and to relapse into Judaism. He knew well the great danger to which they were exposed of apostatizing altogether, and of thus coming short of the heavenly and eternal rest which the Gospel reveals, after the example of their forefathers; who, because they believed not God's sure word of promise, died in the wilderness, and were excluded from the possession of the land of Canaan. This was the critical condition of these Hebrews who had embraced Christianity; and it was their peculiar liability to renounce their Christian principles and privileges which drew forth from the writer of the epistle so many stirring and stimulating exhortations to stedfastness. And whilst I readily admit that amongst ourselves, there are professing Christians always to be met with, who, notwithstanding all their present religious advantages, and all their past avowals of attachment to Christ, are likely to forsake his cause, and to forfeit the blessings of his salvation, whenever temptation arises, and who, therefore, need to be warned and exhorted; still I could wish it to be distinctly understood, that unbelief and doubts are different things, and that, generally speaking, they are experienced by totally different descriptions of people.

We must not forget that mere professors are in reality unbelievers. Many of them do not so much as *know* what it is that they profess to *believe*. And the more intelligent and sincere of them only give the assent of their *understandings* to certain Christian truths, whilst their *hearts* and *lives* remain alike unaffected by them. They are strangers to that renovating power of the Spirit of God which alone brings the sinner into the enjoyment of salvation. They are destitute of that divinely wrought faith in the Lord Jesus Christ, which purifies the heart, and overcomes the world, and works by love. And inasmuch as these merely nominal Christians possess no true faith, I cannot suppose them to be subject to doubts. In regard to their character and conduct as men, there will be found amongst them many grades both of worth and of unworthiness. But as professed believers in Christianity, it is lamentably true that their lives are spent, for the most part, in perfect unconcern about the Saviour and his great salvation. They do not think of God. They do not see the evil of sin, nor feel it to be a burden. They care not for the things that belong to their everlasting peace. They realize not that dread tribunal before which they must one day appear. As it respects the Gospel, either as a system of doctrine or as a rule of practice, it can be no breach of charity to say of such professors, that they are dead while they live. And to hear them complain of being harassed with doubts, would strike us as something quite unusual, and out of character.

The most careless of professors, however, are occasionally visited with compunctions of conscience for professing what they neither understand nor value, and for violating the engagements under which they bring themselves by the reception of Christian ordinances; and in these circumstances it may naturally enough happen that their minds are disquieted by fearful apprehensions. They may even be compelled at times to struggle under convictions of guilt, so strong that they cannot stifle them. And when the unwelcome thought is forced upon them, that they have despised their religious privileges, and abused the goodness of God, and neglected the loving Saviour, it would be strange indeed, if they were not filled with alarm. But such a state of conviction and compunction, uncheered by any ray of Gospel light, and unaccompanied by any Gospel hope of pardon, is never to be confounded with the fears and doubts which often disturb the true Christian.

I ought still farther to remind you that it is by no means uncommon for mere professors, while sitting under a faithful ministry, to be pricked in their hearts as with a sharp twoedged sword. Their sins rise up before them in fearful array. Their danger is felt to be great, and were they to give utterance to their secret desires at these searching moments, we should hear them anxiously exclaim, like the Philippian jailor of old, "What shall I do to be saved?" They are partially awakened; but the work does not go forward. They dread to encourage it. Their convictions stop far short of conversion. They cannot make up their minds to forsake sin, and to follow Christ. They quench the Spirit; and they never become "new creatures in Christ Jesus." The inward conflict, however, to which they have been subjected, increases their own self-condemnation. This is a very important result. Conscience is more enlightened, and its upbraiding voice is less easily silenced than before. And on this account it is not surprising that such persons should sink into fits of despondency, or be overwhelmed with dismay, in the anticipation of death, judgment, and eternity. But we should commit a grievous mistake were we to rank them amongst doubters. Before their awakening they were troubled neither with fears nor with doubts, because they did not seriously think either about sin or about salvation. And after they have been somewhat awakened to a sense of their sinful and perilous condition, and are obliged to think of the consequences, the very dismay into which they are thrown, and the despondency which they indulge, clearly prove that they give themselves up for lost. They are conscious of having no faith in the Saviour, and therefore they dare not entertain the hope of salvation. Were they in a state of doubt, they would feel themselves to be comparatively blessed; but doubts they have none. Had the question been put to them, previous to their awakening, "Are you living for eternity? What are your prospects beyond the present uncertain life?" in all probability the answer would have been, "Let us enjoy ourselves. Why trouble us with such questions? We hope all will be right at last." It is indeed a rare thing to meet with anyone, I mean among the unenlightened and unrenewed, who does not express the hope of getting to heaven. This hope is, indeed, a mere fool's fire. But such as it is, it is cherished without hesitation. It is unclouded by a doubt. And it is worthy of notice, that the same undoubting, unhesitating disposition marks the judgment which they pronounce against themselves, when a partial awakening has filled them with terror and alarm. Their false hope has now entirely failed them, and they have nothing else on which to rest. Let precisely the same question be asked as before, and the anguish of their souls will give increased decision to their reply— "Our case is hopeless." But how widely removed is this from a state of doubt, which must necessarily be characterised by indecision and uncertainty. The doubter, if never comfortably assured of his salvation, is never wholly deprived of the hope that he may be saved. The doubter perseveres in keeping hold of Christ, and nothing can induce him to let go his hold; and thus, although he is much tossed and agitated with suspense, because of the weakness of his faith, he never entirely loses the sustaining persuasion that he has some footing on the only true "foundation." The doubter is, indeed, often involved in thick mists and heavy clouds as he travels onwards in the journey of life; but there is always some star to guide his progress, and to shine, however dimly, on his future prospects. The darkness of despair belongs not to doubts, but to unbelief.

In making these statements, I trust you will acknowledge that I have not exceeded what is actually true; and in short, my friend, the more you reflect on the subject which I have brought under your review, I am satisfied it will become the more obvious to you, that those persons who are honestly distressed with doubts in reference either to any department of divine truth, or to their own spiritual and eternal welfare, must be distinguished from merely nominal Christians. Doubters are something more and something better than mere professors. But then we must be sure that they who represent themselves as labouring under doubts, are honest, and not hypocritical, in the complaints which they make, because it is just as easy, and just as possible, for people *to profess themselves to be doubters*, as it is to profess that they are believers, when they are not, and know that they are not. And it is much to be feared that within the bosom of the Christian church we have at least some false professors of doubts, which are not felt, as well as many false professors of the faith, which is not believed.

Before proceeding to notice the various kinds of doubts that are most prevalent, I have deemed it of importance to free the subject from unnecessary embarrassment, by first of all ascertaining to what description of Christians those who are afflicted with doubts belong; I mean whether we are to regard them as real or nominal Christians. And now, throughout the present and the subsequent letters I request you to remember that, for the reasons already assigned, I am disposed to look upon doubters in general as genuine believers in the Lord Jesus Christ, and as the chosen and adopted children of God. It is true that their doubts have brought them into a spiritually unhealthy and unhappy condition, or, at all events, give indications of their being in such a condition. They are feeble and fainthearted. Their faith wants vigour. Their love wants ardour. Their hopes want brightness. Their joys and consolations have almost departed. But still they exhibit some symptoms of spiritual life. They hate sin. They love those who love the Saviour. They desire to serve and please God. Nor are they entirely destitute either of faith, or love, or hope, or joy. In all these respects they differ from mere professors. And therefore we must recognise them as Christian brethren, and on no account withhold from them the love to which, as brethren in the Lord, they are entitled; nor yet the sympathy, and the counsel, and the encouragement, of which, as brethren in distress, they so greatly stand in need.

And now, my dear friend, in soliciting your attention to the various kinds of doubts that are prevalent among religious people, I am certain you will not expect me to attempt even an enumeration of all the shades of doubt which slightly tinge, or deeply blacken, the experience of individual Christians. Nor is it my intention to advert to those manifold conscientious scruples in reference to points of doctrine or of practice, with which men's minds are so frequently perplexed, and which prove stumblingblocks in the way of their belief and obedience. Those who desire a guide as to the rightful office and the profitable exercise of *conscience*, will do well to consult a very elaborate and philosophical work, entitled *Ductor Dubitantium*, by Dr. Jeremy Taylor; and for others, who are at a loss to decide how they should act in many instances, and whose minds are harassed with painful, though honourable, fears of endangering their own souls, or wounding their Divine Master, by unlawful or inconsistent conduct, there are standard books of casuistry, such as Pike and Hayward's *Cases of Conscience*, which may be perused with advantage.

The observations I have to offer must necessarily be general and not specific. I therefore propose to cast all doubts into two classes,—*First*, Such as respect God himself, and his revealed word. *Second*, Such as respect our own interest and belief in what God has been pleased to reveal and promise. These different kinds of doubts must again be divided into other two classes. *First*, Such as are only occasional and temporary. *Second*, Such as are systematical and permanent. And I trust it will appear to you that this classification is sufficiently comprehensive for practical purposes; but you will please to observe that the *latter* division, which I have proposed, differs in nowise from the *former*, in regard to the *kind* of doubts, of which we shall have to treat; but only in regard to their *degree* or *duration*.

Of the two classes of Doubts, then, to which my observations are to be confined, *the First in order is that which has respect to God himself and to his revealed word*. And I am greatly mistaken if your own experience does not testify to the melancholy fact, that doubts of this kind are by no means uncommon. Is not your own mind, on many occasions, disturbed by them? Doubts which are felt at the moment to be alarming, and which are afterwards characterized as horrible, do seize upon you with the suddenness and surprise of an electric shock, and almost deprive you of personal identity. I cannot be far wrong in supposing that sometimes you have doubted whether there was a God at all; or, if he really does exist, whether the Bible gives you a just representation of his personal attributes, and of his moral government of the world. It is also probable you have been frequently staggered in regard to particular events in providence. You see the wicked prospering like a green bay tree, while the righteous are trampled under their feet, and visited with sore afflictions. You see an unaccountable admixture of good and of evil wherever you turn. And you realize all this so constantly and so painfully in your own little history, that your faith gives way, and you dare to doubt the wisdom, or the rectitude, or the goodness of Him who presides over all.

At other times you may have been irresistibly constrained to question the claims of the Bible to divine inspiration, or to hesitate in admitting the veracity of its records, or to doubt whether the version which you possess is a genuine copy of the originals. The multiplicity and variety and richness of the divine promises have arrested your special attention. But instead of fleeing to them as an overflowing fountain of strength and consolation, which is your usual practice, you are now and then tempted to doubt the truth of His promises, who cannot lie; or His faithfulness to perform them, who is omnipotent. Yea, I must add, as a thing by no means impossible, that you may have been tempted to reject the Gospel of your salvation as a cunningly devised fable, and to doubt the reality of the incarnation and atonement of the Son of God; and thus to launch yourself into an ocean of uncertainty whether Jesus Christ our Lord is able and willing to save you. These are seasons of spiritual wretchedness; for whilst all the pillars of your faith are thus shaken at the very foundations, it is as vain for you to cherish any sure or comfortable hope of life everlasting, as it is to expect the brightness of a meridian sun at the dead hour of night.

Do not complain, my dear friend, of the freedom I have used in exposing to view, what you could have wished to remain concealed. If you feel shame as well as sorrow in acknowledging that the picture I have drawn is too true in all its outlines, rest assured that your case is not singular. I frankly own that similar doubts do occasionally darken and distract my own mind. And from conversations on the subject with a variety of Christian people in different parts of the country, and of different ages, and sexes, and attainments, I am brought to the conclusion that your experience and mine is by no means uncommon. Indeed, I may say, that, on this point at least, it is in painful harmony with the experience of the people of God in general.

I have incidentally hinted that these distressing and dreadful doubts may proceed from the Tempter. At a future stage of our discussions, it will be necessary for me to advert to *the causes* in which doubts of both classes have their origin: at present my object has been simply to state, as an undeniable fact, that doubts of the first class are prevalent. This fact is the more remarkable, as no Christian can allege a deficiency of proof for the existence of God, or for the divine authority and authenticity of the Holy Scriptures. Sceptics may still cavil—Christians dare not. The proof is overwhelming. No book has ever undergone so sifting, I might say, so torturing an examination, at the hand of foes as well as of friends, as the Bible has done. And it is most satisfactory to know that every objection which has been raised in every succeeding age, has directly tended to multiply the accumulating mass of evidence in favour of its high and exclusive title to be called, what it truly is, *the Word of God.*

But although the publications on all the various departments of Scripture evidence are numerous, yet it cannot be denied that the number of Christians who peruse either learned or popular treatises on the subject, is comparatively small. The men who study theology as a profession, have their attention directed to this large and important branch of sacred literature, as a matter of course. For it is indispensably requisite in those who are destined to become the public conductors of the worship of God, and expositors of his word, that they themselves be thoroughly established in the belief that "holy men of God spake as they were moved by the Holy Ghost," 2 Pet 1:21; and that what they committed to writing contains a true revelation of the character, and of the works, and of the will, of that Self-existent and Almighty Being, whose creatures we are, and to whom we all stand responsible. The ordained ministers of the Gospel, beyond all other Christians, need to be well and always armed with ready arguments to defend the truth against the assaults of its enemies, and to "answer every man that asketh them a reason of the hope that is in them, with meekness and fear," 1 Pet 3:15. So must they likewise be well furnished, as stewards of the manifold mysteries of God, for the great work of the ministry, whereunto they are called. And surely their qualifications would be very incomplete, if, when they hear of any of the people of their charge being harassed with doubts regarding truths of fundamental importance, they were unable to expose the unreasonableness of such doubts, and to assist in building them up in their most holy faith.

It is the case, however, that in our days there is very little preaching on the evidences of divine revelation in general, or of the Christian religion in particular. Such preaching may be useful to persons of a sceptical turn of mind; but in my opinion it will never be of much use to Christian people, who are occasionally afflicted with that description of doubts, whereof alone I now write. And the reason is simply this. Although you, or I, or others, are annoyed with these intruders, which perplex and unsettle our minds at the time, still in our deliberate judgment we are convinced, not only that there is a God, but that he is as truly the God of the Bible as he is the maker of heaven and of earth. Our deliverance from the darkness in which these sad doubts envelope us, must be wrought out by other means than arguments, even of the most conclusive kind. And, besides, as it rarely happens that ministers are apprised of the doubts under which their people may be labouring, they cannot so much as attempt to apply a remedy. In truth, such doubts as we are now alluding to, are suffered to lie hidden in the inmost recesses of the heart, and are seldom divulged even to the nearest and dearest of our friends. And all who are troubled with them can declare that they do not arise from dissatisfaction with the evidences. They are not intentional. They are involuntary. And persons who are conversant with the whole body of Christian evidences, are just as liable to be assailed by them, as the most uneducated and simple-minded of the children of God. To the learned and the unlearned, these doubts come unbidden and unlooked for. They are unwelcome guests. So long as they remain, they are disliked and dreaded. And their departure is hailed with joyous gratitude, as a release from the tormenting oppression of a strong and cruel enemy.

You will recollect my remark, that excepting professional men, there are few Christians who consult books on the evidences; and yet it is rather a striking fact, that those who devote none of their time to this branch of study, will, generally speaking, be found as stedfast in the belief of the inspiration, and authenticity, and genuineness of the Scriptures, as the most patient and laborious scholar can be. I grant that the superiority of the latter over the former would be great in conducting a connected and powerful line of argument against any sophistical or artful opponent. But so far as the satisfaction of their own minds is concerned, the one is as much at rest as the other can possibly be; and indeed the likelihood is, that the plain unlearned Christian has, in this respect, an advantage over his erudite brother, whose faith may have lost somewhat of its simplicity, and whose mind may have become in some measure contaminated, by familiarity with the opinions of all sorts of heretics and infidels, as the result of his much reading. And if you have ever reflected on this interesting subject, perhaps you will agree with me in thinking, that, as in professedly Christian countries, and especially in our own, we are trained from infancy to regard the Bible, and to speak of it, as a book like no other—as a holy book—as the word of God; so the impression thus early made, becomes lasting. It may not always grow with our growth, and strengthen with our strength. But it is too deep to be easily eradicated in afterlife. In this way the bulk of professing Christians acknowledge the Bible to have had a divine origin, without having ever dreamt of examining its claims, and they would be sorely puzzled for an answer were they required to furnish a distinct and satisfactory proof of what they profess to believe. It is otherwise, however, with those who are Christians in sincerity, and not merely in name: for, whilst they retain and venerate their early impressions, they have had superadded thereunto the teaching of that same Holy Spirit by whom the Holy Scriptures were originally indited. These heaven-taught Christians discern the stamp of truth on every page of their Bible. And in its whole character, and contents, and structure, when opened up and applied to their minds by the Spirit of Truth, they discover an irresistible evidence of its being a true revelation given to man, for the wisest and most gracious purposes, by the God of creation, and providence, and redemption. They do not require to travel through many volumes in search of what are called the *external* evidences. These, indeed, are abundant, and they are of great value too, in a certain sense. But the *internal* evidence is so perceptible, and withal so satisfying, that the vast majority of Christians seek for no other. And still it is true that almost every individual amongst them has to tell of times, thank God they are often only moments, when the most hateful and hellish doubts, regarding all the truths he holds most dear to his soul, unhinge the firmness of his faith, and spread a covering of horror over all his hopes and prospects.

I do not know how it has been with you, my friend, but I enjoyed the unspeakable advantage of having God-fearing parents, whose desire and delight it ever was to inculcate early lessons of piety, and, to the utmost of their ability, to imbue the hearts of their children with the principles of true godliness. I can recollect being taught, when very young, not only to read, but even to handle the Bible with reverence; so that it always stood alone, and was never mixed up with the little books of amusement, which constitute a portion of the playthings in every nursery. No: the Bible was not to be played with. The Bible was the book in which God speaks to us—the great God who made us, who made all things; the holy God who cannot look upon sin; the just God who cannot but punish sin; the good God who sent his only begotten Son into the world to save sinners. The Bible was God's book; and it tells us about God; and about sin and salvation; and about heaven and hell: and the Bible never was to be touched or looked upon as a common thing. This was a part of my nursery education. And I feel even now when well-advanced in life, that I owe a deep debt of gratitude to those earthly parents, who, from childhood, instructed me in the fear of my Father who is in heaven, and inspired my youthful heart with a holy reverence for his holy word.

Having said this much about myself, while yet a boy, I trust you will forgive my adding that, when sovereign grace arrested me amidst the follies and gaieties of youth, and taught me, ere I had reached my manhood, that knowledge of the only true God, and of Jesus Christ whom he hath sent, which is life eternal, I then began to understand, and to relish, and to value the Holy Scriptures, and to feel in my heart what I had hitherto from education only acknowledged with my lips, that they are "given by inspiration of God," 2 Tim 3:16. This was an important and delightful conclusion at which to arrive. But I read no works on the evidences, until I became a student in divinity. And as I continued a stranger to doubts up to the period, when through mercy I was brought as a convinced and humbled sinner to believe in the one provided Saviour; so I have found ever since that my whole course of reading on the subject of evidences has had no power whatever either to prevent the intrusion of sceptical doubts into my mind, or to dispel them after they have effected a lodgment.

I submit these statements, in reference to the workings of my own mind, merely as an individual and specific illustration of the general principles laid down in the preceding pages, and which appear to me to be correct. In regard to the frequency, or the multiplicity, or the frightfulness, or any other peculiarity of the doubts which respect God himself and his revealed word, it ought to be readily conceded that there are many varieties in the experiences of different Christians, as also, that there are many variations in the experience of the same Christian at different periods; but yet a sameness is found to exist, such as might be expected among the children of one family, and which warrants the persuasion that none of the redeemed and adopted children of God are altogether exempted from doubts of *the first class*, according to our proposed division. Such doubts are experienced by the whole family during their present state of trial; and there are seasons when even the best established and most matured Christians are doomed to suffer under their attacks. This kind of doubts, however, may be compared to the passing clouds which obscure the sun only for a very little while. These seasons of doubt resemble the violent storms, which are only of occasional occurrence, and of short duration. Yes, my friend, after dwelling on the distress and horrors in which doubts of this class so often involve true and stedfast Christians, it is very refreshing and cheering to think that they are never permanent; nor are they permitted, as is the case with doubts of the other class, a place in any system of personal and practical religion of which I ever heard. No Christian, indeed, could live for any length of time under their deadening influence.

The sum and substance of my observations amount to this, that doubts of the first class, which respect God, have these two peculiarities. In the first place, *they are common to all Christians*, whether learned or unlearned, whether young in the divine life, or mellowed with a rich and lengthened enjoyment of the Holy Spirit's power to enlighten and sanctify and comfort. And, in the next place, *they never assume a fixed or systematic character*. Like the lightning whose flashes vanish almost as soon as they have surprised and dazzled us, these doubts come suddenly, and cause alarm; but happily, they are transient visitors. In some instances the visits may be more frequent, and more painful, and of longer duration than in others. But it is not too much to say, that for the most part, *they are only occasional and temporary*.

The second class of doubts to which we must now give some consideration, have respect to ourselves—that is, *to our own belief in, and concern with, that revelation which God has been pleased to make to man.* This is very different ground from that which we have just left; and were a minute examination to be attempted, we might chance to meet with incidents of sufficient interest to occupy many pages. Having already, however, devoted so large a portion of my Letter to the doubts which have respect to God, and which, I do believe, are less noticed, or, at any rate, less spoken of, than their importance would entitle them to be—my remarks must now be more brief than otherwise I had designed. But this is the less to be regretted, inasmuch as our selfishness is ever apt to give a greater prominence than enough to those doubts which directly concern our own present comfort and everlasting well-being; and on this account they are made the gloomy theme of many of the private thoughts, and social conversations of Christian people.

The doubts which belong to this Second Class have extensive ramifications. They shoot out in numerous directions, and assume an almost endless variety of forms and aspects. But they are all found to centre in a tacit or avowed uncertainty on the subject of *personal salvation*. That a subject so infinitely important should command supreme attention, and excite the most intense anxiety, is not only altogether right and proper, but it is in the highest degree desirable. Would to God that we saw among our friends and neighbours, and felt within ourselves, far more of this kind of anxiety than we usually either see or feel! And when a thing so great as everlasting salvation is at stake; salvation from sin and death and hell; a salvation only procured by the blood-shedding of God's own Son; a salvation which exalts fallen man in dignity and glory far above the angels who have kept their first estate; I say, my dear friend, when the salvation which is by the faith of Jesus Christ is contemplated negatively and positively, we can scarcely wonder at the doubts which arise in the minds of anxious inquirers, whether it is possible that they are participants of so boundless a blessing. There is, on the one hand, a strong natural thirsting after immortality and happiness. On the other hand, conscience joins issue with the Bible, in declaring that our sinfulness justly subjects us to misery and death. And when we contrast the promises of pardoning mercy to the penitent, with the threatenings of divine vengeance against the wicked, it is nothing strange that the mind should sometimes vacillate betwixt hope and fear, and sink into a state of doubt whether we are exercising a true, or deceiving ourselves with an imaginary, faith in the only Saviour of sinners.

I would not be understood as offering any apology for doubts. It rather falls within my object, in admitting their existence, to mourn over their extensive prevalence and their pernicious influence. But I have been led, in some measure, to explain how easily we are ensnared by them, in consequence either of imperfect views of the Gospel, or of a weak and wavering faith. Be this as it may, I imagine the fact is unquestionable, that, of those who seldom or never doubt, or profess to doubt, that our Lord Jesus Christ is a divine and all sufficient Saviour, there are very many who seldom or never are free from perplexing and painful doubts about their own salvation.

It thus appears that there is an obvious propriety in drawing a line of distinction between the doubts which have respect to God, and those which have respect to ourselves. And yet I willingly admit that this distinction is rather conventional than real. For, as the greater necessarily includes the lesser, so at the times, when there is a felt misgiving of the fixedness of our faith in those parts of the Divine character and of the Gospel revelation in which, as guilty creatures, we are most particularly interested—there will be a corresponding misgiving in the persuasion we were previously enjoying of forgiveness and safety. The moment we suspect the truth of God's promise, it becomes impossible, with any kind of consistency, to hold fast the hope of eternal life. And perhaps it is nothing more than just, although it may be resented as unkind, to say, that many of those who entertain doubts of their personal salvation, deceive themselves in thinking that their faith firmly embraces all that God has been pleased to reveal and promise. For it strikes me as a sound logical deduction, that a full and unhesitating belief of the mercy of God in Christ Jesus, will bring into the believer's mind a sweet and satisfying enjoyment of that promised mercy which his sense of sin makes so desirable to him. And, in this way, an assured hope of salvation will naturally accompany an assured faith in God the Saviour.

But let us not involve ourselves, or the subject of our present correspondence, with any metaphysical niceties or knotty disputations. I have said there is *a propriety* in distinguishing betwixt the one class of doubts and the other. There is *a convenience* in it too. And I think, also, it is not destitute of *some foundation in truth*. My own feelings, for instance, tell me it is a rare thing to be much, if at all, taken up with our own present spiritual condition or future prospects, when temptation beclouds the mind, and raises a storm of doubts respecting God himself. To a Christian man there is something so inexpressibly awful in the bare possibility of the Bible being stript of its inspiration, or of his having no God before whom to bow, and no Saviour on whom to rely, that it overwhelms him entirely; and for the time this one doubt possesses his mind to the exclusion of all that is selfish. In like manner, we know that, from a diseased mind, or even from bodily disease partially impairing the mental faculties, and perhaps from various other causes of a less ostensible nature, Christian people are sometimes so completely swallowed up in personal anxieties, as to judge from their own feelings, that the doubts which disturb them have no reference whatever to the revealed truths which are the objects of faith, but are altogether confined to their own belief of these truths, or rather to their own interest in them as believers. But, in making these concessions, which justify our adherence to the ordinary method of separating the doubts which directly affect the divine character and revelation, from those which more directly affect ourselves, I cannot renounce the opinion already expressed, that, amongst doubting Christians, the number is great who labour under self-deception in supposing that *their* doubts extend not beyond the one point of their own personal salvation; and in the next Letter I shall explain the scriptural grounds on which this opinion is rested. Nevertheless, we must give these doubters credit for sincerity, in the professions which they make. And, with few exceptions, we hear them all professing a firm belief in the inspiration of the Scriptures, and in the great truths which are there revealed. They believe in the grace and love of God as well as in his justice and holiness. They acknowledge that the Lord Jesus Christ is a perfect Saviour, and say they do not doubt his power and willingness to save to the uttermost all who come unto God by him. They express entire satisfaction with the meritorious completeness of his atonement, and righteousness, and intercession. And they receive without hesitation the whole record of his sacrificial sufferings and death; and of his glorious resurrection and ascension. But they declare that the spring of their disquietude and uncertainty lies within themselves. And what they doubt is, whether *they* are partakers of the grace of God, and the objects of his electing love; whether God is reconciled *to them* in Christ Jesus, having freely pardoned *their* unnumbered offences. They doubt whether the divine Saviour has saved *them* from the wrath to came; or sanctified *them* by his holy Spirit of promise; or given *to them* eternal life. Or, what amounts to the same thing, they cannot satisfy themselves that *they* have come to Christ in compliance with his gracious invitation. They know how blessed and happy is the condition of those who do believe in him; but they discover not *in themselves* the evidences of a true and living faith; and therefore they are in doubt whether *they* really are resting on the right foundation, and making the crucified Redeemer *their* only confidence and hope.

The description now given is necessarily general. You could not expect me to detail special cases. The strength and intensity of the doubts, as well as the frequency of their recurrence, and the particular truth or truths assailed by them at the time, may be all as various as are the mental temperaments, and the Christian attainments, and even the personal appearances, of the individuals suffering under their influence. And certainly it is much to be lamented for their own sakes, and for the sake of Christ, and of his cause in the world, that we have so many *doubters* amongst those who bear the name, and ought to be enjoying the privileges, of *believers*.

The doubts which respect ourselves, and which we rank in the second class, differ in some important features from those to which I have directed your attention as belonging to the first class. Did it so happen that these doubts were as universally disliked and dreaded, and were as occasional and temporary, as are the doubts which have respect to God; then, although the persons affected by them were far more numerous than they are, I am sure that less dishonour would be done to God, and less injury to Christians themselves.

I do believe that the most assured and holiest of Christians have, now and then, a short-lived doubt of their being in a state of grace, shooting through their minds like a poisoned arrow. It takes them by surprise, and wounds them sharply; but they know where to find the healing balm, and they soon recover their lost assurance. And even with regard to Christians who are not at the time assured of their spiritual safety, or who, it may be, never have attained that assured faith in the Saviour which should yield them the assurance of salvation, I know it to be the case that many groan under the discomforting pressure of their doubts, and earnestly desire deliverance. Their situation excites compassion; and concerning them we have good hopes that their day of deliverance is not distant. But it is not so with all doubting Christians. Some there are, from whom we cannot withhold an acknowledgment of brotherhood in Christ, who are, nevertheless, so indifferent about their growth in grace, and so regardless of spiritual comfort, and so reluctant to break up their connection with the world, and to live in close communion with God, that they allow their doubts to become *permanent*, and seem contented to remain in this unhealthy condition, without attempting any resolute or continuous efforts to burst asunder their chains and fetters. Their case is not a hopeful one; but God in mercy may rouse them from their present supineness; and an enlarged supply of the Spirit of all grace will urge them onwards to the happy knowledge that they have passed from death unto life, and are accepted in the Beloved. And there are others who appear much more alive to their spiritual concerns than the persons just alluded to; but we cannot speak of them as being in a better or more hopeful condition. I believe they really seek to walk with God in the way of his commandments and ordinances. They take pleasure in hearing the Gospel preached, and in Christian converse with those who are the followers of Jesus. They are watchful over their general conduct, and desire to live as for eternity. There is much about them to call forth our commendation and esteem; but through the delusive power of some strangely perverted notions on the doctrine of assurance, they give a deliberate and determined preference to a state of doubt. The doubts entertained by this description of Christians must be denounced as worse than any already specified, because they are *systematical*. They are adopted and advocated from choice. They are sanctioned and encouraged as an element in the religion which they profess. Thus they intentionally continue doubters during the whole period of their religious life, and complacently bring forward their doubts as evidences of Christian humility and diffidence. If you have never chanced to meet such people you will wonder at this statement. And well you may. But I can answer for its accuracy. For I have been in places where doubts of this very obnoxious cast are plentiful; and where the men who stand out the most conspicuous from amongst their neighbours, as the highest professors of godliness, and the loudest talkers about Christian doctrines and privileges, are the foremost to condemn that strong and simple faith to which our blessed Saviour ever awarded his warmest approval; and to patronize those baneful doubtings which Jesus rebuked, when he said to Peter, "O thou of little faith! wherefore didst thou doubt?"

And here I must recall to your remembrance a remark thrown out in the introductory part of this Letter, when winding up the proof that doubters are something more and better than mere professors or unbelievers. I there supposed it possible that men might profess doubts, which they do not actually experience, just as we know that multitudes profess a creed which they do not believe. When, therefore, we hear of sensible and pious people being all their life long doubtful whether they are partakers of that faith in Christ Jesus which justifies, and sanctifies, and saves a sinner; and systematically maintaining the utility, and also the desirableness of a state of mind so unscriptural, and unhealthy, and unhappy, we can hardly refrain from suspecting their honesty. And if they are in their hearts enjoying confidence towards God as having freely pardoned all their sins, and being at peace with them through Jesus Christ, whilst with their tongues they speak of their doubts and fears, merely with the view of gaining from men a false reputation for humility, then do they subject themselves to the charge of hypocrisy. In either case, whether they are honest or hypocritical in formally countenancing those doubts, in themselves or in others, to which certainly the oracles of unerring truth give no countenance, their condition cannot, in the nature of things, be spiritually prosperous. And to me it appears to be all the less enviable, and the more to be deplored, on account of the light and knowledge of which it is understood that this particular class of doubters is possessed.

I have now finished the observations I had intended to submit to you on the doubts belonging to the second class, which I believe to be prevalent in the Christian community. But lest there should be any misconception of the strong terms in which I have repudiated doubts, I beg to assure you that my earnest aim and desire is, not to check genuine humility and to foster spiritual pride and presumption, but precisely the reverse. The professed disciples of "the meek and lowly" Jesus should diligently cultivate a spirit of truest and deepest humility at all times; and by all means it is their duty to abstain from placing "confidence in the flesh." But it is equally their duty to rejoice in the Lord, and to rejoice always. They are not required to rejoice in anything *they* have done or can do, but in what has been done in them and for them by the sovereign grace of our Lord Jesus Christ. But they who doubt of their interest in the Saviour and in his great salvation, and especially they who intentionally and systematically continue in a state of doubt all their lives, never can, or, at least never ought to rejoice. Gloom and melancholy best befit those who are in doubt whether God smiles or frowns upon them. And the existence and continuance of their doubts, so far from evincing the humility which becomes a sinner saved by divine grace, are proofs that the heart in which they dwell has not yet entirely surrendered itself to the obedience of Christ. Yes: they are proofs of that heart still maintaining a disguised independence of Him who is our *only* Saviour; who is *all* our salvation; and who never will become the peace-giving guest of any heart until self is crucified and wholly cast out.

After the exposition which has been given of the different kinds of doubts that are prevalent among Christians of all denominations, and the different ways in which they are manifested, it is quite necessary that we should institute some inquiry into their various exciting causes, and likewise into the most efficient remedies that can be applied either for their prevention or removal. This interesting and important department of the general subject will demand our careful consideration, but not until I have placed before you, in the six following Letters, a tolerably minute analysis of the very pernicious influence which these doubts exercise over the feelings and conduct of Christians towards God, and over their own characters and comforts, and over the men of the world, who fortify themselves in their own evil practices and prejudices, in consequence of the inconsistencies and the moroseness which are so common amongst the professors of Christianity.

May God stablish our hearts with grace, and ever keep us stedfast in the faith and obedience of Christ Jesus, that we may enjoy the light of his reconciled countenance, and the comforts of the Holy Ghost.

I remain, yours, etc.

LETTER 4

THE PERNICIOUS INFLUENCE OF DOUBTS
I. THEY DISHONOUR GOD

This branch of our general subject is extensive.—Doubts are deformities in the character of a believer.—But the Church of Rome acts as their advocate and apologist.—So do the Oxford tractarians.—So do some evangelical ministers in our Reformed Churches.—Three propositions illustrative of the pernicious influence of doubts.—I. They are dishonouring to God.—II. They are prejudicial to the Christian character and comfort of the doubter.—III. They exhibit the religion of Christ to the world in a false and forbidding aspect.—The *first* proposition claims our present attention.—Doubts having reference to salvation, either as it is revealed in Scripture, or experienced by the believer, dishonour God.—To doubt his veracity and faithfulness is a great offence; and is commonly followed by doubts of his wisdom, his love, his righteousness, and even his omnipotence.—God is most dishonoured by the doubts of spiritually enlightened men.—The case of Saul and the Amalekites.—Under the Gospel, the divine command is to believe in the Saviour.—Disobedience or doubt disparages all the attributes of God, and incurs his displeasure.

My dear Friend,

We now advance to the elucidation of a very extensive and important branch of our general subject; and I think it must be admitted, that the pernicious influence of doubts, which is felt by so many persons, and manifested in so many ways, is deserving of our most serious attention, on account not only of its diversified and insinuating operations, but especially of its very practical bearings.

It appears so evident that doubts are in their own nature marks of imperfection in the exercise of faith, and consequently, that they must be as blots and stains in the character of a believer, that, were we not so much accustomed to anomalies and inconsistencies among professing Christians, it would be difficult to imagine how any men or body of men, should have the boldness to act as their advocate, and even as their apologist. You are aware, however, that the Romish Church systematically encourages her members to entertain doubts respecting points of Christian doctrine, as well as respecting their own spiritual state and prospects. This seems to arise out of two principal causes: the first of which is, the undue importance attached to what are called the traditions of the church, to the great disparagement of the Holy Scriptures; and the second is, the desire of the priesthood to strengthen and uphold their unwarrantable power over the consciences of the people. The Oxford tractarians, too, in perfect consistency with their semi-popish principles, have expressed themselves very strongly on the difficulty, or almost impossibility, as they imagine, of escaping from doubt in regard to any one department of divine knowledge, or of Christian hope. But are you aware that even some evangelical ministers in our Reformed Churches are the avowed supporters and abettors of doubts? I do not mean to impugn the conscientiousness of their motives. I feel assured that their object is neither to exalt themselves, nor to detract from the authority of the pure and infallible word of God. They are certainly labouring under mistaken views. But at present I merely state the fact, that, in our own highly-favoured land, we have pastors who seem to dread an assured faith, and the assurance of personal salvation, as they would the entrance of some dangerous epidemic amongst their flocks. How you are affected by the existence of such a state of things I do not know; but I confess it does appear to me to be very strange, and very wrong, and very much to be deplored. And, although it might be somewhat presumptuous to determine the cause to which it ought to be assigned, yet it is another melancholy fact, which cannot be contradicted, that, in certain districts of the country, the prevailing religion of the people is so overrun with what our good old reformers stigmatized as "a doubtsome faith," that a man's Christian attainments and excellence are actually measured and judged of by the doubts which he entertains of his own Christianity! This too does appear very strange, and indeed it is also very absurd. But whether these people would meekly submit to have their Christianity doubted by friends and neighbours around them, is a delicate question, which may be left to themselves to answer. It is by no means my intention to throw down the gauntlet, and involve myself in controversy with any class of persons. I have no delight in controversy, and most earnestly desire to avoid a disputatious spirit and manner in treating the subject on which we are now about to enter. I trust you will give me credit for wishing to contend against doubts, rather than against doubters. And, unless your own mind is so blinded by prejudice as to be wholly impervious to the light of truth, I hope to succeed in proving the three following propositions, as illustrative of the pernicious influence of doubts:—

First, they are dishonouring to God.
Second, they are prejudicial to the Christian character and comfort of the doubter.
Third, they exhibit the religion of Christ to the world in a false and forbidding point of view.

The truth of any one of these particulars, when clearly realized, should be sufficient to guard us against the indulgence of a doubting spirit, and to convince us that those must be greatly in error who deliberately cherish doubts in themselves, or in other Christians. But when all those particulars are seen and felt to be true, then surely their combined effect must be strongly condemnatory of doubts.

Of the three propositions enumerated above, the *first* and the *third* require no lengthened demonstrations. They are almost self-evident. For the sake of distinctness, however, to each of them a separate letter will be devoted. But the *second* proposition comes into direct contact with the whole extent and variety of Christian experience, and cannot so speedily be discussed. It brings us into a large and interesting sphere of investigation, which ought not to be superficially treated. It leads to inquiries about the nature and tendencies of many of the most vital gospel truths on which we can meditate. And therefore you must not quarrel with me, although the proofs and illustrations, which it may be needful to adduce, should extend over a succession of letters.

The pernicious influence of doubts is the one subject at present before us. But as it has various aspects, it is only right that we should first of all view it in its aspect towards God. This aspect is twofold. Doubts dishonour God, which sufficiently indicates their evil nature; and doubts subject us to his righteous displeasure, which certainly is an unequivocal evidence of their evil consequences. You will therefore expect me to show *in what way, and to what extent, doubts are dishonouring to God*. But to prevent mistakes, allow me to remind you, that I speak only of those kinds of doubts, which claimed our attention in the former letter;—doubts which respect God himself, and his revealed word; or doubts which respect our own interest in what he has revealed and promised; including the two classes of occasional and temporary, and systematic and permanent, into which such doubts were divided. Or, perhaps it may be convenient to narrow these restrictions still farther, and to confine our thoughts to doubts which respect God in the character of a Saviour, and ourselves as partakers of his salvation. Indeed, the doubts about which we are at this time to institute some inquiry, have an exclusive reference to the subject of salvation, either as it is revealed in the Scriptures, or as it is impressed upon the heart and life of the Christian. And by keeping this in remembrance, we shall avoid the necessity of subsequent explanations, and likewise preserve our minds from much perplexity and confusion. But still there needs be no hesitation in affirming, that the doubts entertained by any true believer, whether they have reference to the character of God as the sole author of salvation, or to the state of the Christian himself as the recipient of salvation, are most dishonouring to God.

Now, my dear friend, it may not be improper to remark, at the commencement of the illustrations I have to offer you, that, as *the divine character*, in its glorious completeness, consists of many distinct attributes or properties, *so the divine revelation* given by God to man, as a whole, is made up of many separate parts. And it is only in the careful study of the separate truths which are revealed to us, and of the several attributes which belong to God, that we can attain a comprehensive knowledge and a firm belief of the divine revelation, or of the divine character. But our study of the inspired volume is often very defective. Hence it is that many Christian men, who have a general belief of the truth of the Holy Scriptures as a whole, are nevertheless chargeable with harbouring doubts about some of its particular statements; and whilst in a general way, they believe in the God whom the Scriptures alone make known to us, they give indulgence to many doubts in regard to some one or other of his essential attributes. I do not recollect to have heard of any Christian doubting the holiness of God. But to cherish secretly in their bosoms, and even openly in words to give utterance to their suspicions of his veracity and faithfulness, of his wisdom and knowledge, of his goodness and love, of his rectitude and righteousness, yea, even of his almighty power, is, alas! by no means uncommon. And it is in these ways that doubting Christians dishonour the God of their salvation.

I have placed *the veracity and faithfulness* of God at the head of this list, because doubts respecting this one moral attribute will necessarily open a door for doubts respecting every other attribute of his character. I place it foremost because, if I may so express it, he has taken especial pains to obviate the incredulity of our sinful hearts, and to inspire our confidence in the entire truthfulness of his own character, and also of those declarations and promises of his word which so brightly reflect the nature of his desires and dispositions towards us. The inspired psalmist could say to his Lord, "Thou hast magnified thy word above all thy name," Ps 138:2. Hence if we really wish to honour God, we must believe his word, without suspecting his sincerity. We must respond without hesitancy to the truth of what he tells us of himself, and of all that he reveals concerning ourselves. To pick and choose among his testimonies and his promises is a most offensive and unwarrantable mode of procedure. To receive some portions of Scripture because they harmonise with our own ideas and inclinations, and to reject others because we cannot comprehend and appreciate them, is to place the glorious Majesty of heaven on a level with erring and shortsighted mortals upon earth. How very unbecoming,—nay, should I not rather say, how sinful is such conduct! Surely they who profess to believe that the Bible is an *inspired* book, bring themselves under an imperative obligation to acknowledge the stamp of immutable and eternal truth upon its every line and letter. It behoves us to know and acknowledge, not merely that the Bible contains a true revelation from God, but likewise that the things revealed are true, and that he who reveals them is himself the God of truth. Here you will observe that I have grouped together three things which are distinct, and which may be separated from each other. There is, first of all, the book; then its contents; and lastly its author. And were we dealing with the production of a human mind, you would at once perceive how possible it is to admit that such a man is the author of such a work, without feeling satisfied with the accuracy of his views and statements. We believe it to be true that he is an author; but we may have good reasons for questioning the truth of what he has written. And even were we satisfied on this point,—did we believe that truth pervades the whole volume, we might be justified in withholding from the author an implicit reliance on his veracity. A man who is notorious for duplicity may, nevertheless, tell an unvarnished tale. A man who has earned for himself the disreputable character of a liar, may sometimes speak or write what is strictly and altogether true. But the Bible is the production of the divine mind, and we need to beware what judgments we form either of its contents or of its author. "All Scripture is given by inspiration of God." All Scripture is solemnly and truly designated *"The Word of God."* What was repeatedly testified from heaven to the apostle John, in reference to some of the sublime visions and revelations with which he was favoured, may, with propriety, be applied to the whole inspired volume,—"These words are true and faithful,"—"These sayings are faithful and true,"—*"these are the true sayings of God,"* Rev 19:9; Rev 21:5; Rev 22:6. And every Christian should retain fresh in his recollection the memorable prayer in behalf of his disciples which our incarnate Lord addressed to his invisible Father, "Sanctify them through thy truth; thy word is truth," John 17:17. *"Thy word is truth."* How emphatic is this short sentence! How replete with preciousness! How sweetly it encourages our faith! But, oh! how completely it puts our doubts to shame and silence! The holy men, too, who lived in early times, and who possessed only a part of that blessed book, with the whole of which we are intrusted, held the word of God in the highest estimation. Agur, the son of Jakeh, has said, "Every word of God is pure," Prov 30:5. *"Pure."* How beautiful is this expression! Pure as the crystal stream, without one atom of defilement! Pure as the refined metal, without one speck of dross! Pure as truth itself, without the smallest admixture of error! The psalmist evidently delighted in the same idea. His language is, "The words of the Lord are pure words; as silver tried in a furnace of earth, purified seven times," Ps 12:6. "Thy word is very pure; therefore thy servant loveth it," Ps 119:140. And to this idea of the most perfect purity, he adds, in other psalms, that of an unchanging and never-ending permanence: "The Lord is good: his mercy is everlasting: his truth endureth to all generations," Ps 100:5. "Happy is he that hath the God of Jacob for his help; whose hope is in the Lord his God, which made heaven and earth, the sea, and all that therein is; which keepeth truth for ever," Ps 146:5-6. It is instructive to notice in these passages how powerfully the eternal truth of God is introduced to confirm our confidence in his goodness and mercy; in the help he promises, and in the hopes he inspires. *"He keepeth truth for ever."* What a rock is this for us to rest upon! He never forgets his promise. His covenant stands fast for aye. He is faithful to every word. His sayings, like himself, are subject to no mutation. *"His truth endureth to all generations."*

Even Balaam, the soothsayer, who loved the wages of unrighteousness, and who did not enjoy the advantage of any written revelation whatever, was constrained, through the inspiration of "the Spirit of truth," to exclaim, "God is not a man, that he should lie; neither the son of man, that he should repent: hath he said, and shall he not do it? Or hath he spoken, and shall he not make it good?" Num 23:19. And unless we submit to the impulses of the same Spirit,—unless we cordially entertain the same exalted conceptions of his veracity and faithfulness, we withhold from God that honour which he justly claims from us, and to which not even the doubting Christian dare deny that *He* is most justly entitled.

The Bible is like no other book. Of it alone the unmixed and undoubted character is truth—threefold truth. The book is truly a revelation from heaven: it is no imposture. Its contents are all "faithful and true:" there is neither mistake nor error to be found in it. And of the author we can say, that he is the only true God, and at the same time the God of truth only,—the God with whom it is impossible to err or to deceive. Unenlightened and unconverted men may, by the exercise of their rational faculties, attain the conviction that "the Scriptures are given by inspiration of God," and yet they may remain ignorant of the spiritual truths which are revealed in these Holy Scriptures; and also ignorant of the true character of God himself. But we are not speaking of such persons. Doubters are spiritually enlightened men. The grace of God has visited their souls, and chased away their natural darkness. Their understandings have been opened to understand the Scriptures. The truths of God's word, and the truthfulness of God's own character, have been applied to their hearts and consciences by the power of the Holy Ghost. And yet they do not stand fast in the faith, and quit them like men. They fall away from their stedfastness. They yield to the insinuating and pernicious influence of doubt. Oh! how grievously such persons dishonour the God of their salvation! They forget that his forgiving grace is altogether spontaneous and gratuitous; and that the salvation of sinners by Jesus Christ is a work already finished and complete. They reason with themselves about the veracity of the Scripture statements. They shrink from relying on the faithfulness of the divine promises. They become suspicious of God's infinite wisdom. They are doubtful whether they are the objects of his love in Christ Jesus. They quarrel with the righteousness of his providential dispensations. They question his very power to pardon or to save. And, in all this, the dishonour done unto God is greatly increased and aggravated by the grace he has already bestowed upon them, and by ingratitude for what they have actually been made to experience of the renovating and comforting power of "the truth as it is in Jesus." The defect, in most cases, lies not so much in their knowledge as in their faith; and this is another circumstance which renders their doubts the more culpable. We must make large allowances for persons whose scriptural knowledge is very limited. But the great mass of doubters cannot plead ignorance of Gospel truths. They know much, but they also doubt much. Their faith is not commensurate with their knowledge, and their doubts hinder them from walking up to the measure of light which they enjoy. They resemble men in a mist, who cannot see afar off; and to whom surrounding objects appear of unnatural magnitude, and in distorted forms and proportions. The dense and deceitful atmosphere of doubts imparts an undue importance, and a dangerous prominence to what concerns their individual comfort and safety. In the matter of salvation, they are so engrossed with selfishness that their views of God's character become dim, and they perceive not how his object is to promote and secure his own glory, when he reveals himself as the Saviour of sinners. And in dishonouring him by their doubts of the exceeding riches of his grace in Christ Jesus, and by their ingratitude for his former lovingkindnesses towards them, they also subject themselves to his righteous displeasure. "O thou of little faith: wherefore didst thou doubt?" How mild is the rebuke! but its very mildness makes it the more pungent. Oh! how marvellous is the patience, and forbearance, and longsuffering of God! With a father's heart he pities his faithless, erring children; and yet it is vain to expect a love like his among the most loving of earthly parents. His ways are not as our ways. His thoughts are not as our thoughts. He deals not with us after our sins. He rewards us not according to our iniquities. He multiplies pardons, and delights to show mercy, even for his own name's sake.

I have some apprehension that you will think me too general in these observations. But, to say the truth, it was my intention to be general, and to confine myself to what may be termed first principles. This seemed to be the likeliest method of exposing the deceit which Christians, whose tendencies are towards the indulgence of doubts, not unfrequently practise upon themselves. They believe the Bible to be the word of God, and with this very limited amount of belief they are too prone to rest contented. But in point of fact this is only an initiatory step. What is chiefly required of them is to believe the truth of all that the book reveals, and, still farther, to believe that everything revealed to us comes from that glorious God with whom nothing is impossible excepting the possibility of any deviation from truth. And I fondly hope it has been made apparent that doubts respecting the divine veracity and faithfulness are the evil root from whence so many other doubts spring forth to dishonour the word and the character of God.

But should you wish it, my dear friend, it is easy to be more particular; and perhaps it is necessary also to a full and correct treatment of the subject we are considering. I might, therefore, proceed to arrange, under the several divine attributes specified above, some selected texts which clearly exhibit the leading truths revealed to our faith, and with the belief of which our salvation stands connected. But as it is desirable to avoid prolixity, it may serve the purpose just as well to fix upon one important passage of Scripture, which presents us with a living exemplification of dishonouring God by a suspicious, or fearful, or doubting spirit.

The case of Saul and the Amalekites is quite in point. Samuel the prophet said unto Saul, "The Lord sent me to anoint thee to be king over his people, over Israel: now, therefore, hearken thou unto the voice of the words of the Lord. Thus saith the Lord of hosts, I remember that which Amalek did to Israel, how he laid wait for him in the way, when he came up from Egypt. Now go and smite Amalek, and utterly destroy all that they have, and spare them not; but slay both man and woman, infant and suckling, ox and sheep, camel and ass." In compliance with this terrible commission, Saul mustered his forces, and waged a successful war. He utterly destroyed all the people, but he spared alive not only Agag, the king of Amalek, but likewise the best of the spoil. "Then came the word of the Lord unto Samuel, saying, It repenteth me that I have set up Saul to be king; for he is turned back from following me, and hath not performed my commandments. And it grieved Samuel, and he cried unto the Lord all night." As soon as the king and the prophet met, Saul said unto Samuel, "Blessed be thou of the Lord: I have performed the commandment of the Lord." So low were his views of the obedience which God claims, and so thorough was his self-deception in the matter, that he considered himself entitled to commendation for having faithfully executed the divine injunction. But Samuel answered him, "What meaneth then this bleating of the sheep in mine ears, and the lowing of the oxen which I hear? And Saul said, They have brought them from the Amalekites; for the people spared the best of the sheep and of the oxen to sacrifice unto the Lord thy God." Here it will not escape your notice that Saul's infringement on the express command of God is ascribed to a religious motive. The reserved cattle were to be sacrificed in thank-offerings to *him* who had given them victory over their enemies. This *seemed* to be a praiseworthy action. But God had said, "Utterly destroy all that they have, and spare them not;" and he cannot tolerate disobedience from any motive, or for any purpose. There must be no reservations of any kind or degree. God is jealous of his own honour. To indulge our own inclinations, or to act upon our own wisdom, in opposition to his declared will, must be offensive to him, under whatever plea it is done. The obedience which God requires must be prompt and complete, as the sequel of the narrative so solemnly teaches us. "Then Samuel said unto Saul, Stay, and I will tell thee what the Lord hath said to me this night."—"The Lord anointed thee king over Israel. And the Lord sent thee on a journey, and said, Go, and utterly destroy the sinners the Amalekites, and fight against them until they be consumed. Wherefore then didst thou not obey the voice of the Lord, but didst fly upon the spoil, and didst evil in the sight of the Lord?"—"Hath the

Lord as great delight in burnt-offerings and sacrifices, as in obeying the voice of the Lord? Behold, to obey is better than sacrifice, and to hearken than the fat of rams. For rebellion is as the sin of witchcraft, and stubbornness is as iniquity and idolatry. Because thou hast rejected the word of the Lord, he hath also rejected thee from being king," 1 Sam 15:23.

We cannot read this portion of sacred history without seeing that Saul did indeed dishonour God. And yet most readers, I apprehend, will feel a kind of secret disposition to exculpate the king in some measure, and to lament the severity of the sentence passed upon him. Do not these feelings arise from the consciousness that our own obedience is defective, and from an unwillingness to submit ourselves either to the charge, or to the consequences of dishonouring God? But be this as it may, it was after listening to the prophet's remonstrance, and to the awful sentence which followed it, that Saul ceased to extenuate his disobedience, and was induced to make confession of his guilt:—"I have transgressed the commandment of the Lord." And he even goes so far as voluntarily to confess in what way he had been drawn aside from the path of duty: "I feared the people, and obeyed their voice." He then entreats for pardon, and desires to worship God. With these requests the prophet did at last comply. But Samuel was very reluctant publicly to appear again as the friend of Saul, because he said, "The Lord hath rent the kingdom of Israel from thee this day, and hath given it to a neighbour of thine, who is better than thou. And also *the Strength of Israel will not lie nor repent; for he is not a man, that he should repent.*"

When God issues a command, it cannot be recalled. When he passes a sentence, it cannot be revoked. God is not a man, that he should repent, or change his mind. His word is law. His counsel shall stand. His will must be obeyed. To suppose him insincere or changeable, and on this supposition to withhold obedience, is to do him the utmost indignity and dishonour. "*The Strength of Israel will not lie nor repent!*" Had Saul firmly believed the divine command under which he was laid, and entertained adequate ideas of the purity of God's word, and the immutability of God's character, he never would have yielded to the solicitations of the people to spare the best of the spoils. Had he not harboured doubts of the veracity and faithfulness of God he could not have consented to obey the voice of the people. It was in doing so that he dishonoured God, and involved himself in disgrace and ruin. His punishment was all the heavier, on account of the high place and power to which he had so recently been exalted. But the very honours which God had spontaneously heaped upon Saul, in making him "the head of the tribes of Israel," added much to the dishonour done to God by his ungracious and ungrateful disobedience.

An individual case, such as that of Saul, should be used as a mirror, into which we may look for the purpose of beholding the deficiency of our own faith, the dishonour which our own doubts cast upon God, and the serious losses to which our consequent disobedience subjects us; and I have called your attention to it at this time for the sake of applying to our own circumstances the principle which it develops.

It is true we have not Samuel nor any of the holy prophets addressing us personally, and with the living voice, in the name of the Lord of hosts. But we do possess the inspired Scriptures. When we read them, we read the very words of God. When we hear them, we ought to hear his voice. In them *he* speaks to all who read or hear. In them *he* utters his solemn commands, his kind invitations, his faithful warnings, and his exceeding great and precious promises. There *he* reveals himself in the glorious harmony of all his attributes as a just God and a Saviour. *He* commends to us his love, which passeth knowledge, in sending his Son into our world to suffer the deserts of our sins—to suffer in our stead, the just for the unjust, that he might bring us unto God. *He* bids us behold the Lamb of God, who taketh away the sin of the world, that our consciences may be relieved from the burden of conscious guilt. *He* tells us that he was in Christ, reconciling the world unto himself, not imputing unto them their trespasses, that we may accept the reconciliation, and enjoy peace with God through our Lord Jesus Christ. *He* encourages us to trust in him who knew no sin, but was made sin for us, that we, who have no righteousness in ourselves, might be made the righteousness of God in him. And that unbelief, and suspicions, and doubts of every kind, might be left without excuse, *he* confirms his word with his oath, for the satisfaction of poor faithless sinners, and assures us with all the solemnity and sincerity that belong to the divine character, that in Christ Jesus we have an all-sufficient and perfect Redeemer; and that in his propitiation for sin, and in the righteousness he has wrought out for sinners, there is a complete, and everlasting, and entirely gratuitous salvation.

This is a summary of the Gospel of the grace of God, which he commands us to believe. It is indeed a blessed Gospel. Is it not also a blessed command? Only believe in the provided Saviour, and the provided salvation is yours. But multitudes despise alike this blessed Gospel, and this blessed command to believe it. And it is much to be deplored, that, among those who have been taught to value the Gospel, and who have grace to believe it, there are many whose faith is too weak to raise them superior to doubts, and whose sense of the value of salvation is not sufficiently powerful to secure their entire, and humble, and thankful dependence on the Saviour. Like Saul, they believe the command that is given to them; but like him, also, they fall short in its performance. They believe that the Lord Jesus Christ is the gift of God's love, and the Saviour of sinners; but they doubt whether he is their Saviour, and whether God loves them. The word of the Lord declares, he that believeth shall be saved; but they doubt *the veracity and faithfulness* of him "*who cannot lie.*" It is written, that God hath commended his love towards us, in that while we were yet sinners Christ died for us; but they doubt *the grace and goodness* of him who is *love* itself. It is written, that Christ crucified is the wisdom of God unto the salvation of every one who believeth; but they doubt *the wisdom* of him who is "*the only wise God.*" It is written, that the righteousness of God which is by the faith of Jesus Christ is manifested by the Law and the Prophets; but in the matter of their own justification they doubt *the righteousness and rectitude* of him who is "*righteous in all his ways.*" And it may happen that they even doubt *the power* of *the Almighty* to give efficacy to the way of his own devising for the salvation of sinners.

In these, and such like ways, doubting Christians dishonour the God who reveals himself in the Scriptures of truth as the God and Father of our Lord Jesus Christ, in whom, and through whom, he is the God of all grace, and the God of our salvation. Oh! it is a sad thing that they who have the character of believers, should so often exhibit the spirit of doubters! It is very sad that any of his redeemed and adopted children should doubt the grace and love of their heavenly Father! It would indeed be incredible, were it not so extensively true, that those who know themselves to be guilty and helpless, and who, for that very reason, should the more gladly grasp at promised mercy, do nevertheless recoil from the promises, and hesitate to rest upon the word of God,—their own merciful and gracious God. Were a fellow-creature to be so treated by us,— did we challenge the accuracy of his statements, or call in question the sincerity of his promises, how keenly would he feel the insult! how forward would he be to resent the affront! But if that fellow-creature has been our special friend, and, in many ways, and at many times, given us convincing proofs of his goodwill and kindness, oh! how deeply his feelings would be wounded, were we to doubt the purity of his motives, as well as the truthfulness of his words! Such conduct would be stamped with infamy; and it would exclude us from the respect and favour of honourable men. And yet such detestable conduct towards a fellow-creature but feebly represents that dishonour which doubting Christians are continually heaping upon their best friend,—their loving and bleeding Saviour!—their patient, and forbearing, and forgiving God!

Christians in general are not anxious enough to show to the world that they are the children of faithful Abraham. How strangely the dishonouring doubts of which we have been speaking contrast with the glorifying faith which distinguished the father of the faithful, "who against hope believed in hope!" "And being not weak in faith, he considered not his own body now dead, when he was about an hundred years old, neither yet the deadness of Sarah's womb: he staggered not at the promise of God through unbelief; but was strong in faith, giving glory to God: and being fully persuaded that what he had promised he was able also to perform," Rom 4:19-21. The case of Abraham is very condemnatory of doubts and of doubters. It shows us clearly what all Christians ought to be, as the case of Saul showed us what too many Christians are. And surely it is most desirable ever to remember that we dishonour God and as effectually withhold from him the glory that is his due, by our fears, and suspicions, and doubts, as we really honour and glorify him by a firm belief of all that he says, and by an unstaggering reliance on all that he has promised.

I am fully persuaded that many doubting Christians have not the most distant intention of dishonouring God, and would be slow to admit that they do so. They shrink from the charge when it is brought against them. They are upheld by a consciousness of its injustice. And they persevere in asserting that it is neither the word nor the promise of God which they doubt, but only their own participation in the grace which bringeth salvation, and in that hope of eternal life which God has given to them that believe in the Lord Jesus Christ.

In dealing with characters of this description, it may be readily granted that those whose doubts have a direct reference to the truth of revelation in general, or to any one revealed truth in particular, bring *a more direct* dishonour upon God, than others do who honestly believe, or think they believe, that "all Scripture is given by inspiration of God," but who stand in doubt of themselves, whether they have so believed in the Saviour whom the Scriptures reveal, as to secure their forgiveness and acceptance with God. There is nothing more, however, than a difference in degree, between the two classes of doubters. For as the assurance of personal salvation is an inferential deduction from an assured faith in the revealed Saviour; so a doubt on this most deeply interesting topic is also inferential from a weak and wavering faith. And I very specially wish you to perceive, that if any sinner comes to the assurance of his own salvation in any other way than by simply and stedfastly believing the testimony of God concerning his Son, he is forsaking the only sure foundation on which so great a hope can be warrantably rested. I say this deliberately, and it well merits the prayerful consideration of all doubters. At the same time it is quite true that our professed faith is utterly worthless unless it produces "the fruits of righteousness," and makes us "careful to maintain good works." But whenever we begin to survey the amount of our good works, and to estimate the value of the fruit which we bring forth, *as evidences of our possessing a genuine faith in Christ Jesus*, we place ourselves between two snares. On the one hand, we may conscientiously form so low an estimate of our best performances, as to be driven farther away than ever from that personal assurance which ought to be desired by every Christian; or, on the other hand, we may be dangerously elated by a self-righteous complacency, and tempted to look to something in ourselves as the ground of our assurance, instead of looking with a single eye, to the finished and accepted work of "the Lord our righteousness."

It is scarcely possible to attach too much importance to what I have just stated. For myself, I have long been convinced that this looking to themselves for evidences of their faith is the very thing which brings so many Christians into a state of doubt, and hinders their attainment of a state of holy and happy assurance.* So, likewise, am I satisfied that the true and only scriptural method whereby we can escape doubts, and be assured of our own salvation, is to exercise an assured faith,—I would say, if you will pardon the quaintness of the expression, a *fiducial faith* in the word and promises of God, which reveal to us a divine Saviour, and a complete salvation. If we are to have fewer doubts respecting our own spiritual condition, we must have a firmer *trust in God*. The thing wanting is trust rather than faith; and in this lies the root of the evil. The faith of Christians is too seldom accompanied by trust. With the understanding we believe the Gospel truths which we hear or read; but the heart is kept back from a free and full reliance on the faithfulness of God to accomplish his own word. And, therefore, inasmuch as doubts of personal salvation indicate a very defective reliance upon God, on the part of those who suffer under their cruel bondage, it seems to be a legitimate and rational conclusion that even doubts of that inferential character are greatly dishonouring to the God of truth.

Is it not true, my friend, that, in his blessed word, God gives us many kind invitations, and lays upon us many urgent commands, to believe, in order to our obtaining the salvation which is by Jesus Christ our Lord? And, besides, he affectionately encourages all believers with promises,—rich and varied promises of grace to meet their every necessity. But he addresses all doubters in the language of reproof. "O thou of little faith! wherefore didst thou doubt?" Were this brief sentence engraven on the memories of all Christians, it might

---

*In Henry Martyn's Journal of date 10th June, 1806, the following instructive passage occurs: "I could draw no comfort from reflecting on my past life; and, indeed, exactly in proportion as I looked for evidences of grace, I lost that brokenness of heart which I wished to retain, and could not lie with simplicity at the foot of the cross."—Vol. i p. 456.

prove a salutary warning, and guard many from the dangers to which their proneness to doubt continually exposes them. To lie under the displeasure of God is certainly by no means an enviable condition. No Christian could deliberately wish to be placed in this unhappy condition, or to remain in it. But the displeasure which God sometimes manifests is not inconsistent with his love. He loves all his children with a special love, and always loves them. When they sin, his love constrains him to chastise them, that they may repent. When they doubt his "true and faithful sayings," his love dictates rebuke, that their "little faith" may be increased, and their many doubts removed. But until these gracious ends are accomplished, and so long as his displeasure lasts, the pernicious influence of doubts cannot fail to be painfully experienced.

Neither of us can forget how much of our happiness, in the days of youth, depended on the smile of our parents. That smile was ever felt to send forth its beams of joy into our unsophisticated hearts. And when that smile was withdrawn, our innocent hilarity departed from us, like the radiance of a bright summer day, when the sun is overshadowed by a passing cloud. A frown upon our parents' countenance,—the expression of a father's displeasure, not only deprived us of our wonted cheerfulness and gaiety, but darted sadness into our hearts. Our joy was instantly turned into sorrow. And thus it is with every right-hearted and humble-minded child of God. If his heavenly Father's gracious countenance shines upon him, he enjoys a pure and satisfying happiness. At such joyous seasons he knows by experience what the holy psalmist meant when he says, "In his favour is life," Ps 30:5: and again, "Because *thy* lovingkindness is better than life, my lips shall praise *thee*,"—"My soul shall be satisfied as with marrow and fatness; and my mouth shall praise thee with joyful lips," Ps 63:3,5. These are the utterances of a heart overflowing with delight in God himself. But, in opposition to this, how miserable is his condition! how depressed are his inmost thoughts! how downcast his spirit! when the Christian has no sense of God's favour; when he cannot recognise a sweet expression of love beaming on his Father's face; when he doubts and fears that *he* is not reconciled unto him in Christ Jesus, who is "our peace." And, indeed, it may be that his very doubts have concealed the smile which might have gladdened his heart; that his very fears have caused that frown which fills him with dismay. Yes, it is the doubts wherewith a Christian dishonours and displeases his redeeming God, which by enveloping his mind in gloomy clouds, intercept the cheering rays of divine favour, and interrupt his enjoyment of heavenly love, and hope, and peace, and joy.

The foregoing remarks are applicable to the circumstances of *real* doubters. But you will recollect, in my last letter, I supposed it possible, that Christian people, under the impulse of mistaken motives, might *profess doubts* which in reality they did not entertain. I believe there are such people within the pale of the church of Christ. And in reference to their case, if it cannot be affirmed that they dishonour God *by actually doubting* the truth of his testimony or his promise, it is certain that they do dishonour and also displease him *by falsely professing* to doubt the grace bestowed upon them,—the grace whereby they have believed in the Saviour. Their conduct is sad and shameful. Nor can they either be happy in themselves, or expect to enjoy the favour of God, so long as they practise hypocrisy and deceit under the specious pretence of humility. God loves sincerity. He looks for truth in the inward parts. He requires us to honour him with our hearts as well as with our lips; and to praise him for the grace already received, whilst we pray for continued or increased supplies. And unless our faith enables and disposes us to comply with his injunctions, we do not honour him as the God of our salvation.

I remain, yours, etc.

LETTER 5

THE PERNICIOUS INFLUENCE OF DOUBTS

II. THEY ARE PREJUDICIAL TO THE CHRISTIAN CHARACTER AND COMFORT OF THE DOUBTER

"Them that honour me I will honour," expresses an all-pervading principle of God's moral government—Doubts dishonour, and therefore they injure the doubter.—Proposition II.—"Doubts are prejudicial to the Christian character and comfort of the doubter,"—illustrated in six particulars.—First, Doubts engender *harassing anxieties, and needless fears*.—Trust in God is the great antidote to anxiety.—"Fear hath torment."—God says, "Fear not."—The doubter neither trusts nor obeys.—Second.—Doubts rob the Christian of that *abiding peace with God and with himself*, which he ought to possess.—The Gospel is preeminently a message of peace.—The want of peace is a great spiritual privation.—Third.—Doubts deprive Christians of *the heavenly joys* connected with a strong faith.—The Saviour's dying desire for his people was that their "joy might be full."—The Gospel a message not only of peace, but also of joy.—The doubter cannot rejoice.—Objections anticipated as to the number of doubters, and the evil influence of doubts.—Concluding reference to the peace and joy, of which our Lord speaks in his valedictory discourse.

My dear Friend,

No reasonable person will deny that there is an established relationship between the Creator and his creatures. And we are warranted to regard the declaration made by God, on a special occasion, and in reference to the conduct of special individuals, as involving a grand general principle, which pervades his whole moral government. To Eli, the high priest of Israel, there came a prophet, saying, "The Lord God of Israel saith, I said indeed that thy house, and the house of thy father, should walk before me for ever; but now the Lord saith, Be it far from me: *for them that honour me I will honour; and they that despise me shall be lightly esteemed*," 1 Sam 2:30.

The honour which God claims may be expressed in one word. It is that he should be *trusted*. We ought to confide, not only in his protecting power, but in his sincerity and faithfulness. To obey what he enjoins, to receive as true what he reveals, and to wait patiently for the performance of what he promises, are bounden duties which arise out of our creature condition; and by our confidence and obedience in discharging these duties we honour God.

But as sinful and fallen creatures, we do not and cannot give unto God that honour which is his due. Instead of approaching him with loving confidence, conscious guilt prompts us, like our first parents, to seek, if possible, to flee from his presence. His love does not reign in our hearts, as a governing principle. His glory is not the one object, for the promotion of which we live and labour. And therefore we forfeit the blissful benefits which he has connected with our cheerful and uniform obedience. God does not honour us when we do not honour him. Still, like a tender and compassionate parent, he desires the happiness of his children; and desires too that we should seek our happiness in *himself*, and not in any created good;—in the enjoyment of his own favour; in the experience of his own lovingkindness. And the redemption which is by Jesus Christ, the incarnate Son of God, is designed to remedy the evils which sin has introduced into our world. The remedy is marvellous in its effects, as well as in its origin. It satisfies the claims of God's justice against sin, and averts his righteous wrath from the sinner. It delivers man from sin itself, and from the wages of sin, which are misery and death. It restores him to holiness and to happiness. It does so partially even here, and hereafter the blessing will be complete. The love of God, which is so illustriously displayed in this remedial scheme, begets reciprocal love in every sinner who believes it. And the Holy Spirit is promised to instruct us in the knowledge of these great truths,—to open up these mysteries to our understanding, and to bring us to the obedience of faith. On the part of God, the grant of redemption must be wholly ascribed to *his own sovereign and spontaneous good pleasure*; and on our part the reception of it is *only by faith*. In this simple and efficacious way, God brings more glory to himself by our redemption, than by our original creation. And believers in the great Redeemer are placed under stronger obligations by their redemption than by their creation, to glorify God in their bodies and in their spirits, which are his.

The redemption of sinful creatures furnishes brighter and more endearing discoveries of the character of God, than possibly could have been done by the creation of innocent creatures. And now by redemption man is exalted to a higher and more intimate relationship with God, than naturally belongs to him, or than even those angelic beings enjoy who have never sinned. This is marvellous indeed. And on this account the redeemed of the Lord resemble the favoured children of a family, on whom a fond father delights to bestow the richest of his gifts, that they may ever bask in the balmy beams of his affection, and rejoice in the fulness of his own joy. But a moment's reflection should convince us that whilst *faith* realizes and enjoys all this graciously provided blessedness, *doubts* drive it to a distance, and, to a greater or less extent, deprive us of its sanctifying enjoyment.

Doubts, as we have seen, are very dishonouring to God. They cast unworthy and ungenerous suspicions on his veracity, on his wisdom, on his love, on his righteousness, and even on his omnipotence. For this very reason, we may be sure, that they injure the Christian who yields to their influence. They are indicative of a spiritually unhealthy condition. And, in their practical operation, they dim the lustre of the Christian character: they relax the energies of Christian devotedness: they interrupt the harmony of Christian fellowship: they impede the flow of Christian consolation. The Christian who doubts whether he is a believer in Christ, or whether God will give him grace to believe, is incapable of serving God with zeal, with constancy, and with delight. He toils rather like a slave, oppressed and fettered with heaviness of heart, than like a son, animated by filial trust and affection. In point of fact he is not honouring God with his confidence; and God is not honouring him with his enriching blessing. The life of faith in such a man is not extinct, but it is at a low ebb. In a certain sense and measure, it is not too much to say, that he is despising God;—despising his goodness, by not opening his heart to its thankful reception;—despising his grace by doubting its absolute freeness and exceeding riches. He may not know how basely he is acting towards God, and he may not intend to act so. But the very doubts which he entertains are conclusive proofs that he lightly esteems the sacredness of his authority, and the truthfulness of his word, and the faithfulness of his promise. No marvel, then, that he should feel himself to be lightly esteemed of God, and left to learn by bitter experience, that

Doubts are prejudicial to the Christian character and comfort of the doubter.

This is the second of the three propositions which it was proposed to explain as illustrative of *the pernicious influence of doubts*. And I feel warranted to attempt an ample explanation, because the selfishness of our nature makes us peculiarly sensitive to whatever concerns our own peaceful prosperity, whether it be in things temporal or in things spiritual.

The six following particulars will embrace the various observations to which I must bespeak your patient and indulgent attention. And, if I do not greatly err, the doubting Christian himself will be unable to deny, that each and all of these particulars are most unfavourable to his exhibition of a truly Christian character, and to his enjoyment of true Christian comfort.

1. Doubts engender many harassing anxieties, and many unnecessary fears, in the doubter's mind.

2. They rob him of that abiding peace with God, and peace with himself, which the Christian ought to possess.

3. They deprive him of those heavenly joys which are connected with the exercise of a strong and stedfast faith.

4. They cool the ardour of his love to God and man, which is the mainspring of all holy and acceptable obedience.

5. They obstruct and repress that spirituality and heavenly-mindedness, by which the Christian should be distinguished and adorned.

6. They damp and darken the brightness of his hopes for eternity.

First, then, I remark that there is no escape from harassing *anxieties*, and unnecessary *fears*, when a Christian doubts either the suitableness and the completeness of the gospel salvation, or his own individual interest in it. In this respect, those who have no thoughts beyond the present life, may be the object of his envy. Whatever are the anxieties and fears of a worldly man, they are confined to "the things that are seen and temporal," and are therefore comparatively trifling. But he who has been awakened to the real importance of "the things that are unseen and eternal,"—who is enlightened in the knowledge of his own sinfulness, and of the holiness and justice of God, without being able, at the same time, to appropriate the forgiving mercy and grace revealed to sinners in Christ Jesus, must be a prey to painful anxiety on the subject of his personal salvation, and to the terrifying apprehension of exposure to everlasting perdition. The man of the world thinks neither of God, nor of judgment, nor of eternity. He eats and drinks, and is merry. But the doubting Christian cannot act so foolishly. He has a sufficient sense of the reality and value of divine truths to attract his thoughts towards them. He thinks of himself as a sinner, and he trembles. He thinks of God as an avenging judge, and he is troubled. His conscious guilt gives activity to the emotion of fear. His uncertainty whether his sins are pardoned, and the righteousness of Christ imputed for his justification, keeps him in continual anxiety. And so long as he remains under the influence of doubts, it is vain for him to expect relief or deliverance from this iron bondage. Every contemplation of his spiritual state and prospects increases the evil. He can even contemplate the wondrous events transacted at Gethsemane and Calvary, and acknowledge the freeness of the love which was there manifested, and the efficacy of the sacrifice which was there offered up, without the experience of much substantial consolation. For still he doubts whether that one sacrifice, once offered, made expiation for his own guilt, and whether he himself is the object of that love divine which prompted the Son of God to die for the salvation of sinners.

For aught I know, you yourself, my dear friend, may be no stranger to the mental perturbation and perplexity to which I have been alluding. At all events, you must have frequently met with Christian people who were suffering under this miserable disquietude. And what I wish to urge upon your conviction is, that it is nothing more than the legitimate offspring of doubts.

In a general way it may be affirmed that anxiety of mind arises out of the feebleness and shortsightedness of our sinful condition. It stands connected with our inability to foresee what awaits us, or to provide against coming inconveniences and distresses, or to secure the continuance of present enjoyments. And the great antidote to this spirit of anxiety is the habitual recognition of God, and a firm reliance upon him, as presiding over all events, and providing for all creatures, and especially as pledged by his voluntary promise to watch over his own adopted children with a peculiar love and care. It is here that the doubter fails. He wants confidence in God as his father and his friend. Did he cast all his care upon God, as he is exhorted to do, in the happy belief that God cares for him, 1 Pet 5:7, oh! then, from what a heavy burden would he be released! And did he obey the injunction of St. Paul, "Be careful for nothing; but in everything by prayer and supplication, with thanksgiving, let your requests be made known unto God," oh! then, how sweet and soothing would be his experience of that "peace of God which passeth all understanding!" Phil 4:6-7. That blessed peace would *keep* his heart and mind through Christ Jesus:—keep him in the possession of an undisturbed and perpetual calm, to the exclusion of all anxious thoughts and careful solicitudes. Oh! how desirable to enjoy such a tranquil state of mind! and how desirous should every Christian be to believe that Gospel which confers so great a blessing! But the doubter forfeits this blessing. He does not cast the burden of his cares upon his God, because he hesitates to believe that God really cares for him. On this account his harassing anxieties are not removed, and like a cankerworm they gnaw the very core of his happiness. They unhinge the mind; they warp the judgment; they irritate the temper; they interrupt the natural play of the affections; they cause much inward dissatisfaction, which shows itself in the outward conduct; and just as indulgence is given to this unhappy disposition, there is an infringement on that sweet serenity of mind, which is a continual feast. Nor is this the only deprivation which the anxious Christian undergoes. It is true, indeed, that he suffers the loss of Christian comfort; but his Christian character also is impaired. So far from shining as a light in the world, other men can discern in him nothing more than the faintest traces of that contentment, and patience, and fortitude, and cheerfulness, which ought to distinguish the true believer. All this comes of doubts, and clearly proves how pernicious is their influence.

Our *anxieties* are chiefly directed to something beyond the reach of our own skill or control,—something independent of ourselves,—something, above all, that is wrapt up in the secrets of futurity. And it often happens that people make themselves and others wretched with anxiety about what is in itself excellent and desirable. Our *fears*, on the other hand, are connected with some real or imaginary evil, and for the most part are awakened only by an apprehension of danger, either immediate or impending. There are exceptions to this, however; and in some cases fear must be ascribed simply to the weakness of our nature. But whilst our *guiltiness* exposes us to many evils, and surrounds us with innumerable dangers, it is our *consciousness of guilt* that gives power and poignancy to the emotion of fear. How truly the apostle John says, "Fear hath torment," 1 John 4:18. But the Gospel is designed and fitted to deliver us from every kind of torment. And it should excite our gratitude that the expressed object of so many of its counsels and exhortations, and warnings and promises, is to allay those fears which we are so prone to indulge, and which are so destructive of our happiness and comfort.

The stedfast believer, like other men, is liable to attacks of disease. He may also be involved in difficulties, or be beset with enemies, or be cast down by the severity of his trials. For these, and similar reasons, he, as well as others, might become fainthearted and fearful. But his faith in God and in his word bears him up, and keeps his spirit tranquil. He hears the oft-repeated declaration of Jehovah, "Fear not; for I am with thee."*
He believes these encouraging words. He stays himself upon his gracious and omnipotent God. And thus he feels privileged to say with the psalmist, "Yea, though I walk through the val-

ley of the shadow of death, I will fear no evil, for *thou* art with me: thy rod and thy staff, they comfort me," Ps 23:4. "God is our refuge and strength, a very present help in trouble; therefore will not we fear though the earth be removed, and though the mountains be carried into the midst of the sea; though the waters thereof roar and be troubled; though the mountains shake with the swelling thereof," Ps 46:1-3. The man who is built up in a scriptural persuasion that through grace he is saved by the faith of Jesus Christ, and that God for Christ's sake is on his side, ought to enjoy exemption from fears of every kind, except the holy fear of offending his gracious God, and a watchful fear of falling from the stedfastness of his faith. Again, with the psalmist, he can exult, "The Lord is on my side; I will not fear: what can man do unto me?" Ps 118:6. And the confiding language of St. Paul becomes his own: "If God be for us, who can be against us? He that spared not his own Son, but delivered him up for us all, how shall he not with him also freely give us all things?" Rom 8:31-32. This love of God in Christ Jesus is the strong tower to which the believer may always repair; and from its heights he can look down without dismay on every form of evil that presents itself. God is with him at all times; and leaning securely on the omnipotence of His love, he can alike survey, without alarm, the blackness of the clouds above him, or the number of assailing foes from beneath. He knows his fortress is impregnable; and there he sits, and sings in humble, holy triumph,—

> "Let troubles rise, and terrors frown,
> And days of darkness fall;
> Through *him* all dangers we'll defy,
> And more than conquer all."

*The reader is referred to the following passages:—Gen 15:1; Gen 21:17; Gen 26:24; Gen 46:3; Exod 14:13; Deut 1:21; Josh 1:9; Isa 35:4; Isa 54:4; Lam 3:57; Ezek 3:9; Dan 10:12; Matt 10:31; Luke 2:10; Luke 8:50; Luke 12:32; Rev 1:17.

It well deserves your notice, my friend, that this calm and dignified superiority to fear is no presumption on the part of a true believer. Thus to conduct himself is enjoined as a positive duty. It is the divine Saviour who commands his disciples, "Let not your hearts be troubled, neither let them be afraid," John 14:27. It is their covenant God who says to his own redeemed people, "O Israel, fear not, for I have redeemed thee; I have called thee by thy name; thou art mine. When thou passest through the waters, I will be with thee; and through the rivers, they shall not overflow thee: when thou walkest through the fire, thou shalt not be burnt; neither shall the flame kindle upon thee. For I am the Lord thy God, the Holy One of Israel, thy Saviour."—"Fear not, for I am with thee," Isa 43:1-5. And he who obeys the command, enjoys the promised protection.

But how fares it with the doubting Christian? Alas! he cannot divest himself of his fears. He is in bondage to the fear of death, and of every evil that threatens the injury of his person or his property. And above all, he fears that God is not his God: that Christ is not his Saviour: that salvation is not his portion, and that the heavenly kingdom will never be his home. He cannot get quit of inward discomfort. He is a stranger to the peaceful security which is connected with a simple reliance on the veracity and faithfulness of God. And his own experience should teach him, that the tendency of all doubts is to distress the mind, and to deteriorate the character of a Christian, on account of the slavish and servile fears which they so certainly engender.

As a child of God the doubter debars himself from the privileges of his heavenly Father's family. He fears he shall not find access with acceptance to his Father's life-giving presence. He fears he has no right to eat of the children's bread, and to share their joys. He does not enjoy "the glorious liberty of the sons of God;" and therefore he fears to cherish that "spirit of adoption," whereby, with holy delight, a poor sinner may cry unto God, "Abba, Father."

As a servant, he groans under a perpetual bondage, and knows nothing of that "perfect freedom" which belongs to the service of God. He doubts his Master's love to him. He fears his services are not accepted in the Beloved. He fears he cannot evade his Master's displeasure.

As a Christian warrior, he hesitates to take the field. He shrinks from a determined conflict with the flesh, the world, and the devil. Instead of realizing the arm of the Almighty as outstretched for his defence; instead of buckling on the impenetrable armour which is so graciously provided; instead of placing himself under the banners of the "Captain of our salvation," and thus courageously fighting the good fight of faith, having his heart fired with the hope of success, and his eye fixed on the crown of glory, he yields to the feeling of his own weakness. He is dismayed at the bare idea of encountering his spiritual enemies. He is afraid to expect help from above. His many fears enervate him; and he is overcome by the mere anticipation of failure and disgrace.

Or, if we look upon the doubting Christian as a pilgrim, travelling to the better country, it is apparent to himself, and to his companions by the way, that he walks neither with buoyant step, nor with exulting heart. His knees are feeble, and his hands hang down, Heb 12:12. His progress onwards to the rest which remaineth for the people of God is slow indeed. Instead of rejoicing, he trembles at the thought of reaching the termination of his journey. He has no assurance of a welcome to the mansions which Christ has gone to prepare. No: the doubter cannot adopt the triumphant language of the apostle, "For we know that if the earthly house of this tabernacle were dissolved, we have a building of God, an house not made with hands, eternal in the heavens," 2 Cor 5:1.

Thus it is evident, that, however secure the final salvation is of all who have been given unto Christ of the Father, yet he who doubts the grace bestowed upon him, and the hope set before him, cuts himself off from the purest and noblest pleasures enjoyed by men in this world, and is incapacitated for serving God *"without fear,* in holiness and righteousness before him, all the days of his life," Luke 1:74-75. This is the result of doubts, and strikingly shows how powerful and how pernicious is their influence.

But, surely, it is not the will of God that any believer should be harassed with anxious thoughts, and tormented with fearful forebodings. All are the objects of divine compassion. And it is especially to the weary and heavy laden that the Saviour's invitation is given, "Come unto me, and I will give you rest." We cannot mistake the meaning of this sweet promise. The Saviour here seems to say, "Believe on me with an assured faith, as able and willing to pardon all your sins, to protect you from every enemy, to deliver you from every evil, to provide you with every needful blessing, for time and for eternity. Only come to me, and you shall certainly find rest. I will relieve you of the heavy burden of your cares and anxieties; I will chase away your painful and alarming apprehensions; I will cheer and comfort your hearts with heavenly cordials; I will strengthen you with might in the inner man, and make my grace sufficient for you under all circumstances. Only come unto me; for this is the rest, and this is the refreshing." And oh! how sad that doubts should render the kind invitation and the precious promise of our Lord so ineffectual in the experience of multitudes!

Second. The doubting Christian is robbed of that *abiding peace*, peace with God, and peace of conscience, which is one of the most direct and blessed effects of faith in the Lord Jesus Christ.

The apostle Paul says to his Roman converts, "Therefore being justified by faith, *we have peace with God through our Lord Jesus Christ,*" Rom 5:1. This one blessing of peace is so characteristic of the dispensation under which we live, that the Saviour was predicted of old under the title of "the Prince of peace," Isa 9:6. And in reference to the object of his mission to this earth, it is written, "How beautiful upon the mountains are the feet of him that bringeth good tidings, *that publisheth peace*; that bringeth good tidings of good, that publisheth salvation; that saith unto Zion, Thy God reigneth!" Isa 52:7. The whole mediatory work of the incarnate God may with the utmost propriety be designated *"The Gospel of Peace."* Our world was the seat of a fearful rebellion. Mankind was not only in a state of hostility against God, but they were at war with themselves, and with one another. And when the Saviour was born, the very angels of heaven, anticipating the successful issue of his enterprise, sang, in rapturous strains, "Glory to God in the highest, and *on earth peace*," Luke 2:14. In beautiful harmony with such an announcement at his entrance into the world, were the sentiments expressed by himself at his departure from it. In the last discourse he addressed to his sorrowing disciples, he bequeathed to them peace, his own peace, as a dying legacy. *"Peace* I leave with you; *my peace* I give unto you: not as the world giveth give I unto you. Let not your heart be troubled, neither let it be afraid," John 14:27.

In these blessed words of our Lord you will please to observe that he contrasts the peace which he gives with the anxieties and fears which are natural to sinful men, and with the distress and disquietude to which he foresaw that his disciples would be exposed. After apprising them of the peculiarly painful circumstances which were to accompany his own departure out of the world, and also of all the varied hardships and persecutions which awaited themselves, he most kindly says to them, "Let not your heart be troubled, neither let it be afraid." And at the close of his discourse, he says, "These things I have spoken unto you, *that in me ye might have peace*. In the world ye shall have tribulation; but be of good cheer: I have overcome the world," John 16:33. To have such counsels, and from such a friend, and at such a solemn and affecting moment, could not fail to be very soothing and consolatory. But the disciples would feel, and our Lord himself would know, that it is utterly beyond the power of mere words, even from his lips, to allay the fears to which the difficulties and dangers that were coming upon them might give rise. How precious then is the legacy of the dying Saviour! *"Peace I leave with you. My peace I give unto you."* Although the Saviour has gone to heaven, yet he left peace behind him. And although his followers must expect to meet with troubles and tribulation in the world, still their Lord and Master gives them peace. This divine gift, this gracious bequest, supplies the oil which alone can smooth the troubled waters of a present life, through which the Christian must pass ere he can reach the haven of everlasting rest. This is the only true composer of our anxious minds: this is the one effectual antidote to every fearful emotion, by whatever cause excited.

Oh, my friend, what a blessed thing is peace! how unspeakably blessed the peace which Christ himself enjoys!—the peace which Christ himself bestows! And this peace ought to be the present and the permanent possession of all true Christians. It is not a blessing which is ours merely by promise: it is not something which we are privileged to hope for at a future period. Had we no more than the prospect of peace, even for that we should have cause to give thanks, and rejoice. But how much greater are our obligations when peace is put into our possession! Of all who are justified by faith, the apostle affirms, "*We have peace* with God through our Lord Jesus Christ." Believers have a right to it; and they ought to be in the enjoyment of it. Nor will they ever be left to mourn the want of it, if faith be kept in proper exercise. The believer's own experience testifies to the truth of the apostolic declaration. He is persuaded that Christ is his own peacemaker. He realizes the efficacy of his blood to reconcile us unto God. He feels that God is absolutely reconciled unto himself. He is assured, sinner though he be in himself, that he is accepted of God in the Beloved,—accepted as righteous only for the righteousness' sake of Him who is "our peace." And everyone who is thus justified, and whose strength of faith gives him the knowledge of his justification, enjoys a substantial and satisfying peace of mind. He has received what Christ gives. He has entered into the possession of what Christ bequeathed. He knows the reality of that peace which the world can neither impart nor impair. He can tell you that it is "the peace of God, which passeth all understanding." It is peace from God: it is peace with God. And, oh! who can estimate the worth of such a treasure!

The work of Christ as our surety, when understood and believed, subdues the natural enmity of our hearts against God; and calms the inward passions which sin has made so tumultuous and ungovernable; and pacifies the clamorous upbraidings of a guilty conscience. Hence the believer cleaves to God as his best friend, and ceases to dread him as his greatest foe. He desires to have a single eye to his glory at all times. He aims at submission to his will in all things. His faith in the Saviour of sinners purifies his heart. It strengthens him to resist the cravings of his own earthly and sensual inclinations, as well as the crafts and assaults of the devil. It gives him victory over the allurements of the world, and keeps in subjection that sinful selfishness of his nature, which is ever running counter to all God's revealed commandments, and also to all his providential dispensations which wear an afflictive aspect. And thus it is, that, as the Gospel itself is a message of peace, so the belief of it confers on the believer the experience and the enjoyment of peace.

But it is a melancholy fact, that the mass of mankind do not believe the Gospel which is preached to them, and know nothing of that true peace—peace with God and peace of conscience, which is of more value than thousands of silver and of gold. And it is a humbling fact, that, even among Christian people, multitudes are robbed of this precious treasure, by means of the doubts which they entertain. Where doubts prevail, it is not possible that real tranquillity should be enjoyed. And, alas! this evil influence is too well known to those who have now lost the peace which once they did possess. The number is not small of those who can say with the poet,

> "Where is the blessedness I knew,
> When first I saw the Lord?
> Where is the soul-refreshing view
> Of Jesus and his word?
>
> "What peaceful hours I once enjoy'd!
> How sweet their memory still!
> But they have left an aching void
> The world can never fill."

Other Christians, who never have attained to peace, are not in a condition to comprehend the full amount of their privation. And yet it ought to be sufficiently intelligible to them all, that the natural effect of doubts, whether they respect the reality of Gospel blessings, or our own participation in them, is to let loose upon us the terrors of conscious guilt, and of a broken law, and of a righteous Judge. There is no sense of pardon in that mind where doubts predominate; nor is there any settled assurance of God's love. In most cases of this kind there is no peace at all; and the peace which may be experienced is at best unsteady and defective. Doubts not only obscure the cheering sunshine of the Gospel from the weak believer's view, but it sometimes happens that they brighten his conceptions of that holy law which demands a perfect obedience. Thus as he loses sight of Christ, who is "the end of the law for righteousness to every one who believeth," Rom 10:4, he finds himself immersed in spiritual darkness, and becomes a prey to mental disquietude, perhaps to despondency, or, it may be for a time, even to despair. While his doubts retain their mastery, his uneasiness cannot be removed. It is only in the stedfast faith of Jesus Christ, that any sinner can have either peace of mind, or peace with God. True and faithful are the words of Scripture: "Thou wilt keep him in perfect peace, whose mind is stayed on thee, because he trusteth in thee," Isa 26:3. How important it is to have our minds *stayed on God*! Let this, my dear friend, be the attainment to which you and I are ever pressing forward; for assuredly the measure of our peace will always be in proportion to the exercise of our trust.

Third. The doubting Christian is robbed not only of peace, but *of joy in God through our Lord Jesus Christ*.

The Gospel is emphatically a dispensation of joy. It is indeed a great truth which the angel of the Lord declared to the shepherds of Bethlehem, when he said, "Fear not; for behold I bring you *good tidings of great joy*, which shall be to all people; for unto you is born this day, in the city of David, *a Saviour*, which is Christ the Lord," Luke 2:10-11. And this anointed Saviour, whose coming into the world was celebrated with songs of rejoicing by the very angels of heaven, did not leave the world without fully explaining to his disciples the purposes of his mission, and the consequences of his departure. And "these things," he said, "have I spoken unto you, that my joy in you might remain, and *that your joy might be full*," John 15:11.[3]

The things to which our Lord refers in this place, concerned both himself and his people, as may be seen in reading over this his last and most precious discourse, which begins with John 13, and goes on till the close of John 16. What he said respecting himself had reference not only to his sufferings and death, but to his resurrection and glory; not only to his going away, but to his coming again, and to the promise of the Comforter, the Spirit of truth, during his absence. And what he said respecting his people, had reference not merely to their future prospects as heirs of the glory to be revealed, but to their present privileges and duties. It must be confessed that these things are to us of paramount importance. We should study them diligently, as containing a comprehensive summary of Gospel doctrine, and of Gospel practice. And it should be our earnest desire that our Lord's gracious design may be accomplished in regard to ourselves. "These things have I spoken unto you, *that my joy in you might remain, and that your joy might be full.*"

Thus it is manifest that the Gospel has not produced its legitimate and intended effects, where joy, even a fulness of permanent joy, is wanting. The joy of a true believer is like a perennial fountain. Outward circumstances may obstruct the natural ebullitions of his joy, and divert it from flowing in its accustomed channels; but they cannot shut up the fountain. Our Lord, whilst speaking to his disciples of his gracious design, that their joy should be full, did not conceal from them the hard treatment they might undergo as his disciples. "In the world ye shall have tribulation." But he immediately adds, "Be of good cheer."—Let no prospect of outward suffering daunt you. Let not your heart be troubled. Let not your spirits sink. Let not your joy be interrupted or diminished. "Be of good cheer; I have overcome the world," John 16:33. In this retention of joy, even in the midst of abounding tribulations, there is something which worldly people cannot understand; but the true believer has an experimental knowledge of it. It is probable that the disciples themselves, when listening to our Lord's valedictory discourse, would imagine that he spoke of impossibilities. But after enduring a plentiful measure of the world's hatred and persecution during a long lifetime, it is most instructive and encouraging to find them testifying, from personal experience, to the truth of their Lord's declaration.

The apostle John, for instance, nearly sixty years after the Saviour had ascended into heaven, expresses the similarity of his reason for writing his first Epistle, with that which our Lord has avowed in delivering this memorable discourse:

"And these things write we unto you, *that your joy may be full*," 1 John 1:4. So likewise the apostle James commences his Epistle with these words, which fall so strangely on the ears of those who know not the truth as it is in Jesus: "*My brethren, count it all joy* when ye fall into divers temptations; knowing this, that the trying of your faith worketh patience," James 1:2-3. And Peter takes up the same subject in very animated strains. After blessing God for the glorious hope to which we are begotten by the resurrection of our Lord Jesus Christ, he says, "Wherein *ye greatly rejoice*, though now for a season, if need be, ye are in heaviness through manifold temptations; that the trial of your faith, being much more precious than of gold that perisheth, though it be tried with fire, might be found unto praise, and honour, and glory, at the appearing of Jesus Christ; whom having not seen, ye love; in whom, though now ye see him not, yet believing, *ye rejoice with soy unspeakable, and full of glory*," 1 Pet 1:6-8. This is a remarkable testimony; and there is another in an after part of the same Epistle, which is not less remarkable, as a bright evidence that the joy which the Gospel of Jesus imparts to the believer, bursts through all outward hindrances, and sustains his spirit under the greatest weight of worldly calamity and suffering. "Beloved, think it not strange concerning the fiery trial which is to try you, as though some strange thing happened unto you; *but rejoice*, inasmuch as ye are partakers of Christ's sufferings; that when his glory shall be revealed, *ye may be glad also with exceeding joy*," 1 Pet 4:12-13.

I might refer you also to very many passages in the Epistles of St. Paul, but it is unnecessary. Even in the Old Testament times, when the Gospel was preached only under types, and shadows, and prophetic intimations, it clearly appears that joy and gladness was the blissful portion of all whose faith in God, as merciful and gracious, inspired their hearts with confidence towards him. The language of the psalmist is in perfect accordance with that of our Lord and his apostles.

"But let all those that put their trust in *Thee rejoice*: let them *ever shout for joy*, because *thou* defendest them: let them also that love thy name *be joyful in thee*. For thou, Lord, wilt bless the righteous: with favour wilt thou compass him as with a shield," Ps 5:11-12. And in all ages of the church, and amongst all classes of established Christians, we know that the power of divine grace has so completely triumphed over the weakness of natural feeling, that streams of holy joy have gushed freely from many hearts that were sad and sore with this world's tribulations.

"As sorrowful, yet always rejoicing," is indeed the Christian's motto. But when a Christian doubts the promises of God, or the work which Christ has accomplished, or his own interest in the great salvation, he finds that this of itself is a painful addition to his other sorrows, and the Gospel brings no joy to him. He does not experience peace with God, and therefore he is afraid to rejoice. Peace and joy are closely blended together in the affairs of life, as they are also in the religion of Jesus. When neighbours quarrel, and have long lived in a state of alienation and enmity, their reconciliation causes joy not only to themselves, but to all connected with them. And when nations have been at war with each other, wasting property, and shedding human blood, and spreading desolation and distress far and wide, it is notorious that the mere rumour of peace diffuses universal gladness: and when at last preliminaries are concluded, and articles are signed, binding the contending parties to a friendly intercourse, is it not true that the cessation of hostilities is welcomed with delight, and the din of war is hushed amidst the demonstrations of national rejoicing? But those who disbelieved or doubted the news of peace could not participate in the widespread joy. Thus it is that every rebellious offender against God, when he is brought to know the reconciliation that has been effected by the great Mediator, and when he believes that God is at peace with him, and when he feels himself delivered out of the hands of his enemies, and rescued from the pit of perdition, is so constituted that he cannot but rejoice. He rejoices in what has been done *for* him; and he rejoices in what has been done *in* him; because if God has become his friend, he also has become the friend of God. The reconciliation is mutual. His conscience tells him that he is no longer a rebel—that he is now a loyal subject. And the Spirit of God bears witness with his own spirit that he is a child of God. For this cause he rejoices in God, and in the salvation of God. It is his privilege to do so, and it is his commanded duty to do so. "Rejoice in the Lord alway, and again I say, Rejoice." Oh blessed command! But how can the doubter obey this apostolic command? How can he *rejoice in the Lord* at all? And how can he *rejoice alway*? He fears the Lord is still his enemy. He fears his sins are not yet pardoned. He fears he has no title to the promised inheritance. He fears the gates of heaven are not open to him. He fears his everlasting portion may be with the devil and his angels. He doubts the "good tidings of great joy" which the Gospel announces: and his doubts debar his enjoyment of that continual joy which the Gospel is fitted and designed to impart. It is in vain for such a man that Jesus himself has said, "These things have I spoken unto you, that my joy in you might remain, and that your joy might be full." And oh what a renewed proof does this furnish of the pernicious influence of doubts!

In addition to the afflictions which are the common lot of man under the existing dispensation, the Christian has to expect afflictions connected with his profession of Christianity. We have been forewarned by our Lord—"In the world ye shall have tribulation;" and an apostle has declared, "It is through much tribulation that we must enter into the kingdom of heaven." But amidst these tribulations the assured believer can "be of good cheer," because he knows that his Lord has overcome the world. And amidst whatever afflictions he is visited withal, his faith brings in abundant consolations and rejoicings for his support. Thus every rightly exercised Christian should be able to say with St. Paul, "As sorrowful, yet always rejoicing." But is it not a sad privation that the doubter undergoes? He too has his trials and tribulations, not only as a man, but as a Christian man. He has not, however, the supporting and the cheering experience of gospel principles, and privileges, and promises, and prospects, as he ought to have. In his heart there is no fountain of holy joy; or, at any rate, his doubts have so sealed up the fountain that it sends forth no refreshing streams. He is downcast and disconsolate. The doubter's motto seems to be, "Always sorrowful, and never rejoicing." The little faith which he possesses, and which in itself is a very precious possession, although he knows it not, so far from making him a happier man than others who have no faith at all, only goes to deprive him of such happiness as the world has to give, without allowing him to participate in the true peace and substantial joys of the Gospel. Surely this is a state of mind most destructive of Christian comfort, and very unfavourable to that advancement in personal holiness, towards which it becomes the Christian continually to aspire. And into this unfavourable and uncomfortable state he is brought by doubts. Doubts are injurious to spiritual health, and, of course, to spiritual happiness. They dishonour God, and they bring their own punishment along with them. They fill the mind of the doubting Christian with anxieties and fears; they rob him of peace and joy in believing.

In my next Letter (p. 109) I shall resume the consideration of this subject, and point out the pernicious influence of doubts in cooling the ardour of the Christian's love to God and man. But I cannot close the present Letter without anticipating an objection to what has now been stated. It is not unlikely that you incline to the opinion that I have overrated the number of doubters in these last days in which we live, and exaggerated the evils of a doubting state of mind; as perhaps you seldom meet with Christians so full of anxieties and fears, and so destitute of peace and joy, as I have described. Now, I at once admit that there does seem to be an increasing number of active and enlightened Christians, and a great deal of healthy and cheerful Christianity. I trust much of it is genuine. But it must be recollected that this is a day of high profession, and that, according to the old proverb, "it is not all gold that glitters." By all means let us look around us with charitable eyes, and judge of others with a charitable heart. Let us be thankful for the exertions made to spread the blessings of the gospel at home and abroad, among Jews and Gentiles. Let us be thankful for an increase of ministers, both in the established Churches and among the Dissenters, who preach evangelical doctrine, and for an increased attendance on their ministrations. But, I imagine, we should greatly err were we to conclude, that, amidst the multitudes who are thus so busy with societies and sermons, personal religion is generally in a prosperous condition. If we are really to have anything like an approach to the truth on this point, we must enter into close conversation with professing Christians of different communions, and in different classes of society. And if your observation at all coincides with mine, we shall both agree that it is rare to fall into a company of experienced and well-established Christians, whose heartfelt delight is to tell what the Lord has done for their souls, and to show forth the praises of Him who has called them out of darkness into his marvellous light. The conversation of Christians one with another, in these times, is seldom of an experimental and edifying character. And, indeed, have you not often seen that the introduction of a spiritual or a searching remark silences an entire gathering? So long as the conversation is about churches and chapels, and ministers and missionaries, and schools and committees, and what may be called the mere outworks of religion, all tongues are eloquent; but how few are to be found who acknowledge the work of God's Spirit on their own hearts, and who use their tongues to speak of their wondrous privileges and glorious prospects, as the Lord's redeemed and adopted children!

I think you will not deny that it is comparatively a rare thing to meet with Christians who humbly but frankly say with St. Paul, "I know in whom I have believed, and am persuaded that he is able to keep that which I have committed unto him against that day," 2 Tim 1:12. And if this is the true state of the case, we are left to conclude that the great mass of Christian people are not assured of their own salvation. In other words, they are doubters in a greater or less degree. Still you will tell me that amongst this great mass of doubters, you seldom hear confessions of the doubts under which they labour, or of the spiritual distress which their doubts occasion. This may be quite true; but silence does not prove the absence either of doubts or of distress. The fact is, that most persons are naturally and properly slow to divulge their inward conflicts. I believe that painful and long-continued efforts are sometimes made to conceal what is passing in the heart. And besides, it should be remembered, that by far the greater number of those who suffer under the evil influence of doubts, although they may never be blessed with assurance of salvation, are not always in a doubting state. They endeavour to avoid thinking or talking of their spiritual condition as much as possible. When engaged in the affairs of the world, they are apparently as tranquil, or cheerful, or free from anxieties and fears, as other people are. It is only when their ordinary occupations are interrupted by some striking dispensation of Providence, or when some particular truth is carried home with power to their consciences, that the concerns of their souls engage their special attention. And when they are constrained to examine into the state of their affections towards God, and their interest in the Saviour, and their hopes for eternity, then it is that doubts arise to trouble them. But they generally keep their troubles to themselves. It is not the less true, however, that such seasons of doubting do occur, and are always more or less marked by the painful absence of gospel peace and joy, and by the more painful presence of alarm, or dismay, or despondency. But I wish it also to be clearly understood, that the composure and serenity of mind, which such persons at anytime enjoy, is not that peace which Christ gives to his people, and which their faith receives from him. Neither should the mirth and pleasantry in which at times they indulge be mistaken for that "joy in God through our Lord Jesus Christ," which only flows from a sense of our forgiveness and reconciliation.

In conclusion, allow me once more to quote the blessed words of our Saviour in his last discourse with his disciples, "These things I have spoken unto you, that *in me ye might have peace*. In the world ye shall have tribulation: but be of good cheer; I have overcome the world." And again, "These things have I spoken unto you, that *my joy in you* might remain; and that *your joy might be full*." To complete the antithesis in this beautiful sentence, the words "in me" must be supplied in the latter clause, "*your joy in me*." Here, then, there is a double joy spoken of—a reciprocal and mutual joy. The Saviour not only designs and desires that his people should have joy in him, and that their joy should be always full, and never suffer diminution; but that his own joy in them might remain. This deserves particular notice. The Saviour does rejoice over every sinner given to him of his Father, and rescued from the captivity of Satan, and renewed by the Holy Ghost, and grafted into the true Vine. But where there are so many doubts of the grace bestowed, and such a want of love, and so little fruit-bearing, how can his joy in them remain? He knows how destitute they are of soul prosperity. He marks the little progress they make towards the heavenly goal. He does not, indeed, withdraw his love from them; but the blessed Saviour must view such doubters with feelings of pity rather than of pleasure. Instead of rejoicing in the victories which their faith would achieve, he mourns over the spiritual dangers and defeats to which their doubts continually expose them. Nor can their joy in him be full, whilst they doubt their covenant-union with him, and are destitute of the sense of his forgiving love. Neither can they experience that heavenly peace which is only to be found in Christ, and which is only to be received from him by faith, and which is so needful to sustain and cheer the Christian amidst the world's sorrows and tribulations. And thus the merciful purpose for which the Saviour uttered so many precious and gracious words is frustrated by the doubts of his own disciples.

I remain, yours, etc.

LETTER 6

DOUBTS ARE INJURIOUS TO THE CHRISTIAN CHARACTER AND COMFORT OF THE DOUBTER

IV. THEY COOL THE ARDOUR OF HIS LOVE TO GOD AND MAN

Love a most powerful emotion.—*God is Love.*—Love causes all the sweet harmony of heaven.—Love is the mainspring of all holy obedience.—Whatever impairs the energy of love must be detrimental to personal godliness.—We love God, because he first loved us.—Faith makes us holy and happy.—Doubts mar both our holiness and our happiness.—Scriptural illustrations, Gal 5:5-6: "Faith worketh by love."—The Thessalonians commended for their "work of faith, and labour of love."—When their faith grew exceedingly, their love towards each other abounded.—Love is the fulfilling of the law.—Simon the Pharisee and the woman that was a sinner.—St. Paul's prayer for the Ephesians, that they might "know the love of Christ," in order that they might "be filled with all the fulness of God."—Precepts in harmony with that prayer.—The doubting Christian slow to offer this prayer, and to obey these precepts.—Sanctified love leads to the devoted service of God.—Our love to God whom we do not see, is manifested by love to the brethren.—The Gospel inculcates the most expansive benevolence.—Weak faith, and still more, doubts, make us unprofitable servants.—The consciousness of loving Christ, and being loved by him, greatly elevates the Christian's character, and contributes to his spiritual comfort.

My dear Friend,

In the preceding Letter (p. 83), I gave you three distinct illustrations in proof of the general proposition, that doubts are prejudicial to the Christian character and comfort of the person who entertains them. I trust it has been explained to your satisfaction, *first*, that doubts engender many *harassing anxieties*, and many *unnecessary fears* in the mind of the doubting Christian: *second*, that they rob him of that sweet and abiding *peace with God and with himself* which he ought ever to possess: and *third*, that they deprive him of those *heavenly joys* which are connected with a strong and stedfast faith.

In advancing now to the *fourth* illustration, which you will recollect was to this effect, that *doubts cool the ardour of the Christian's love to God and man*, I feel that the subject has sufficient magnitude and importance to occupy an entire Letter.

Love, you are aware, is a very powerful emotion. Its workings within the human breast shed a most benign and heavenly influence over the human character. "God is love;" and therefore it should be our holy ambition to exercise and cherish this godlike emotion, because the assimilation of man to his Maker, is the very perfection of his nature. Love, besides, is the mainspring of all holy and acceptable obedience. It sanctions no rebellious feelings. It sympathises with no discordant words. It tolerates no sinful actions. It silences every murmur. The harps of heaven are attuned by love to their melodious harmony. It is love that softly and sweetly constrains the celestial intelligences to unhesitating and universal compliance with the will of heaven's great Lord. Among them no jarring sound is heard. How blest this earth would be, how blest each heart would be, were love to predominate also among men! If, then, it should appear, on examination, that doubts impair the energies and the activities of this our strongest motive to run in the way of all God's commandments, it must follow, as a necessary sequence, that they are detrimental to the Christian's advances in holiness. And, for this reason, you will at once perceive how closely connected is the topic, on the consideration of which we are about to enter, with the promotion of true peace, and practical godliness, among professing Christians.

Surely you do not need to be reminded of the prompt determination with which it behoves us to repel every enticement to relax the vigour of our faith, and the constancy of our obedience. For whilst it is undeniable, that God, with most affectionate earnestness, desires the happiness of his redeemed people, we must never forget that he does so always in strict accordance with their personal holiness. The love and peace and joy and hope, for the production of which the Gospel of Christ so richly provides, can only be enjoyed when our faith in the great realities of the Gospel is in exercise. It is when simply believing the grace and goodness of God revealed to poor sinners, that these pleasurable and elevating emotions are awakened. And when God requires of us to believe, and even when he enables us to trust in himself, as reconciled to us in Jesus Christ, we must beware of supposing that he designs to feed and nourish in us a selfish indulgence of these delightful emotions. The glory of God, and not our own happiness, is the object which we ought directly to have in view. Under the gospel, as truly as under the law, God maintains his superiority, and lays upon us an obligation to honour him with our confidence and our obedience. He commands us to believe in his incarnate Son, "the Saviour, who is Christ the Lord." And it is when we obey his command, that we are made happy: it is in the very act of believing in *him*, whom *he* hath sent to bless us, that we receive the blessing.

More particularly I would observe, that the gospel of our salvation, which so clearly manifests the wondrous love of God to the guilty, never affects us with a sense of gratitude, or inclines us to obedience, or imparts to us any power to obey its many exhortations to holiness of heart and life, until we have believed that we ourselves, in the midst of all our sinfulness and guilt, have been the objects of this love of God in Christ Jesus, which is so marvellous. It is not God's method of dealing with us, to constrain us to be happy whether we will or no, that thereby he may induce us to follow after holiness. On the contrary he wishes us to be holy in order to secure our happiness. He wishes us to be holy because he himself is holy. Yea, he desires that we shall serve and honour him, not from any motives of selfishness, but from a principle of holy love. The very reason why we are so often and so earnestly urged to believe the unparalleled love of God, is just because the belief of his love to us will beget a reciprocal love in us. And thus faith not only carries us forward to that cheerful obedience which God most justly claims, but at the same time awakens within us those emotions which are essential ingredients in our happiness. It is faith which warms our hearts with the *love* of God, and puts us in possession of the *peace* of God which passeth all understanding, and fills us with *joy* in the Holy Ghost, and brightens our *hopes* of the glory which is to be revealed in us. But inestimable as these gospel blessings are; elevating and sanctifying as these delightful emotions are, we are not permitted to seek after love, and peace, and joy, and hope, merely as a source of personal gratification. The grace of God which teaches us to deny all ungodliness and worldly lusts, teaches us also to deny ourselves, and to take up the cross, that we may be daily followers of the Lord. And our measure of spiritual enlightenment must be small indeed, if we do not perceive how reasonable it is, that, in the gospel plan of salvation, the honour and glory of God should have a place prior and superior to the personal happiness of men.

Self-love, however, must not be confounded with selfish love. Self-love is not necessarily sinful, nor is it inconsistent with supreme love to God, and with disinterested love to our fellowmen. But selfish love is a usurper and a tyrant, which admits of no rival: and selfishness of every kind is one of the many hateful forms of sin which the Gospel of Christ is intended to subdue. The Gospel would be a very defective remedy for the evils under which we labour, unless it revealed deliverance from the power of sin, as well as from its punishment. But the remedy is complete. We may rest assured, therefore, that if the belief of the Gospel did not sanctify us, so neither would it save us. And we know, on the authority of Scripture, and by experience, that faith in a Saviour crucified for sin, purifies the polluted heart of him who believes. He is made free from sin, and has his fruit unto holiness, and the end everlasting life. But as doubts hinder that full exercise of faith in God's forgiving love, which is the glory of the Gospel, so, of necessity, they cannot but cool the ardour of the Christian's love to God and man, and thus they injuriously interfere alike with his personal godliness and his spiritual comfort.

I do not ask you, however, to rest satisfied either with my assertions on this point, or with reasonings of any kind. Here, as in former Letters, I refer you to the unerring standard of Scripture.

In writing to the Galatians, St. Paul says, "For we through the Spirit wait for the hope of righteousness by faith; for in Jesus Christ neither circumcision availeth anything, nor uncircumcision; *but faith which worketh by love,*" Gal 5:5-6. This testimony is decisive of the fact, that the faith of Christ Jesus is essentially an operative principle. It worketh in the way of love to God and man. And this faith manifested in acts of love is what alone avails for our acceptance with God;—what alone warrants "the hope of righteousness." The apostle is speaking in the context of our justification; and by this expression, I understand him to denote that peculiar hope of God's favour, both here and hereafter, which belongs only to them that are justified, not by the works of the law, but by the faith of Jesus Christ, whose righteousness is imputed unto them; "for God hath made him to be sin for us, who knew no sin, that we," who are sinners, "might be made the righteousness of God in him," 2 Cor 5:21.

In this portion of Scripture it is of importance to observe how the faith in Christ which excludes works of the law from all share in the matter of our justification in the sight of a holy God, is nevertheless productive of good works, whereby God is glorified in our sanctification. It is very far from being what St. James condemns as a dead faith. Gospel faith works. It is active and energetic; and it "works by love." It receives the love of God revealed to us in Christ Jesus, his best, "his unspeakable gift:" and love is the return which it makes. "We love him, because he first loved us," 1 John 4:19. How perfectly natural is this! And how beautifully it exhibits the divine adaptation of the Gospel to our mental constitution, as well as to our sinful circumstances! The simple belief of God's love to us effects a great and instantaneous change. It rectifies the moral disorders which sin has occasioned. It compels us, without any physical force, but by an irresistible spiritual compunction, to lay down the weapons of our rebellion. We abandon the service of sin and Satan. We tender allegiance to *him* who assures us of pardon and of welcome. We cease to be his infatuated enemies. We become his willing servants; his loving and obedient children. And as it is obvious that the more fully we realize and appropriate the "manner of love which the Father hath bestowed upon us, that we should be called the sons of God," the more ardent and active will be our love to him so it is equally certain that whatever paralyses our faith, must necessarily impair the fervour of our affection, and the devotedness of our obedience. For this reason, whenever we begin to doubt whether the Gospel of the grace of God is not, after all, a cunningly-devised fable; or whether, at least, we ourselves are the objects of that love of Christ which passeth knowledge; then, although it remains as true as ever that "God is love," and that "in this was manifested the love of God towards us, because that God sent his only-begotten Son into the world, that we might live through him," we ourselves are no longer stimulated and sanctified by this love as we used to be, before doubt supplanted faith. Our affections toward God grow cold. A grateful sense of obligation is wanting to impel our obedience; and languor and lukewarmness creep into all the services we may still continue to render him.

But I wish you also to observe in what an interesting way the apostle here links together "the hope" for the accomplishment of which "we through the Spirit wait," with "the faith which worketh by love." From which connection of faith, hope, and love we gather this great truth, that they all spring from one source, and are all means for the attainment of the same end. They come *from* God, and are designed to bring us *to* God. They are the productions of his own sovereign grace, and they must all redound to his own glory in the sanctification of those to whom they are imparted. Thus it is warrantable to conclude that there is no safety in indulging a hope of eternal life which is not based on such a faith of God's word, as prompts to loving obedience; and still further, that, in some proportion to the sincerity and constancy of the obedience which does flow from faith and love, will be "the assurance of hope." These three Christian graces assist each other in their separate actings; and as they embrace and intertwine, their united strength enables the Christian to walk worthy of his high vocation, and to adorn the Gospel of God his Saviour.

The condition of the Thessalonians, as described by St. Paul, is quite in point: "We give thanks to God always for you all, making mention of you in our prayers; remembering without ceasing your work of faith, and labour of love, and patience of hope in our Lord Jesus Christ," 1 Thess 1:2-3. Here the activity of Christian principle appears in full force, and the excellency of the Christian character is, in few words, portrayed with great correctness. Faith leads to acts of piety towards God, and of benevolence towards man. Love sweetens and lightens all the labour, so that it is never felt to be burdensome. And the hope which is set before him, (as we shall more largely explain in a subsequent Letter,) stimulates the believer to endure with patience every present cross and hindrance; and, in defiance of all opposition, to persevere unto the end in the work of faith, and in the labour of love.

I dare say it may have frequently occurred to you, in reading both of the Epistles to the Thessalonians, that the members of that church seem to have attained a very high degree of Christian perfection. St. Paul addresses them with peculiar tenderness, and in terms of strong commendation. He found no occasion to point out errors, or to administer reproof. But he praises God on their behalf in the most fervent strains, as in the verse which has been already quoted from the commencement of the first Epistle, or as in the following quotation from the second Epistle: "We are bound to thank God always for you, brethren, as it is meet, because that your faith groweth exceedingly, and the charity (love) of every one of you all toward each other aboundeth; so that we ourselves glory in you in the churches of God, for your patience and faith in all your persecutions and tribulations that ye endure," 2 Thess 1:3-4.

You will excuse my introducing these quotations. Indeed, I trust that you unite with myself in finding it a profitable employment to contemplate such a bright pattern of what Christians ought to be. But it is needful for me to make yet another quotation; for the Holy Ghost, under whose inspiration the apostle wrote, has guided him, not only to delineate the character of the Thessalonian Christians as a pattern worthy of our imitation, but likewise to explain in what way, and by what means, this lovely character had been formed and matured. Adverting to the circumstances in which their faith, and love, and hope had originated, he writes to them, "For our gospel came not unto you in word only, but also in power, and in the Holy Ghost, and in much assurance"—"and ye became followers of us, and of the Lord, having received the word in much affliction, with joy of the Holy Ghost," 1 Thess 1:5-6. This explanation is very emphatic. There was a great work of the Holy Ghost amongst them, bringing down every lofty imagination, and removing ignorant prejudices, and imparting teachableness, and commending the salvation of the cross to their consciences with irresistible power. And who can doubt that in every case in which the Gospel is listened to and received with the same humble docility, and with the same holy joy, and believed with the same convincing assurance of its truth, exactly the same effects will be produced? Thus we learn that the indulgence of doubts will certainly raise an insuperable barrier in the way of our attaining that unwavering stedfastness and joyful activity in the Christian life, by which the Thessalonians were distinguished; and that if we really expect or desire to abound in the work of faith, and in the labour of love, it must be by the Gospel coming unto us "in power, and in the Holy Ghost, and in much assurance."

Other parts of Scripture, as might be expected, furnish instructive examples of this combined influence of faith, hope, and love, in leading to decision of Christian principle and practice. For instance, you may carefully peruse Rom 5:1-5. The whole passage brightly displays the high and holy privileges connected with justification by faith, but I request you especially to observe what preeminence is assigned to *love*. The apostle mentions the undeniable truth that believers are privileged with peace, and joy, and hope, enabling them even to "glory in tribulations;" and he accounts for all these blessed and extraordinary effects by simply adding, *"because the love of God is shed abroad in our hearts."* And in his first Epistle to the Corinthians, St. Paul concludes an eloquent description of the meek, and humble, and self-denying, and disinterested, and, in short, heavenly nature of true Christian charity or love, by saying, "And now abideth faith, hope, charity, these three; but the greatest of these is charity," 1 Cor 13:13. It was then quite natural for him to add, "*Follow after charity.*" And this admonition is addressed to all Christians.

Thus, my dear friend, if we honestly desire to serve God with a perfect heart and with a willing mind, and to shine before men in the beauties of holiness, we must diligently cultivate that assured faith in Christ Jesus which worketh by love; for love is the mainspring of all holy obedience. Our Lord and Saviour, who is the great Prophet and Teacher of his church, has said, "Thou shalt love the Lord thy God with all thy heart, and with all thy soul, and with all thy mind. This is the first and great commandment. And the second is like unto it, Thou shalt love thy neighbour as thyself. On these two commandments hang all the law and the prophets," Matt 22:37-40. And with this broad and unequivocal declaration of the Master, agrees the sentiment expressed by his servant Paul: "Owe no man anything, but to love one another; for he that loveth another hath fulfilled the law. For this, Thou shalt not commit adultery, Thou shalt not kill, Thou shalt not steal, Thou shalt not bear false witness, Thou shalt not covet; and if there be any other commandment, it is briefly comprehended in this saying, Thou shalt love thy neighbour as thyself. Love worketh no ill to his neighbour, therefore *love is the fulfilling of the law*," Rom 13:8-10.

I do consider it a very pleasing duty to refresh your memory and my own with these sweet sayings of Christ and of his apostle, because they exhibit true religion in all the loveliness of its heavenly origin, and not as an irksome yoke of bondage, nor as a system of restraint and asceticism; and likewise because they plainly teach us, that what God prescribes and commands, does not consist in that self-righteous and negative morality which passes current in the world, nor in the cold formalities of outward rites and ceremonies, but has its seat in the heart, and, in regard both to God and man, is altogether dictated by love. Yes; it is love to God that must bring us into his presence as worshippers, and keep us from every species of idolatry, and from all manner of profanity, and also from sabbath desecration. And it is love to our fellow-creatures that must regulate our feelings as well as our conduct towards them. For without love there is no fulfilling of the spirit of the law, however strictly the letter of it may be observed; and without love there is no obedience that is well-pleasing unto God, however plausible or praiseworthy it may be in the estimation of men. But you very well know that by nature we are all destitute of this love, being the enemies of God by wicked works, and "living in malice and envy, hateful and hating one another," Titus 3:3. The Gospel of Christ, therefore, by the faith of which our hearts are purified, and the fountain of love, which sin had sealed up, opened afresh within us, is indeed felt and seen to be the wisdom of God, and the power of God, unto the salvation of all who believe it. For, as it was in the love of God to us that the plan of our salvation originated, so it is in our love to God that our salvation is made sure. The love wherewith he hath loved us, when it is experimentally realized, calls into activity our gratitude, and awakens a reciprocal love towards him, and we become new creatures. Enmity and hatred give place to a pure and fervent affection. The commandments of God cease to be complained of as grievous and burdensome. We find obedience to be our happiness. We cordially join issue with the holy psalmist, when he says, "O how I love thy law!"—"How sweet are thy words unto my taste! yea, sweeter than honey to my mouth," Ps 119:97,103. And we can even cheerfully adopt the prophetical language of our Lord himself, "I delight to do thy will, O my God; yea, thy law is within my heart," Ps 40:8. This is salvation. It is deliverance from the usurped tyranny of Satan, and from the debasing power of sin, and from the ensnaring pleasures of this present evil world. It is a blessed thing when faith thus works by love, and constrains us to the ready obedience of all that God requires, and to the patient endurance of all that he appoints. The love which constrains us to serve God with delight and with alacrity, will at the same time make us kind, and courteous, and compassionate, and incline us to "do good to all men as we have opportunity, especially to such as are of the household of faith." And this is holiness. It is that love of God, and that love of our neighbour, on which, as our Saviour says, "hang all the law and the prophets," and which substantially fulfils every moral precept that God has enjoined.

But true as it is that a strong faith in Christ Jesus our Lord begets a strong sense of obligation in the believer, and warms his heart with grateful and adoring love, it is equally true that a wavering faith will be accompanied with less love, and with a feeble sense of obligation. But if the weak faith terminates in doubts respecting either the Saviour's love to us, or our own interest in his great salvation, then these very doubts will go far to extinguish whatever love to him previously existed in the heart; and the doubting Christian will find himself deprived of spiritual strength for the service of God, as Samson was when the locks of his hair were shorn. Besides, there may be, in addition to a weak and doubtsome faith, a very inadequate conviction of our own great guilt and utter helplessness, or of the all-perfect and all-sufficient work of Christ in behalf of sinners; and thus the individual must necessarily be influenced by a low and languid love to his Saviour. All this is finely illustrated in the speech addressed by our Lord to Simon the Pharisee, who was offended when the woman who was a sinner "stood at his feet behind him weeping, and began to wash his feet with tears, and did wipe them with the hairs of her head, and kissed his feet, and anointed them with the ointment." These various actions indicated intense affection towards the Saviour. But Simon knew nothing of the love that was burning in the heart of this woman. He only knew her to have been a sinner, and therefore he wondered that Christ allowed her to touch him. "And Jesus answering said unto him, There was a certain creditor which had two debtors: the one owed five hundred pence, and the other fifty. And when they had nothing to pay, he frankly forgave them both. Tell me, therefore, which of them will love him most? Simon answered and said, I suppose that he to whom he forgave most. And he said unto him, Thou hast rightly judged." Then he presents in striking contrast the unkind and uncivil treatment which he, as an invited guest, had experienced from Simon in his own house, with the unwonted civilities and most affectionate attentions shown to him by this woman, who was a stranger; and he comes to this legitimate conclusion: "Wherefore I say unto you, her sins which are many are forgiven; for she loved much: but to whom little is forgiven, the same loveth little," Luke 7:36-47.

As a general principle, then, we are to understand, that where there is much of the love of Christ in the heart, it is the result of believing in the forgiveness of many sins; and, on the contrary, where there is the belief of little forgiveness, or perhaps a doubt whether there is any forgiveness at all, there will be little love. Now, this is a principle which has a direct and powerful bearing on Christian character and Christian comfort. For in the respective behaviour of the proud, self-righteous Pharisee, and of the poor penitent woman, towards our Lord, there is depicted for our warning, on the one hand, the small and slothful service which is to be expected where there is little love; and for our encouragement, on the other hand, the spontaneous, and devoted, and self-sacrificing services which flow from love when it abounds. And O how anxious should every Christian be that his love may abound, so that he may abound also in every good word and work! And how earnest should every doubting Christian be, by prayer and all other scriptural methods, to obtain deliverance from doubts, whose evil influence is so painfully felt by himself, in the want of that abiding heavenly love, which yields true Christian comfort; and is so plainly seen by others in the imperfections and shortcomings which stain his Christian character!

As another apposite and instructive illustration of the

power and importance of Christian *love*, I would now remind you of St. Paul's memorable prayer for the Ephesians; "that God would grant you according to the riches of his glory, to be strengthened with might by his Spirit in the inner man; that Christ may dwell in your hearts by faith; that ye being rooted and grounded in love, may be able to comprehend with all saints what is the breadth, and length, and depth, and height, and to know the love of Christ, which passeth knowledge, that ye may be filled with all the fulness of God," Eph 3:16-19. This is truly a most comprehensive, and sublime, and marvellous prayer. We might meditate for hours together with much advantage, on the vastness and the preciousness of the apostle's few requests. It is not, however, my present intention to detain you with any lengthened exposition of their meaning. But let us fix our thoughts for a moment on the object of the prayer as a whole. Paul prays for the Ephesians, that they *"may be filled with all the fulness of God."* This is a great, a wonderful request, and, beyond doubt, an extremely important one. We can conceive of nothing so safe, so enriching, so ennobling to any creature, and more especially to fallen and guilty creatures, as to "be filled with all the fulness of God." We never could have dared to make such a request, had not an inspired apostle taught us by his own example. But, in order to the enjoyment of this ultimate object, you will mark how he prays, that they *"may know the love of Christ, which passeth knowledge:"*—just as if the whole fulness of the divine perfections was so concentrated and treasured up in the person and work of Christ, that our experimental knowledge of the Father's love in sending his Son, and of the love of the incarnate Son in dying for our salvation, put us in possession of all that God can bestow. And in order that we may *really* know this love of Christ, although we never can *fully* know it, the apostle prays *"that Christ may dwell in your hearts by faith."* There is something singularly expressive in the *indwelling of Christ*. It implies his permanent presence, affording us the means of continually beholding his excellences, and learning of his wisdom, and sharing in his counsels, and growing in love to him as the consequence of a growing experience of his love to us. And as it is by faith that our hearts are opened to receive Christ, so it is by faith that he *dwells* with us. This strong and stedfast faith must have a gracious origin. It is not indigenous to the heart of fallen man. Therefore the first petition in the chain is, *"to be strengthened with might by his Spirit in the inner man."* The more that Christians study their advancement in holiness, and their enjoyment of spiritual privileges, the more habitually will they pray for the Holy Spirit. As it is through his power that we "abound in hope," so it is in the might of his imparted strength that we have faith to admit and retain Christ, whose presence in our hearts is at once the pledge and the promoter of mutual love; and also the security for our participation in "all the fulness of God." We are assured of this on the testimony of the apostle John, who has said, "God is love; and he that dwelleth in love, dwelleth in God, and God in him," 1 John 4:16. Oh what a marvellous union and communion is this! How condescending on the part of the triune Jehovah to make our hearts his residence! How sanctifying and consoling to us to hold such an endearing fellowship with the Father and the Son through the Holy Ghost! I say, how sanctifying! how very sanctifying is that knowledge of divine love which we obtain when Christ dwells in our hearts by faith! And therefore what can be more prejudicial to our progress in holiness, than the indulgence of those doubts, which hinder the Saviour's entrance into our hearts, or which exclude him after he has blessed us with his gracious presence?

The prayer which has given rise to these reflections, is, it must be admitted, as decidedly a prayer for elevation above the cloudy and cold and barren atmosphere of doubts, as for the full fruition of all the light and warmth and productiveness of a faith which worketh by love. And it ought not to escape your notice, that, immediately after pouring forth this most memorable prayer in behalf of his Ephesian converts, the apostle proceeds to admonish them how they ought to live and act. "I *therefore* beseech you that ye walk worthy of the vocation wherewith ye are called, with all lowliness and meekness, with longsuffering, forbearing one another in love; endeavouring to keep the unity of the Spirit in the bond of peace." And again, "Let all bitterness, and wrath, and anger, and clamour, and evil-speaking, be put away from you, with all malice: and be ye kind one to another, tenderhearted, forgiving one another, even as God for Christ's sake hath forgiven you. Be ye, therefore, followers of God, as dear children; and walk in love as Christ also hath loved us."

These precepts are in admirable keeping with the prayer which preceded them. Nor is there anything in them that is unreasonable. Every Christian must acknowledge that they breathe a very heavenly spirit, and are designed to work in us a very heavenly temper and conduct. Would to God that their observance was more extensively manifested amongst all Christians! There is indeed a lamentable, and I fear at present an increasing lack of love, which is "the bond of perfectness." But sure I am that in our own times it will be the case, as it was in the days of the apostle, that the strong faith which brings into the soul the exceeding riches of the love of Christ, will be the most forward to hear and to obey every apostolic command. We may expect it to be quite otherwise, however, where faith is not exempt from doubt. The man who doubts whether he has been called, can scarcely be expected to feel the obligation of walking worthy of his vocation. And he who doubts whether God has forgiven him, is little likely to be actuated by the Gospel motive to forgive his fellows. And he who doubts whether Christ has loved him, is in a great measure insensible to the duty of loving others. And in the same way I might refer to many of the other preceptive parts of Scripture. But time would fail. And it must be abundantly obvious, from all that I have already stated in this Letter, that the influence of doubts, in checking that glow of affection which naturally accompanies the faith of Christ Jesus, is very great; and, on that account, very prejudicial to the Christian character and comfort of the doubter.

It is not my desire, dear friend, to exhaust your patience; but this love to God and man which faith inflames and feeds, and which doubts smother and subdue;—this holy love which leads to holy obedience, and which is, in fact, the very dawn of heaven here below, deserves some farther consideration. The various views of the subject which have hitherto been submitted to you, are like so many converging lines, which all meet in one point; and in their concentrated light the pernicious influence of religious doubts is rendered very apparent. I am by no means reluctant to hope that the light, emanating from the scriptural illustrations already adduced, has given you a deeper insight than ever into the evil nature and tendency of doubts. Nevertheless, I wish before concluding this Letter, that the vast, I might have said, the unspeakable importance of the love of Christ in the Christian's heart, as a practical principle, should be more distinctly and forcibly stated than it yet has been.

Everyone knows that love, as an affection of the human mind, is most potent in its operations. The scriptural declaration is in strict harmony with actual experience,—"Love is strong as death;" and again, "Many waters cannot quench love, neither can the floods drown it; if a man would give all the substance of his house for love, it would utterly be contemned," Song 8:6-7. With the most unwearied service we cheerfully wait on the object of our affection; and with delighted eagerness we obey his every command, and even anticipate his wishes to the utmost of our power. Love is lavish in its gifts, and never thinks it gives enough. Love is prompt to suffer any privation, to undergo any hardship, to make any personal sacrifice; and in all that it does or suffers for the beloved object, it enjoys a real satisfaction and delight. In thus strongly expressing myself, you cannot say I am overstating the truth. The daily occurrences of real life,—the endearing intercourse of those who are knit together in the bonds of disinterested friendship, the hallowed attachments of conjugal and parental affection, the warmth and devotedness of betrothed hearts,—all testify that this picture of love is not at all too highly coloured.

Allow me, then, to ask, whether this affection of the mind, which is so powerful when directed to natural objects, should be strengthened or weakened when it is directed to the divine Saviour?—whether it should be stronger or weaker, when purified and ennobled by divine grace, than when polluted and debased by sin? There can be only one answer to these questions. Our reason and our conscience both reply, that, as enlightened and sanctified men, our love even towards earthly objects should be fervent in proportion to its purity; and that our love to Christ should be undivided and supreme. In the Holy Scripture this truth is openly declared, to which there is a secret response within our own bosom. The Saviour himself hath said, "He that loveth father or mother more than me, is not worthy of me; and he that loveth son or daughter more than me, is not worthy of me," Matt 10:37. And St. Peter says to those whose faith and hope were in God, "Seeing ye have purified your souls in obeying the truth through the Spirit unto unfeigned love of the brethren; see that ye love one another with a pure heart fervently," 1 Pet 1:22.

Now, my dear friend, I know not how you may be affected by these remarks, but in writing them I feel self-condemned. In this case there is an awful and a melancholy difference between what one ought to be, and what one actually is. I thank God for the measure of grace bestowed upon me; because I do know that by his grace all the ties of nature are strengthened and sanctified, so that I have a greater and a holier affection for my kindred according to the flesh, than otherwise I should have had; and also far more of benevolent interest in mankind at large, and of sympathy towards all who are in any distress; dependent of that special love for fellow-Christians, which is a distinctive proof of having "passed from death unto life." But I do not feel that my love comes nearly up to the high standard of Gospel requirement. Oh! it is *very* difficult to love one's neighbour as he loves himself. Nor am I prepared to lay down my life for my brethren. And yet the beloved and loving apostle John hath placed on record these words, "Hereby perceive we the love of God, because he laid down his life for us; and we ought to lay down our lives for the brethren," 1 John 3:16. Might he not rather have said, that we ought to lay down our lives *for God*? In saying so he would have reiterated the sentiment which he had often heard from the lips of his divine Master. But, in a subsequent part of the same epistle, while still expatiating on the duty and the blessedness of love, he obviates this very objection. "If a man say, I love God, and hateth (or withholdeth love from) his brother, he is a liar; for he that loveth not his brother whom he hath seen, how can he love God whom he hath not seen?" And in reality we manifest our love to God, in every expression of love to our fellow-creatures, and especially to our fellow-Christians. But the apostle's argument is addressed to our common sense. We are daily experiencing the difference, in the effect produced by what we actually see, and what we merely know by report. And as God is necessarily out of sight, (although we ought always to realize his presence,) there is a convincing propriety in drawing out our affections towards those with whom we are associated, as partakers of the same humanity, as occupiers of the same world, and as the offspring of the same heavenly Father. The whole inhabitants of heaven live together in love, as one united and harmonious family. And the Gospel of Christ excites my admiration, in its fitness to restore to this earth that element of universal love, which sin has partially, and, for a season, destroyed. The Gospel teaches me to love the whole human race, because they are the creatures of God, and because he loves them. And it teaches me to love all true Christians with brotherly kindness, because our Lord Jesus Christ owns them as his brethren, and regards every act of kindness done to them, as something done unto himself. This is a duty imposed on me by the highest authority, and to the discharge of which I am urged by the strongest motives. The duty is in itself most delightful. Never am I happier than when the glow of love is felt within, and when my passing hours are filled up with words of kindness, or with acts of benevolence. And I expect that your own experience corresponds with mine. But the duty is too often neglected, and, at best, it is very inadequately performed, because the great motive to its performance is not sufficiently felt. And I am much mistaken if you too are not ready to join in this humiliating confession. The truth is, that although we do not doubt either the truth of the Gospel salvation, or our own interest in it, yet our faith at best is so weak, and we live so little in the exercise of faith, that the unparalleled love of God in Christ Jesus is too seldom and too feebly realized, to constrain us either to love him with all the heart and soul, or to love our neighbour as ourself. Verily it behooves us to acknowledge with shame and sorrow that we are unprofitable servants.

But our unprofitableness—our shortcomings—and all our unnumbered offences, only render the love of God to us the more conspicuous and amazing. The one short Scripture assertion, *"God is love,"* may well supply us from day to day with the most edifying and peace-giving meditations. And the difficulty which we must have encountered in such meditations, has been marvellously removed, in compassion to our limited capacities; for whilst God is a spirit and invisible, whose nature surpasses our comprehension, "the man Christ Jesus" is revealed to us as "the image of the invisible God." On him of whom Moses and the prophets, as well as the evangelists and apostles, have written so largely, we ought ever to fix our thoughts; for in the whole lovely character and mediatorial work of our Saviour, we are furnished with the brightest display of God's wondrous love to guilty men. Christ is the only ladder by which our thoughts can rise to a scriptural knowledge of the true God. Christ is the only medium through which God is seen as a just God, and yet a Saviour. Christ, is the only revealer of God's hatred of sin, in combination with his love to sinners. Thus when we think of God, and of his love to us, there is a necessity for our thoughts centering in Christ; in whom, as our Surety and Redeemer, we have the encouraging assurance, that the love of God has made for our salvation the greatest sacrifice that even God himself could make; and dispenses to us the most inestimable benefits that even God himself can bestow. And did we habitually and impressively realize this love of God to us, which is infinite, and inexhaustible, and unchangeable, and everlasting;—did we experimentally comprehend its truth, although it has an incomprehensible breadth and length and depth and height;—and did we really know its efficacy, although it passeth knowledge;—I am sure we should then have no cause to complain of cold hearts, although we might still feel that the most affectionate and devoted service we can ever render to God, is a very worthless and inadequate return for his spontaneous and surpassing love to us.

Our wisdom then, and our safety too, lies in the maintenance of a strong and stedfast faith in Christ. Faith is nourished and kept in exercise by Scripture reading, by meditation, and by prayer. It is good to have the mind well stored with the rich treasures of divine truth, on which we may meditate by day or by night, when we are stretched on our beds, or when we sit in the retired chamber, or when we walk by the wayside. And, by the example of an inspired apostle, we are taught to pray to God, "to be strengthened with might by his Spirit in the inner man; that Christ may dwell in our hearts by faith." In the use of such prayers, we come to know and comprehend his love, and to be animated by its all-constraining power. It is when we are "rooted and grounded in love," in consequence of the indwelling of Christ, that we catch the martyr's spirit, and become prepared even for a martyr's sufferings, and are enabled to rejoice in hope of the martyr's crown. And oh! how wondrously it elevates our Christian character, and how essentially it contributes to our Christian comfort, to feel assured of the Saviour's love to us, and, at the same time, of our own love to him! In such a state of mind, our lives would not be unmarked by works of faith, and labours of love, and patience of hope. The power of divine grace would be magnified in us; and we should be able to adopt as our own, the noble sentiments, and the triumphant language of St. Paul: "It is Christ that died, yea rather, that is risen again, who is even at the right hand of God, who also maketh intercession for us. Who shall separate us from the love of Christ? shall tribulation, or distress, or persecution, or famine, or nakedness, or peril, or sword? As it is written, for thy sake we are killed all the day long; we are accounted as sheep for the slaughter. Nay, in all these things we are more than conquerors through him that loved us. For I am persuaded that neither death, nor life, nor angels, nor principalities, nor powers, nor things present, nor things to come, nor height, nor depth, nor any other creature, shall be able to separate us from the love of God, which is in Christ Jesus our Lord," Rom 8:34-39.

In the next Letter I shall continue my observations on the pernicious influence of doubts, and, for the present, I express my hope that as you value Christian consistency, and desire prosperity of soul, you will avoid that evil influence to the utmost of your power.

Believe me ever, etc., etc.

LETTER 7

DOUBTS ARE INJURIOUS TO THE CHRISTIAN CHARACTER AND COMFORT OF THE DOUBTER—Continued

V. THEY CHECK HIS SPIRITUALITY AND HEAVENLY-MINDEDNESS

Spirituality and heavenly-mindedness are Christian duties, privileges, blessings.—"To be spiritually-minded is life and peace."—Highly desirable that spirituality should be universal among Christians.—But doubts obstruct and repress it.—Distinction between spirituality and heavenly-mindedness.—This latter word does not occur in Scripture; but it has a scriptural meaning.—In the New Testament, "heaven" is often significant of blessings to be enjoyed upon the earth.—The word "heavenly" is peculiar to the Gospel dispensation.—"The patterns of things in the heavens" contrasted with "the heavenly things themselves," Heb 9:21-23.—"The heavenlies" proved to be the Christian Church.—Gospel privileges, and Gospel precepts.—Heavenly-mindedness described.—Exemplified in the active life of our Lord himself, and of his servant St. Paul.—Heavenly-mindedness is attainable—but only by a life of faith.—Doubts are destructive of it.—Thus they manifest their pernicious influence on Christian character and comfort.—Concluding observations on the frequent use of the expression, "in the heavenlies," in St. Paul's Epistle to the Ephesians.

My dear Friend,

The more narrowly we look into the subject, the more evident it becomes, that doubts raise up many formidable barriers in the way of the Christian's progress heavenward, and greatly hinder his enjoyment of those spiritual privileges and blessings which rightfully belong to every believer in the Lord Jesus Christ.

To be spiritually-minded, and to be heavenly-minded, are not merely duties to the performance of which we are bound by the strongest obligations: they are privileges in the appreciation of which we ought to delight: they are special blessings for which we ought to render thanks to the Giver of all good—"the Father of lights, from whom cometh every good and perfect gift."

What we generally call spirituality, is a state of mind peculiar to the people of God. It never manifests itself among the ungodly. It is something even altogether distinct and distinguishable from the sanctimoniousness with which self-righteous formalists and hypocritical professors of religion either deceive themselves, or try to deceive their fellowmen. But heavenly-mindedness is a step still farther in advance. I believe it is the highest point of Christian character on earth. Its attainment, therefore, should be the object of our holiest ambition, as it elevates our souls to sweet communion with God, and places us on the verge of heaven itself. Doubts, however, as I am now to explain, tend *to check that spirituality* which ought ever to distinguish the Christian, and *to counteract that heavenly-mindedness* to which it is alike his duty and his privilege to aspire. This is a new point of view, in which I purpose to exhibit the baneful influence of doubts on Christian character and comfort. And I trust you will not be displeased, should my observations be directed more fully to the heavenly, than to the spiritual state of mind.

In order, then, the better to estimate the greatness of the loss to which the doubting Christian is subjected, it may be of advantage that we endeavour to ascertain, as correctly as we can, what is the proper meaning of heavenly-mindedness. And it will at once occur to you that this expression, which is so current amongst religious people, and the very sight and sound of which is so pleasing to our eyes and ears, is never used by any of the sacred writers. It is not a scriptural expression. But in the Epistle to the Romans, we meet with something very similar to it. The apostle says, "To be spiritually-minded is life and peace." In the margin of our Bibles a different translation is placed at our option—"The minding of the Spirit;" and as to the right interpretation of what this means, we are much assisted, not only by the other clause of the same verse, which is antithetical, but by the whole context.

If you turn to Rom 8, you will find St. Paul, at its commencement, is describing the blessedness of an experimental knowledge of the Gospel. The believer in Jesus Christ is represented as possessing "the Spirit of life," and having been "made free from the law of sin and death." For such a man there is now no condemnation, because he is said to "walk," which means to conduct himself,—to live and act, "not after the flesh, but after the Spirit." Here, then, according to the apostle, is the grand distinction between the believer and the unbeliever; between the regenerate and the unregenerate; between the natural and the spiritual man; "For they that are after the flesh do mind the things of the flesh; but they that are after the Spirit the things of the Spirit." And it is immediately added, "For to be carnally-minded," or, as it is in the margin, "the minding of the flesh," "is death; but to be spiritually-minded," or, the minding of the Spirit, "is life and peace." There can be no mistaking of the sense in which St. Paul employs the terms, "the flesh," and "the Spirit," standing as they do in direct opposition, the one to the other. "The Spirit" summarily denotes that whole renovation of heart and life,—that *new man* in Christ Jesus, which constitutes the true Christian. "The flesh," on the other hand, is descriptive of human nature in its sinful and unrenewed condition, which is elsewhere emphatically called *the old man*. It follows, therefore, that "the minding of the flesh" must not be understood in the restricted signification of a mere concern for our bodily comfort, nor of a lawful attention to the business of the world, because these things are not in themselves sinful; and yet it is expressly declared, that "to be carnally-minded is death." Nor can "the minding of the Spirit" be fairly interpreted as synonymous with the application of our own mental faculties to the comprehension of those truths which the Spirit of God reveals, or to the wondrous modes of his operation, because for such mental exercises no supernatural enlightenment is required, and yet it is expressly declared, that "to be spiritually-minded is life and peace."

But our chief inquiry is into the real meaning of the word φρονημα which is translated "minded," or "the minding;" and I may mention that it occurs nowhere else in the New Testament than in this passage which we are considering, although the verb from which the substantive noun is derived is of frequent occurrence, and is differently translated in different places. Thus, in the immediately preceding verse we read, "They that are in the flesh *do mind* (φρονοῦσιν) the things of the flesh." Again in the rebuke which our Lord administered to Peter, "Get thee behind me, Satan, for thou art an offence unto me; for *thou savourest* (φρονεῖς) not the things that be of God, but those that be of men," Matt 16:23. And so in the apostolic exhortation, "*Set your affection* (φρονεῖτε) on things above, not on things on the earth," Col 3:2. These are sufficient proof that though the translations of the same word vary, there is great similarity in their sense; and from these three specimens we gather that the verb signifies, not merely to be acquainted with, or to reflect upon, or to give the mind's attention to, any object, but to do so willingly and with satisfaction, or to have a relish and delight in the doing of it. The derivative noun ought, in fairness, to be allowed a corresponding signification. And thus we easily come to understand how "the minding of the Spirit," that is, the wisdom and knowledge in divine truths which the Spirit of God imparts, and which is accompanied with feelings of holy delight therein, distinguishes a prosperous Christian from an unregenerated and carnally-minded man, whose wisdom and knowledge are conversant only with the things of this present evil world, and who ever finds his pleasure in the things that are evil.

A spiritually-minded man devoutly acknowledges the personality of the Holy Ghost; meekly submits himself to his instruction in the things of God and of Christ; meditates much on his mighty workings, which are like the wind, that bloweth where it listeth; earnestly desires the witness of the Spirit with his own spirit; has a holy relish for spiritual exercises; and finds in them a true and satisfying peace. Would to God that you and I, my friend, had a deep and abiding spirituality! And, oh, how desirable it is that all Christians should be spiritually-minded! Then should we see a visible separation betwixt the church and the world—betwixt them that fear God, and them that fear him not. But you must be sensible, from your own experience, how directly any relaxation in the exercise of a stedfast faith, and still more, how the least giving way to a spirit of doubt, tends to check the rise, or the progress, or the continuance of that spirituality, which is so consistent with Christian character, and which contributes so essentially to the enjoyment of Christian comfort.

But it was my proposal to condemn doubts as a sad hindrance, not merely to spiritual-mindedness, but chiefly to heavenly-mindedness. And I selected the one term in preference to the other, because I imagine that when we speak of a man being heavenly-minded, something different, and something more is intended, than when we speak of his being spiritually-minded. The difference, however, is only in degree, and not in kind; for I admit that the two words have a close affinity, as have the two descriptions of character to which they refer. But if I mistake not, there is a distinction between them, which lies in this, that in the religion to which we give the name of heavenly-minded, there is a more glorious liberty, and a nobler elevation of soul, and altogether a greater measure of cheerful resignation to the will of God, and of placid joyfulness in his service, than is usually ascribed to spiritual-mindedness; which rather conveys the idea of a self-denied and subdued temperament, of a contrite and strict and watchful inward discipline, and altogether of a religion that is pure and peaceful, rather than elevated and joyous. This, however, is only an opinion, which you may value at what it is worth. At all events, I trust you will so far coincide with me, as to award to heavenly-mindedness the nearest approach to perfection that is ever experienced or ever exhibited on this earth. And as, for this very reason, it is the more likely to be assailed by doubts; so is it likewise the more evident, that great is the loss which the Christian suffers, when doubts hinder him from attaining, or from preserving, that high and holy frame of mind, which is the pledge and the prelude of heaven.

Although I have said that *heavenly-minded* is a word which is not to be found in the Holy Scriptures, yet the *use* of the word is perfectly warrantable; and by a little careful research, we may also discover that it has a scriptural *meaning*.

In the Old Testament we have frequent mention of "heaven," or "the heavens," as a part of the material universe, and as the throne or special residence of *him* whose presence is everywhere, and who is the Creator and Preserver of all things. But it is in the New Testament alone that we find this word used as significant of spiritual blessings, and *descriptive of a state of blessedness to be enjoyed on the earth.*

The Gospel of our salvation by the Lord Jesus Christ is

very often and most emphatically called, "the kingdom, or the reign of heaven;" and I conceive it is in connection with this cheering revelation of divine grace, that God Almighty is designated "our heavenly Father." Indeed, the word *heavenly* is peculiar to the Gospel dispensation. We do not meet with it in the writings of Moses or the prophets, but our Saviour makes use of it on some occasions; and as it is quite a favourite word with St. Paul, it may be both interesting and instructive to investigate, in what sense, and for what purposes, it is employed.

Now, my dear friend, you will not be offended should I suppose, that, as it was for a long time with myself, so it still is the case with you, that you consider it a matter of indifference whether you say, "our heavenly Father," or "our Father which is in heaven." You have been accustomed to look on these two modes of expression as embodying precisely the same truth. And so, in regard to the passages in the epistles where the word "heavenly," or "heavenlies," is introduced, you have thought it might answer just as well, and would have conveyed exactly the same meaning, had some adaptation of the word "heaven" been used. After mature reflection, however, I am persuaded that we sadly miss the mark, in thus confounding ideas that are in themselves distinct. And now I feel constrained to believe that the expression "in heaven" is designed to fix our thoughts on *a certain locality*, whereas the word "heavenly" is designed to fix our thoughts *on some moral quality or attribute*. Thus, when we read of our Father which is *in heaven*, we ought particularly to think of *the place* of his residence; but when we read of our *heavenly* Father, we ought rather to think of *his character*;—of some peculiar feelings and dispositions towards us, his guilty creatures, which entitle him to this appropriate and endearing appellation. On the same principle I conclude that when St. Paul, in his writings, uses the word "heavenly," we must not understand him as referring us to transactions or enjoyments in the actual heavens, as a locality separated from the earth; but merely as describing in the strongest language the surpassing excellence and preciousness of those privileges which are connected with the Gospel of Christ, and which are enjoyed, even on this earth, by every genuine believer.

The one passage which first arrested my attention as a key to all the others where this word occurs, is in the Epistle to the Hebrews. At Heb 9:21-23, we read, "Moreover, he (Moses) sprinkled likewise with blood both the tabernacle and all the vessels of the ministry. And almost all things are by the law purged with blood; and without shedding of blood is no remission. It was therefore necessary that the patterns of things in the heavens should be purified with these; but the heavenly things themselves with better sacrifices than these." Now, in this striking quotation, you will observe that the whole religious ritual which was prescribed by God to the Israelites,—the tabernacle in the wilderness, and afterwards the temple at Jerusalem, with all the furniture, and utensils, and priests, and worshippers,—are here denominated *"the patterns of things in the heavens,"* which it was necessary should all be purged with the blood of the animals appointed for sacrifice: and with this is contrasted what the apostle calls *"the heavenly things themselves,"* which, he says, it was also necessary should be purified, but with "better sacrifices,"—with more precious blood than that "of bulls and of goats." Nor can we doubt for a moment as to his meaning in reference to the "better sacrifices;" for in a subsequent verse, after having adverted to the entrance of Christ "into heaven itself, to appear in the presence of God for us," and to the perfection of his priestly service compared with that of Aaron and his sons, he makes this declaration, "But now once in the end of the world hath *He* appeared to put away sin by *the sacrifice of himself*." Thus we reach the irresistible conclusion, that whatever has been sprinkled with the blood of Christ, and purified thereby, must be "the heavenly things" of which the apostle speaks. And this great truth is repeated in the following chapter, where the apostle proves, that the coming of Christ to do the will of God, and the one offering of himself for sin, has superseded the sacrifices offered under the law, and opened up for believers on earth an acceptable entrance even into "the holiest"—that is, the inner sanctuary, which was the type and figure of heaven itself, Heb 10:19.

I feel myself bordering on the large and inviting subject of the atonement. But it shall be my endeavour to confine my remarks to an explanation of *"the heavenlies;"* and in doing so to study the utmost brevity that is consistent with perspicuousness.

Let me request of you attentively to peruse the whole of Heb 9, with the one which precedes, and with the first half of that which follows. Read the whole passage at once. Indeed, it will answer the purpose still better, if you can read continuously from the commencement of the epistle, onwards till Heb 10:22. And if I do not greatly miscalculate, it will then clearly appear to you, that *the gospel dispensation* is *the reality* of which the law, with all its ceremonial institutions, was only *the example*; for John the Baptist bare witness, that "the law was given by Moses, but *grace and truth* came by Jesus Christ," John 1:17. And still farther, you will find ample grounds for concluding, that *the Christian church*, which is composed of living men in successive ages, who have believed in the Lord Jesus Christ, and who, in their collective capacity, constitute "the house of God," is *the substance* of which the movable tabernacle, in the first instance, and afterwards the fixed temple, were but *the shadows*. Let these grand leading facts be well understood and cordially believed; and then I expect we shall agree in looking to this very earth, on which we now dwell, for the realization of "the heavenly things themselves," which St. Paul contrasts with the mere "patterns." I say, on this very earth, and I add, even at this present time, the exalted title of "the heavenlies" most justly and appropriately belongs to all those persons on whom the blood of the Lamb of God is sprinkled, as well as to the wondrous privileges with which, in consequence of being thus purified, they are invested; because the title, as I trust you are prepared to acknowledge, is descriptive rather of qualities and properties that are of *a heavenly character*, than of any exclusive *place*, where such properties and qualities may be developed.

These great and glorious prospects are lawful food for the nourishment of heavenly-mindedness. But what I wish you to see distinctly, and deeply to feel, is, that even now, under the existing era of grace, there is abundance of Scripture authority for applying to *the Christian church*, notwithstanding the imperfections and disorders that prevail in her, a designation so exalted and honourable as that of "the heavenlies."

And first of all, I must refer you Heb 12:18-29. Read it. The passage is too long for quotation. But you will recollect that the apostle is addressing men who were Christians, but who had been Jews. And in contrasting their former with their present privileges, he uses these remarkable expressions: "But *ye are come* unto Mount Zion, and unto the city of the living God, *the heavenly* Jerusalem, and to an innumerable company of angels, to the general assembly and church of the firstborn, which are written in heaven, and to God the Judge of all, and to the spirits of just men made perfect, and to Jesus the Mediator of the new covenant, and *to the blood of sprinkling*, that speaketh better things than that of Abel." In this long and astonishing enumeration of the spiritual privileges which belong to true Christians, you will be struck with the mention of "the blood of sprinkling" in connexion with "the heavenly Jerusalem," etc., because it shows so perfect an accordance with the passage on which I have already offered some comments. And, above all, you must not overlook the fact, that the apostle speaks in the present tense. He certainly gives a catalogue of very heavenly things. But he does not tell believers to view them as future and far off. No: he pointedly says, *"ye are come."* As believers in the Lord Jesus Christ, who have been sprinkled and purified with his blood, we are admitted into "the heavenly Jerusalem." Although dwelling on the earth, amidst many evils and imperfections, this is nevertheless our real and exalted position,—this is our actual and present privilege. We have been made by grace to sit together with Christ our glorified Lord "in the heavenlies." But, alas! the weakness of faith in all of us, and the doubts which darken and depress so many, do not allow us to realize our true position, or to enjoy as we ought our high and undoubted privilege.

As another illustration I beg you to notice, that, in the foregoing quotation, *the Christian church* is represented as "the city of the living God;" and in exact harmony with this beautiful figure St. Paul says to the Philippians, "Brethren, be followers together of me, and mark them which walk so as ye have us for an ensample;" "for *our citizenship* ($πολίτευμα$) *is in heaven*, from whence we look for the Saviour, the Lord Jesus Christ," Phil 3:17,20. Here, also, the apostle uses the present tense. He says not, Ye are going to heaven, and the time draws near when ye will participate in the immunities of the city of the living God; but even now, whilst still sojourning on the earth, our citizenship is in heaven ($οὐρανοῖς$). And in writing to the Ephesian Christians he introduces the same figure with much magnificence, combining with the city the idea of an house or temple, which is also to be met with in many other parts of holy writ. "Now, therefore, ye are no more strangers and foreigners, but *fellow-citizens* with the saints, and of *the household of God*; and are built upon the foundation of the apostles and prophets, Jesus Christ himself being the chief cornerstone; in whom all the building fitly framed together, groweth unto *an holy temple* in the Lord: *in whom ye also are builded together for an habitation of God* through the Spirit," Eph 2:19-22. And what, I ask, can be more heavenly,—more like heaven, than to be part of the very household of God? What more heavenly than to form a part of that spiritual edifice of which the Son of God is himself the chief cornerstone? What more heavenly than to be an habitation for God to dwell in; a spiritual temple, in which *he* may be continually worshipped with the sacrifices of a broken and a contrite spirit, and at the same time with the peace-offerings of a thankful heart and of joyful lips?

I might adduce a multiplicity of other passages, particularly such as inculcate the real though mysterious union which subsists between Christ and those who are given to him of the Father,—a union which is uniformly represented as subsisting *now*, and which will never be dissolved. Oh, what an honour! what an infinite dignity to be conferred on any creature, and especially on sinful men! You may prosecute this research at your leisure. I need not trespass further on your patience. The examples which have been adduced are amply sufficient to satisfy every person of ordinary candour and reflection, that *the Christian church*, as a whole, and even the individual members of it, blessed as they are, through "the blood of sprinkling," with such nearness of access to God, and such intimate communion and fellowship with him, and such tokens of his love, and such supplies of grace for present necessities, may be regarded as justly warranting the apostolic description, "the heavenly things themselves."

Had I not already detained you on this subject so much longer than I wished to do, it would be interesting in no common degree to inquire in what particulars the Mosaical institutions furnished "patterns" of those truly "heavenly blessings" which are fulfilled unto us by the gospel of Jesus Christ our Lord. But, were it only as a hint to help your own inquiries, I must be permitted just to mention, that, as it is only in Christ that individual believers are complete, and as it is his finished work alone on which the church universal is based, and by which it is upreared, and upheld, and enriched, and adorned; so, unless we can find Christ and his work typically exhibited in the furniture and in the services of the Jewish tabernacle, which for the time being was "the house of God," we should come short of the conviction that they were "patterns of things in the heavens," and that the things of which they were patterns are realized in the Gospel Church. Do, however, take a look into this. Look with the eye of faith, and submit yourself to the guidance of the Spirit of truth; and, assuredly, every principal object that attracts your notice will testify of Christ. You will see him in the mercy seat; in the altar of incense; in the golden candlestick; in the table of shewbread; in the altar of sacrifice; in the victims that were offered; yes, and in the priest who offered them. The more narrowly you examine, the more apparent it will become, that under the Law, the whole solemn religious ritual was but "a shadow of good things to come," and consisted only of "the patterns" of those heavenly realities with which we are favoured under the Gospel. And every fresh discovery of Christian truth lying under these Jewish shadows, and prefigured by these divinely-constructed patterns, will afford essential aid in the correct interpretation of the word "heavenly," whether it occurs in the discourses of our Lord, or in the writings of his apostles.

And now, my friend, if the scriptural illustrations to which I have solicited your attention have any value, we shall understand from them that heavenly-mindedness is something intelligible, and rational, and attainable. It does not consist in the excitement of high religious feeling; nor in visionary ecstasies; nor in fanatical rhapsodies; nor in the vagaries of an uncontrolled imagination. These are in general the accompaniments of ignorance, and of great want of judgment. And although I should be sorry to say that persons who give indulgence to such excesses are altogether devoid of true Christianity, yet there is too much room to infer, that, in their case, the workings of the flesh are more manifest than the workings of the Spirit. Neither does heavenly-mindedness consist in the mental quietness of mysticism; nor in the bodily seclusion of monachism. In order to its exercise, there is no necessity for the abstraction of either body or mind from the place which Providence allots to us here below, or from the personal and relative duties which are incumbent upon us as members of human society. Were all Christians continually shut up within the cloisters of an abbey, or were all the hours of every passing day spent in the retirement of their closets, their light could not shine before men, and they would cease to act on society as the salt of the earth. You may depend upon it, there is a gross error in the notion that we must be monks and nuns, or hermits and anchorites, before we can become heavenly-minded. Another great error it is to imagine that we cannot be heavenly-minded unless our thoughts are continually directed upwards to the literal heavens, and our affections exclusively set on objects that are spiritual and invisible. Far be it from me to deny the duty or the benefit of living above the world whilst we are in it, and of withdrawing our thoughts and affections from objects that are of an earthly and unworthy character. But some pious and well-meaning people seem to forget that the design of the Gospel is to bring heaven down to earth,—yea, to bring heaven into our own hearts. And we have seen that the blessings of the Gospel, as enjoyed by the church of Christ on earth, and even in her present militant condition, are what the Scriptures call "the heavenly things themselves." It is true that amongst our present blessings, as believers, we are called to rejoice in the hope of glory;—the glory of living and reigning with Christ on the earth in his heavenly kingdom; and the still higher glory of heaven itself, when this earth shall pass away like a scroll, when time shall be swallowed up in eternity, and when God shall be all in all. To be allowed such transcendent hopes, and yet to close our minds against their elevating and animating power;—to have such glorious prospects opened up before us, and yet to refrain from their contemplation, would be an unpardonable neglect of some of the noblest privileges which belong to us as the Lord's redeemed. It is strange, indeed, that our thoughts are so seldom turned to these heavenly realities; and most desirable it is that they should form the subject of our more frequent meditations. But what I wish to state is this, that, although these hopes and prospects, which concern the life that is to come, are proper materials for the cultivation of heavenly-mindedness, yet they are not the only materials. Those Gospel privileges and promises and precepts, which concern the life that now is, demand our special and constant attention; and in attending to them, I humbly believe that we shall attain unto heavenly-mindedness, according to the scriptural meaning of the term.

Our impetuous and aspiring spirits may attempt to soar in thought into the highest heavens, and to stretch into the boundless regions of eternity; but these attempts are painfully disappointed. Such flights may be often repeated, but they never succeed. The earth is still our native home, and we find that we cannot leave it. The burden of mortality still presses our spirits downwards, and makes us to "groan within ourselves, waiting for the adoption, to wit, the redemption of our body," Rom 8:23. But oh! how thankful—how very thankful should we be, whilst we cannot as yet go to God, that God promises to come to us; and that although Jesus, in the character of our High Priest, and Advocate, and Forerunner, has passed into the heavens, to appear in the presence of God for us, he nevertheless has given us the cheering assurance, "Lo, I am with you always!" Nor is this all; for the Holy Ghost, who proceeds from the Father and the Son, as a Guide and Comforter, dwells with the church, which is the mystical body of Christ; and dwells also in the hearts of all the many members of the body, inspiring them with the spirit of adoption, whereby they cry, "Abba, Father." What unspeakable privileges are these! Well might the apostle John exclaim, *"beloved, now are we the sons of God, and it doth not yet appear what we shall be."* Let us ponder well the import of these words, while we joyfully respond, "Now are we the sons of

God!" And if through the riches of divine grace we are thus so greatly blessed, notwithstanding our insignificance and guilt;—if we are the sons of God, and the joint heirs with Christ;—if we are reconciled unto God, and accepted in the Beloved;—if we are called, and chosen, and forgiven, and sanctified;—then, surely, "the minding" of these things, is not only what we can understand and attain unto, but what is well fitted to raise our affections above the world, and the things of the world; and to constrain us to live as strangers and pilgrims, who are pressing onwards to the heavenly country.

But there are precepts enjoined by the Gospel, as well as privileges conferred. These precepts, which are so numerous, so varied, so self-denying, and so holy, must not be disconnected from "the heavenly things themselves," which are freely given to us of God. They are all intended to guard us against sin, and to guide us into the practice of holiness. In the Saviour's discourses, and in the apostolic epistles, the fulness and spirituality of the divine requirements are unfolded; and divine strength is promised for the performance of duty. There are duties which we owe to God, and to our fellow-creatures, and to ourselves; and no duty of whatever kind must be neglected; and all duties, whether sacred or secular, whether personal or relative, should be performed in a religious spirit. Think on the prayer which our Lord has taught us: "Our Father, which art in heaven! May thy name be hallowed; may thy kingdom come; may thy will be done *on earth as it is in heaven!*" In heaven the worship of God is universal, and obedience to God is perfect. This is the standard to which we, on earth, are directed to aspire. God is not only the object of our homage, but his revealed will is our law. And with these petitions of the Lord's prayer, the injunction of St. Paul agrees right well. "Whether, therefore, ye eat or drink, or *whatsoever ye do*, do all to the glory of God," 1 Cor 10:31. Now this word, "whatsoever," is as comprehensive as possible. It is a mistake to imagine that no duties are of a religious nature except they directly concern God, such as praise, and prayer, and the study of his word, in private or in public. You do not need to be reminded that the New Testament Scriptures lay down, in plain language, and with great minuteness, how Christians ought to conduct themselves in every situation of life,—as husband and wife, as parents and children, as masters and servants, as rulers and subjects, as fellow-Christians, and as fellow-creatures, in youth or old age, in poverty or affluence, in prosperity or adversity. And you will please not to forget, that so far from exempting us from the ordinary labours and avocations of life, we are expressly enjoined to be "not slothful in business," Rom 12:11. But whilst diligent in our several callings, and labouring with our hands, if need be, to provide for ourselves and our households, so as to owe no man anything but love; we must ever desire, as Christians, to be "fervent in spirit, serving the Lord;" and "whatsoever we do in word or deed, to do all in the name of the Lord Jesus, giving thanks to God and the Father by him," Col 3:17. And I am impressed with the conviction, that heavenly-mindedness may be cultivated, and ought to be manifested, by a careful and constant attention to Gospel precepts, just as successfully as it is in the enjoyment of Gospel privileges.

In confirmation of the foregoing views and illustrations, I might refer to the whole recorded life of our Lord Jesus Christ. None will deny that he was heavenly-minded in the highest degree. But he was a man of faith and prayer; and his was a life of rational and religious activity. We find him in the temple, serving God; but we also find him frequenting the busy haunts of men, and unremitting in the discharge of every social and relative duty. In him precept and example are most instructively combined. And so likewise it was with his apostles. Look to St. Paul. He furnishes a bright example of heavenly-mindedness. But truly he was neither a pious enthusiast, nor a meditative recluse. His life was one of extraordinary labour, and travel, and peril, and activity. Like his divine Master, it was his desire and his delight *to do* the will of God; and in all his doings the glory of God was the end at which he aimed. He was a heavenly-minded man, because his faith was not enfeebled by doubts.

But I must not enlarge. And now should you ask me to bring my observations to a point, and briefly to state my ideas of heavenly-mindedness, I answer readily, that it is the concentration of gospel faith, and love, and hope, and peace, and joy, operating in harmony with an extensive and accurate knowledge of gospel truth, yielding the enjoyment of gospel privileges, and leading to the practice of gospel precepts. It is the minding of the heavenlies. It is savouring the things of Christ. It is contemplating the great salvation with wonder, love, and praise. It is realizing the gracious presence of God through the Spirit, and delighting in the blessings of adoption. It is setting the affections on all the members of the body, which is the church, as well as on the glorious Head himself. It is feasting with holy relish on all the ordinances and appointments of the Lord, which are designed for the spiritual nourishment of his body. It is, in a word, so experiencing the truth, and power, and consolation of *present grace*, as to rejoice in the assurance of millennial blessedness, and of everlasting glory. These are my ideas of heavenly-mindedness. It is characterized by the subjugation of selfishness, by superiority to "the lusts of the flesh, and the lust of the eyes, and the pride of life;" by sobriety and watchfulness, by humility and holiness. It is calm, and cheerful, and catholic. In all respects it befits its origin and its destiny; for from heaven it comes, and it prepares for heaven.

Oh! my dear friend, what a blessed thing it would be, did you, and I, and all Christians, inwardly experience, and evidence outwardly, this heavenly-mindedness which I have endeavoured to describe! It certainly is attainable, and therefore we should never cease to labour and pray for its attainment. But from long experience, I know how hard it is to "live by the faith of the Son of God." I do not allude to the difficulty of renouncing all self-dependences and self-complacencies, in order to be saved by Christ alone. This difficulty, indeed, is only overcome by the omnipotence of divine grace. But after we have been crucified in heart with Christ, and have received from him the principle of a new and holy life, we still find it no easy matter to keep faith in vigorous and habitual exercise; and this must be acknowledged, and at the same time deplored, as a chief cause why so low a degree and so small a measure of heavenly-mindedness is enjoyed even by truly Christian people. If, then, the mere feebleness of our *faith*,— a defect in its actings, rather than in the principle itself, has such a withering and depressing influence, it requires neither illustration nor argument to prove that the existence of *doubt* in our minds must operate to a far greater extent, and in a still more unfavourable manner. Yes, my friend, I suppose we both know, by occasional experience, how painfully and powerfully doubts of our personal interest in the gospel salvation tend to check that holy elevation of soul, and that cheerful devotedness to the service of God, in which we ought to delight, and by which our Christian character should be adorned. Nor is this all. For, whenever these doubts gain the ascendency, we cannot retain that firm hold of the divine promises in which we find our strength. We are deprived of that happy enjoyment of Christian privileges which God designs as a substantial and satisfying consolation to our hearts, amidst all the trials and discouragements of our earthly pilgrimage. We are tossed about from one anxiety and fear to another, like a vessel on the stormy sea, without a pilot or a chart to guide her course unto the desired haven. We cease to enjoy that sweet and refreshing rest in Christ, and in him alone, which is the prelude to heaven itself. And thus, as we have found it to be the case in regard to the gospel blessings of peace, and joy, and love, so likewise in regard to that heavenly-mindedness which is the believer's highest earthly attainment, and which preeminently raises him above the things of the world, we come to the conclusion, that doubts exert an influence which is most prejudicial to the purity of Christian character, and to the promotion of Christian comfort.

I am unwilling to close my Letter without alluding, however briefly, to St. Paul's epistle to the Ephesians, wherein, no less than five times, he makes use of the expression, ἐν τοῖς ἐπουρανίοις, "in the heavenlies." I refer to Eph 1:3, and also Eph 1:20; Eph 2:6; Eph 3:10; and Eph 6:12. In the last of these passages our translators have introduced the word "high," instead of "heavenly;" and in all of them they have withheld the article "the," and added the word "places." By this means, so far from giving perspicuity to the apostle's meaning, which must have been their intention, is there not reason to complain, that they have rather obscured it?

For myself, I do confess, that, when reading of "heavenly places," and "high places," my thoughts are directed upwards from this earth on which we now dwell, and away from the existing state of things here. It is this that makes the passages to which I have referred you so apparently confused, and so difficult of comprehension: and I dare say yourself, and many other Christians besides, have been perplexed from the same cause. But it is obvious that the apostle, at least in two of these passages, is speaking exclusively of the blessings and privileges which believers in Christ *enjoy at present upon earth*. And if we admit that, by the phrase, "in the heavenlies," he meant "the grace and truth which came by Jesus Christ," in contradistinction to "the law which was given by Moses," then I apprehend all obscurity vanishes. You must allow me to quote the passages with this interpretation—"Blessed be the God and Father of our Lord Jesus Christ, who hath blessed us with all spiritual blessings, in the heavenlies, in Christ," Eph 1:3. "And hath raised us up together, and made us sit together in the heavenlies, in Christ Jesus," Eph 2:6. The precious truth which the apostle expresses is simply this, that under *the gospel dispensation,* believers in Christ experience *even now* a fulness of spiritual blessings; and, by their union with the only-begotten Son of God, they so truly participate in his death and resurrection, as to be quickened to a new and holy life, and are exalted to the high honour and dignity of being the sons and daughters of God by adoption. It is in our enjoyment of such "exceeding riches of divine grace," that, amidst many trials and sorrows, and also amidst great shortcomings and imperfections, we are nevertheless "made to sit together in the heavenlies, in Christ Jesus." A still higher exaltation, and still nobler privileges do indeed await the Lord's redeemed in the coming age, for which we daily pray—"Thy kingdom come." St. Paul, however, in the verses quoted, speaks not of things future, but of things present; not of things in heaven, but of things on earth.

In the remaining three of the five passages in the epistle to the Ephesians, to which reference has been made, the difficulty occasioned by substituting heavenly or high places for "the heavenlies," is considerably augmented by the mention in all of them of "principalities and powers," etc., and the necessity in each of them of applying these lofty titles to different descriptions of intelligent beings. But whether the apostle had earthly princes and rulers more particularly in his eye, as in Eph 1:21; or the angelic hierarchy, as in Eph 3:10; or the chiefest of devils, as in Eph 6:12, I do feel it of importance to understand, that there never is any variation of his meaning of "the heavenlies." It would lead me into a long digression, were I to attempt any critical analysis of these verses. But do you study each of them carefully; and I hope you will be induced to think with me, that, in the whole of them, St. Paul, by *"the heavenlies,"* refers, not *to any place or places* apart from this earth, but to *a state of things* now existing "in Christ Jesus," under the gospel dispensation.

I shall only add, that, if we desire successfully to withstand the false prophets and teachers who have molested the church from the earliest times of Christianity—those whom the apostle designates "wicked spirits in the heavenlies," and likewise to wrestle against the rulers of the darkness of this world, it behoves us to be well established in the faith of Christ Jesus, and to have our minds free from the influence of doubt respecting either the sufficiency of his grace, or our own participation thereof. Doubts deprive us of strength, and make us cowards. But we shall fear no evil, and fall before no enemy, when, like St. Paul, we can bless the God and Father of *our* Lord Jesus Christ, because *he hath blessed us with all spiritual blessings*. Oh, how cheering! how sanctifying! may we not even say how heavenly it is to *know* that Christ is ours, and that we are blessed in him!

> In darkest shades, if *he* appear,
> My dawning is begun;
> *He* is my soul's sweet morning star,
> And *he* my rising sun.
>
> The opening heavens around me shine,
> With beams of sacred bliss:
> While Jesus shows his heart is mine,
> And whispers, "*I am his.*"

To praise God for what he is, and for what he has done for us, will constitute the distinguishing employment of heaven; and therefore we may rest assured, that the spirit of praise is essential to heavenly-mindedness upon earth.

Ever yours, etc.

LETTER 8

DOUBTS ARE INJURIOUS TO THE CHRISTIAN CHARACTER AND COMFORT OF THE DOUBTER—Concluded

VI. THEY DAMP AND DARKEN HIS HOPES FOR ETERNITY

Christianity alone reveals eternal life to man.—The resurrection of Christ is the pledge that his people also shall be raised.—The redemption of their bodies from the grave is the great object of expectation, Rom 8:23-25.—It is hope that saves us.—Hope is the anchor of the soul, and heaven is the anchorage.—Heb 6:18-20 explained.—St. Paul's prayer for the Romans, Rom 15:13: it is addressed to "the God of hope," and its object is, that they may "abound in hope."—No Christian can abound in the hope of future glory who doubts his possession of present grace.—The hope of being made meet for the inheritance is essentially different from hoping for the inheritance, because we are made meet.—Remarks on Col 1:12-14.—The power of the Holy Ghost necessary to a strong faith and an abounding hope.—Hope is animating and cheerful: doubts are cheerless and depressing.—Doubters cannot "rejoice in hope of the glory of God."—The potency of hope exemplified in the affairs of the world; and applied to things spiritual and eternal.—The future rewards of the world to come are stimulants to our hope.—For the joy set before him Christ himself endured the cross.—We are to run the race before us, "looking unto Jesus," hoping to be with him, and to be like him.

My dear Friend,

The extent to which doubts are prejudicial to the Christian character and comfort of the doubter, we have considered in a variety of particulars, in the last three Letters. And before concluding this very practical branch of our subject, I must endeavour to satisfy you that—

Doubts damp and darken the brightness of the Christian's hopes for eternity.

I am sure you will concede to Christianity the high honour of revealing the immortal destinies of man. The wisest heathens had no certain knowledge of the future. They could only speculate about the immortality of the soul. Their expectations of surviving the shock of dissolution were vague and powerless. They had no sure and certain hope of any existence whatever beyond the grave, and still less of a holy, and blessed, and never-ending life. But the well-grounded hope of a better state of being in a better world is an essential element in the gospel salvation;—a good hope through grace, of glory, honour, and immortality, constitutes a distinguishing feature in the Christian character. Hence an inspired apostle has declared, that, "if in this life only we have hope in Christ, we are of all men most miserable: but now," he triumphantly asserts, "but now is Christ risen from the dead, and become the firstfruits of them that sleep," 1 Cor 15:19-20. And, in another place, the same apostle, speaking of those true believers who have the fruits of the Spirit, says, "Even we ourselves groan within ourselves, waiting for the adoption, to wit, the redemption of our body;" that is, its redemption from the corruption of the grave. "For we are saved by hope; but hope that is seen is not hope; for what a man seeth, why doth he yet hope for? But if we hope for that we see not, then do we with patience wait for it," Rom 8:23-25.

It is, then, the hope of a glorious and eternal existence,— the hope of a reunion of soul and body in resurrection glory, that reconciles the Christian to his sufferings in the present life. It is hope that even saves him:—saves him from fainting under the frequent discouragements of his earthly toils and conflicts,—saves him from sinking amidst the howling storms to which he is so often exposed here below. It is the hope of help in the time of need, the hope of final victory, the hope of the eternal crown, that saves him from yielding to the pressure of present opposition, and animates him to persevere unto the end. "The hope of salvation" is the impenetrable "helmet" provided for the Christian warrior, along with "the breastplate of faith and love," 1 Thess 5:8; and under the protection of this spiritual armour he fearlessly maintains his ground on the battlefield, and fights the good fight of faith, that he may lay hold on eternal life, 1 Tim 6:12. This hope of salvation is likewise "the anchor of the soul," firmly fastened in the very place where Christ himself hath gone; and thus it imparts to the true believer a delightful feeling of safety, even when he is tempest-tossed and afflicted on this world's agitated ocean. And this hope is well grounded, which makes the Christian so bold and so buoyant. For God himself has given to us his own word of promise, confirmed by an oath, "that by two immutable things, in which it was impossible for God to lie, we might have a strong consolation, who have fled for refuge to lay hold on the hope set before us; which hope we have as an anchor of the soul, both sure and stedfast, and which entereth into that within the veil; whither the Forerunner is for us entered, even Jesus, made an high-priest for ever after the order of Melchisedec," Heb 6:18-20.

This passage must strike you as possessing peculiar force, and as being very appropriate to the subject in hand. I have quoted it without mutilation or abridgment, because it would be difficult to find another so rich in sentiment, and so powerful in expression, or which leaves so little excuse for the doubter. My object is not to write a dissertation on Christian hope, else I might here gather important materials. But you must permit me to glance at the several precious truths which the apostle so beautifully groups together in these few verses.

In the first place, you will keep in mind, that "the hope set before us" is what St. Paul describes to Titus as "the hope of eternal life, which God, that cannot lie, promised before the world began," Titus 1:2; or what he declared more fully before Agrippa to be the hope of the resurrection from the dead, Acts 26:6-8. This hope is spoken of as a "refuge." The fleeing for refuge implies the presence of distress and danger, a sense of the need of help out of ourselves, and an earnest desire for safety. And "strong consolation" is said to be secured to those who actually *"have fled"* for refuge to the hope set before them. Then, mark the character which is given to this hope. It is "an anchor of the soul, both sure and stedfast;" and this anchor "entereth into that within the veil." Here we have most accurately defined those precise two things that are necessary for the preservation of the vessel that is threatened with destruction by the raging winds and waves. Here is not only the good anchor, but likewise the good anchorage. The one without the other would be unavailing. Both are needed, and both are provided; and both have a warranted excellence to inspire the most unhesitating reliance on their adaptation to our case. Unless the anchor itself were "sure and stedfast," its being dropped into good mooring ground would only increase its liability to break; and unless the anchorage were good, the very best anchor would be of little service, in maintaining the position of the ship, and keeping it from drifting. But the strength of the Christian's hope is only equalled by the sureness of its object. His hope is certain and stedfast, because it is founded on "the two immutable things, in which it was impossible for God to lie," even his word of promise, confirmed by his oath! To the Christian, this is the anchor of his soul; and where, within the whole compass of creation, could such another be found? The anchor is of matchless excellence. It never can give way, inasmuch as it is impossible for God to lie. And we have the same certainty as to the unrivalled character of the anchorage. The Christian's hope is not fixed on any earthly quicksands, nor is it confined in its grasp to the shadowy and fleeting objects of time and sense. It "entereth into that within the veil." How beautiful! how exhilarating is this! The two ideas contained in this little sentence are very precious. "Within the veil" is an expression of peculiar endearment and sanctity in the ears of a Hebrew; and it was to Hebrew Christians that the words we are considering were originally addressed. It reminded him of the holy of holies in the Temple, where God sat enthroned on the mercy seat, but from which all were excluded except the high-priest once a year: and he knew that "within the veil" was descriptive of heaven itself, of which the holy of holies was only an earthly pattern. Within heaven, then, where all is stable, and nothing is treacherous,—where all is immutable and blissful and glorious as God himself, the hope of the Christian "entereth," and taketh hold, just as the anchor does of the good ground into which it is dropped. Heaven, then, is the Christian's anchorage, and hope the anchor of his soul. Surely it becomes us to exclaim in admiring gratitude, and with rapturous praise, Such an anchor and such an anchorage!

But the apostle has done much to enlarge our views, and confirm our faith, by adding, "Whither the Forerunner is for us entered, even Jesus, made an high-priest for ever after the order of Melchisedec." Jesus is himself our anchor. He is the Hope of Israel, and the Saviour thereof in the time of trouble. St. Paul says to Timothy that the *"Lord Jesus Christ is our hope,"* 1 Tim 1:1; and to the Colossians he speaks of *"Christ in them, the hope of glory,"* as constituting the riches of the gospel mystery, Col 1:27. Jesus has entered into heaven "for us"—on our behalf—to secure the present and eternal safety of his people. He has gone as our "Forerunner," which gives a security that we shall follow; and that there may be no possibility of failure or disappointment, "he is made an high-priest for ever," to carry on a continual intercession for us; "and he is made a priest after the order of Melchisedec," that in the exercise of kingly power, combined with priestly service, the deliverance of his people from sin and death and hell may be secured, to the honour and glory of God, throughout the endless ages of eternity.

I fear my glance at these immensely rich and most consoling verses has been more rapid than perspicuous. Still I feel pleased with bringing them under your notice, and could earnestly wish that they were carefully and prayerfully pondered by every doubting Christian. But there are two points deserving of special attention. The one is, the foundation on which our hope is to rest—"the two immutable things"—*the promise* of the God of truth, and *the oath* of the God of faithfulness—the two things "in which it was not possible for God to lie." What a foundation is this! How strong! how immovable! how imperishable! And the other point is the avowed purpose of our gracious God in laying such a foundation for our hopes. It is, "that we might have *a strong consolation.*" Oh, how kind and condescending is this! He desires that we, who are naturally full of fears, and without hope, by reason of our guilt and unworthiness, might enjoy the assurance of his forgiveness, and be relieved from every painful apprehension of impending danger, and repose in perfect confidence of attaining the salvation which the Gospel reveals.

The first of these two points of doctrine is calculated deeply to impress doubting Christians with the conviction, how unreasonable are their scruples, how unjustifiable are their hesitations, how culpable their delays, in fleeing for refuge to lay hold on the hope set before them, when God, in the abundance of his mercy, confirms his promise with his oath, for the express purpose of giving *undoubted solidity* to the foundation on which their hopes of life everlasting must rest! And the second very forcibly depicts how great is the loss they sustain, in consequence of their doubts. They debar themselves from the "strong consolation" which God places within their reach. I do not say they are altogether without hope; but just in proportion to the activity of their doubts, their hopes must be faint and uncertain. Instead of participating in that joyous sense of deliverance from danger—in that sweet feeling of safety, which is the mariner's consolation, who has fled from the angry storm, and has cast the well-tried anchor within the well-known harbour, they are still a prey to the raging elements, and cannot divest themselves of the fear of danger. The utmost consolation they can command is only a precarious hope of at last reaching the desired haven. They are tossed up and down on the billows of uncertainty. They are ignorant whether they have fled to the right refuge. They cannot tell whether they have laid hold on the right hope. They are afraid to think that their everlasting all is safely based on the right foundation; and therefore they continue strangers to the "strong consolation" which God has prepared for his believing people. They know that there is rest for their souls in Christ, but their doubts hinder them from entering into that sweet and secure rest. And thus, however precious Christ is to *those who believe* in him, *the doubter* excludes himself from the enjoyment of this precious Saviour.

Every Christian is privileged to "rejoice in hope of the glory of God," Rom 5:2. And if he does not, and cannot entertain this glorious hope, there must be a serious defect in his faith; for "faith is the substance of things hoped for." It gives them reality. It brings them near. It puts us, as it were, in possession of them. And in this consists the very charm of hope, that it soothes and softens all the trials of this present world, by giving us a foretaste of the joys and blessedness of the world that is to come.

> When the star of hope is beaming
> Mildly through the silent sky,
> When its ray of promise, streaming,
> Trembles on the anxious eye,—

> Fears that chill'd the spirit vanish,
> Woes that bound it break their chain;
> Those pure rays descending, banish
> Clouds of doubt, and storms of pain.
>
> Brightly to the gazer's spirit,
> In its light the future shines;
> Bowers of bliss his thoughts inherit;
> Peace for him, her olive twines.*

But this leads me to offer a few remarks on another passage of Scripture, wherein peace, and joy, and hope, as springing alike from gospel faith, are beautifully interwoven. Towards the close of his epistle to the Romans, St. Paul introduces this very comprehensive prayer, "Now may the God of hope fill you with all joy and peace in believing, that ye may abound in hope through the power of the Holy Ghost," Rom 15:13.

The first thing that claims attention here is the character in which God is addressed—"the God of hope"—the God who is the source and the centre of all our hopes; the God at whose disposal is every good and perfect gift; and whose word of promise emboldens us to ask, and inspires the well-grounded hope, that in asking we shall receive. It would be well that we more frequently contemplated God in this delightful character. There is something very encouraging in it. But you will not fail to notice that the apostle has intentionally chosen it on this occasion, because of the especial blessing which he desired that his Roman converts might obtain. He wished them to "abound in hope." He wished them to have large hopes; to have bright hopes; to hope for every promised blessing; to hope with cheerful perseverance; and to hope with undoubt-

---

*These verses are from the pen of the late Mrs. Wallace Duncan, of whom a very pleasing Memoir has been written by her mother.

ing assurance. This was a great request to make; and there is an admirable propriety in addressing it to "the God of hope."

It is rather singular, however, and on no account to be overlooked, that St. Paul does not make it the *direct* object of his prayer, that they should abound in hope. This, indeed, was the end he had in view; and as the most effectual means for the attainment of this end, he prays that they might be filled "with all joy and peace in believing." And oh! what a wonderful petition is this! Had he only prayed that their faith might not fail, that it might be increased, that it might be strong; that would have been asking much: but the apostle's heart was enlarged by Christian love, and he asks great things for those whose stability and holiness he desired to advance. Here he prays for these Christians, as we ought to pray for ourselves and for one another, that their faith might be accompanied with *joy and peace*—with *all* joy, and *all* peace—yea, that they might be *filled* with all joy and peace in believing. And the purpose for which he asks this fulness of peace and joy in the exercise of Christian faith is, that they may *abound* in Christian hope. It is not merely that they might be happy in the experience of present grace, knowing their election of God; but that their utmost expectations of future and never-ending glory might find a sure warrant in the unchanging and unchangeable word of Jehovah. He wishes them to have a continual "respect to the recompense of the reward," like Moses, "esteeming the reproach of Christ greater riches than the treasures of Egypt," Heb 11:25-26. He wishes them clearly to realize their high destinies as the children of God, and joint-heirs with Christ, that like himself they might "reckon that the sufferings of this present time are not worthy to be compared with the glory which shall be revealed in us," Rom 8:17-18. He wishes them to "gird up the loins of their minds, to be sober, and hope to the end for the grace that is to be brought unto them at the revelation of Jesus Christ; that, as obedient children," they may be "holy in all manner of conversation," 1 Pet 1:13-15. He wishes them to be longing for the appearing of their absent Saviour, that they themselves may see him in his glory, and be like him; for "every man that hath this hope in Him purifieth himself, even as *he* is pure," 1 John 3:2-3. He wishes that, as "strangers and pilgrims" in this world, they may be ever looking forward to "the better country," Heb 11:16. And therefore it is that he makes it his petition on their behalf that "the God of hope may fill them with all joy and peace in believing." For assuredly no Christian can "abound" in such sure and certain hopes of future glory, unless his faith be sufficiently strong to yield him "the peace of God which passeth all understanding," and that "joy in God" which is "unspeakable and full of glory."

There is no necessity for my taking up the subject in a metaphysical point of view. It is enough simply to remind you that in our mental constitution there is an intimate connection betwixt the different emotions of hope, and peace, and joy; and I believe it will generally be found true in experience, that the two latter have the precedence of the former. There must be at least some measure of peace and joy, before hope arises to diffuse its cheering influence. And in regard to spiritual things, the whole of these emotions are regulated in their intensity by the measure of our Christian faith.

It will thus be evident to you, that the man whose mind is disquieted, because he believes not that God is reconciled unto him in Christ Jesus, and who is a stranger to the gladdening sense of deliverance from the wrath to come, is not in a condition to indulge the animating hope of "the inheritance that is incorruptible, and undefiled, and that fadeth not away." He may indeed hope *to be made meet for the inheritance*, and this kind of hope is very prevalent. But this hope is far short of what the believer is privileged to entertain; and indeed it is altogether different from that hope which the Gospel sets before us. Instead of hoping even with fear and trembling *for grace to make him meet*, the believer confidently hopes *for the inheritance itself*, knowing that by grace he is already made meet in the faith of Jesus Christ, in whom he has righteousness and strength; and having at the same time a conviction that the firmer and stronger his hope of glory is, the more he will advance in holiness, and in personal meetness for *the enjoyment* of the inheritance.

These observations will lead your thoughts to the first chapter of the epistle to the Colossians, where the expression occurs of being made meet for the inheritance; but it is of no small importance for us to recollect that St. Paul introduces it into his prayer for "the saints and faithful brethren in Christ, which were at Colosse," not as something to be asked or hoped for, but *as a blessing actually conferred, for which he gives thanks*. "Giving thanks unto the Father, who *hath made us meet* to be partakers of the inheritance of the saints in light; who *hath delivered us* from the power of darkness, and *hath translated us* into the kingdom of his dear Son; in whom *we have redemption* through his blood, even the forgiveness of sins," Col 1:12-14. And I know not a surer plan for obtaining an increased fulness of divine blessing, than just to thank God for what he has already bestowed. Is not this our duty?

The doubting and downcast Christian, however, has no such thanksgivings to offer up. He only as yet hopes for the blessings of which a stronger faith would put him in the immediate possession, and afford him a present enjoyment. But his hopes cannot extend into eternity. The want of spiritual peace and joy necessarily checks the uprisings of true Christian hope within his breast. On such a man the encouraging and conclusive argument of the apostle in writing to the Romans is entirely lost. As it concerns himself, he cannot enter into the premises, and therefore he loses the benefit of the conclusion: "For if, when we were enemies, we were reconciled to God by the death of his Son, much more, *being reconciled*, we shall be saved by his life," Rom 5:10. Oh what a power there is in the apostle's "much more!" But he who doubts his reconciliation can cherish no certainty of salvation. He who doubts his interest in the blessings which flow from Christ's death, cannot hope for the glory which is connected with his resurrection life.

Permit me to add, that, as it is of the nature of hope to impart a spirit of buoyancy and cheerfulness which raises a man superior to the depressing influence of circumstances that really are or appear to be trying and unpropitious, so it cannot exist in a mind where the absence of Christian peace and joy tends to encourage despondency, which is the very opposite of hope. If we truly desire to partake of the animating, and elevating, and purifying influence of gospel hope, we shall be anxious to get quit of doubts. If the hope of glory is to exert *any* sanctifying influence on our conduct, or to impart any comfort to our hearts amidst present sorrow and sufferings, then there must be *some* measure of peace and joy accompanying our faith in Christ Jesus. And if our hope is to *abound,* so as to fire us with a martyr's spirit, and in heavenly aspirations to lift us above all earthly clogs and entanglements, then must we feel and acknowledge, with how much of true philosophy, as well as of divine wisdom, the apostle has taught us to pray that "the God of hope may fill us with all joy and peace in believing."

It would be unpardonable, in my remarks on this passage of Holy Scripture, to omit adverting for a moment to that supernatural instrumentality on which the apostle depended for the fulfilment of his petition in the experience of those for whom he prayed. He concludes with these words, "through the power of the Holy Ghost." This sets a great truth before us. If we expect to be filled with peace and joy, we must not lean on our own poor performances, nor must we look too much to human instruments. It is all right to use with diligence the means of grace with which we are favoured; but we must beware of exalting ministers or ordinances above the place which God himself assigns to them. Even his own holy word falls lifeless on the ear, and does not penetrate the heart, without the accompanying power of the Holy Ghost. It is vain for us to attempt filling our own hearts with joy and peace. These are blessings which God alone can give us; and when we do ask them from him, let us expect them to be given only "through the power of the Holy Ghost." And if we desire to "abound in hope," the magnitude of the desire might overwhelm us in confusion and dismay, did we not in faith address ourselves to "the God of hope," and place our trust in "the power of the Holy Ghost," through whom God works in us all good works, and through whom he fulfils all the holy desires which his own free grace has kindled in our hearts. He who gives grace will also give glory. Salvation, in all its stages and departments, is wholly of God. It lies with him to begin, and to carry on, and to complete the mighty work; and the whole is accomplished "through the power of the Holy Ghost."

What I have hitherto advanced on this very short, but very comprehensive apostolical prayer, has been chiefly in the way of doctrinal exposition; but I trust you have all along felt your heart interested in the subject. It may, however, be advantageous to consider specifically the uses to which we should apply the example with which an inspired apostle has here furnished us.

And in the first place, I feel constrained to urge it on you, and on myself, as a great and primary duty, to pray for the Holy Ghost with more frequency and fervour than we are accustomed to do. He is expressly promised to them that ask; and it is impossible to set limits to his "power" in enlightening our darkened minds, and spiritualizing our grovelling affections, and strengthening us mightily in the inner man, and building us up in faith and holiness, and fortifying our minds against the intrusions of doubts. And even when we pray for special spiritual blessings, as it is lawful and right to do, let us remember to expect them, yea, also to ask them, not in the ways and methods of our own devising, but "through the power of the Holy Ghost."

For instance, if we earnestly desire an abiding peace of mind, and a greater measure of rejoicing in the Lord, let us pray to be kept from self-seeking, and self-dependence, and self-satisfaction, for all these are polluted sources; and to be kept stedfast in the faith of the all-perfected and accepted righteousness of our anointed Saviour, through the power of the Holy Ghost; for it is only through this divinely appointed medium that we are certain of success. It was "joy and peace *in believing*" for which St. Paul prayed in behalf of his Roman converts, because he knew well that without believing in Christ Jesus no sinful creature can experience true peace and solid joy, even in a small measure. And if we honestly wish our cup to overflow with these blessings, we must seek to receive them through the same channel. Now, this supplies a useful hint to the established Christian, who is already in possession of joy, and peace, and hope. He must not decline in the exercise of faith, or ever look away from Christ, else his peace will diminish, and his joy will depart, and the brightness of his hopes will be obscured. By all means, let him indulge a holy ambition for continued joy and peace, and even that he may "be filled with all joy and peace;" but let him only expect what he asks in the way of "believing," and "through the power of the Holy Ghost." Thus, also, shall he "abound in hope;" and as a strong and cheerful and rejoicing Christian, the God of all grace shall be glorified in him and by him.

And here, also, the doubting Christian has pointed out to him the certain road to stability and comfort. Instead of wasting his time, and wounding his spirit, by fruitless attempts to find something in himself as a ground of hope that he has passed from death unto life, and is an heir of glory; let him fix his thoughts on God's sure word of promise, confirmed by his oath. Let him fix his affections on God's own Son, nailed to the accursed tree, and yielding up his life a sacrifice for human guilt; let him fix his faith on the reality and on the efficacy of this one sacrifice for sin, and be encouraged to make the prayer of St. Paul for the Romans his prayer for himself. Let him weigh well the meaning of every word employed by the apostle; and whilst he pants for peace, and joy, and hope, let him in faith pour out his heart to "the God of hope," and expect an answer only "through the power of the Holy Ghost." It is thus that his doubts are to be removed by the exercise of his faith, and faith itself will be increased by exercise; then with the increase of faith, he will have joy and peace; and in proportion to his joy and peace in believing, his hopes of glory will brighten and abound.

And in the next place, from the very fact that an apostle offered up such a prayer, and that it has been preserved in the Holy Scripture, we may certainly learn that St. Paul attached a very high degree of importance to the possession, not only of peace and joy, but of abounding hope. Nay, may I not even assert that we are furnished in this apostolical prayer with an example of *what* God would have all his people to ask of him, as well as of that special *mode* of asking, to which I have already referred? And surely, my friend, as peace, and joy, and hope are emotions of the mind so soothing, so refreshing, so exhilarating, as sweetly to counterbalance the cares, and grosses, and sorrows, which continually chequer our earthly pilgrimage, we must be singularly devoid of all right feeling, if we do not besiege the throne of grace for these great blessings; and thank God, moreover, that, as "the God of hope," he himself emboldens us to ask in no measured strains, and for no scanty supplies. It is our happy privilege to appropriate to our own use the very language with which his own holy word supplies us, and to imitate the example which his own holy apostle has set us. Oh! my faithless heart shrinks from this privilege, as if it were presumptuous in me to ask so much; and yet I dare not question the permission which every Christian man enjoys of praying that "the God of hope may fill him with all joy and peace in believing, that he may abound in hope, through the power of the Holy Ghost."

Now, as God himself teaches us to pray for these blessings, and to pray for the largest measure of them, we have an encouraging certainty of his willingness—I might say, of his intention, to bestow them. And more than this: we may be certain that he knows how needful is an abounding Christian hope to cheer us onward with steady and consistent step, under every darkening providence, and amidst the allurements and the hindrances which arise from sin within us, and from the temptations of the world and the wicked one. He is, indeed, a gracious God, who ever desires the happiness of his creatures, and especially of his redeemed and adopted children. And thus, although in serving him here below, our services are all marred by imperfections, so that we cannot survey them with satisfaction, yet would he ever have us to persevere in his service, and to delight in serving him, because this is the path of duty, and God in Christ is himself the rest and the refreshing of our souls. On this account, he wishes us to be filled, not with doubts of his fatherly love, nor with fears as to finding acceptance in his sight, but with all joy and peace in believing, that we may abound in hope. And if it is necessary, in order to serve God with persevering stedfastness, and to take pleasure in his service, that the animating influence of a hope full of immortality, springing out of a peaceful and joyful faith, should pervade our hearts, then it requires no words of mine to show how pernicious, how paralyzing, must be the effects of doubts.

The sentiment expressed by the poet finds a ready echo in the experience of all God's children:

> When I can read my title clear
> To mansions in the skies,
> I bid farewell to every fear,
> And dry my weeping eyes.

How desirable that all Christians should be in this happy condition, and at all times! For surely there is truth in the melancholy contrast by which the workings of doubts are depicted in the following verse:—

> But oh when gloomy doubts prevail,
> I fear to call *thee* mine;
> The springs of comfort seem to fail,
> And all my hopes decline.

Doubts are justly characterized as *gloomy* things. They quench our sense of God's love, and they cast a shade over the light of his reconciled countenance; and thus, the Christian who ought to be rejoicing in God his Saviour, has his heart oppressed with sadness, and all his spiritual energies are impaired. His knees become feeble, and his hands are weakened, Isa 35:3. He loses the blessedness of being "strong in the Lord, and in the power of his might," Eph 6:10. The springs of his comfort *seem* to fail. They have not actually failed. They are still within reach, and as full of consolation as ever. But the doubting Christian has not energy enough to approach the springs. He stands afar off, and looks at them, but dares not to apply their comfort to himself. And, what with the depressing apprehension that he is not a "fellowcitizen with the saints," nor belongs to "the household of God," together with a painful feeling of desertion and discomfort, how can it otherwise be than that his hopes should *decline*? His hopes do not altogether depart. But so soon as clouds conceal their native brightness, they lose their power to encourage and uphold him. Doubts are the clouds which hinder the Christian from realizing the things God has prepared for them that love him. These things are still distant, and, excepting to the eye of faith, they are invisible. The doubter only dimly discerns them: and as he is unable to "joy in God," as reconciled to him, so neither can he *"rejoice in hope of the glory of God."*

You must allow that those Christians are decidedly in an unfavourable state, whose spiritual strength is reduced to weakness, and whose spiritual comfort is nearly dried up, because all their hopes have declined. Doubts must be very injurious when they produce such effects as these. For who does not feel how powerful, and how all-pervading is the influence of hope, even in the common affairs of the world? I mean not the hope which is peculiar to the believer; but hope as one of those affections of the mind which operate, not merely in the formation of character, but in the regulation of conduct. It is true that mankind in general are under the impulse of hopes that are vain or false, and, at best, shadowy and uncertain. But such as they are, only consider how they stimulate to action, and what support they administer under disappointment, and how they smooth down the roughness of life! Without hope men would sink into inanity and sloth. Every person is, some way or other, urged onwards, and upheld in his course, by hope. All are looking forward, living in the future rather than the present, and finding more happiness in the expectation of something which they have not, than in the possession of what they have. The youth hopes to be a man, and to engage in manly pursuits. The man is always hoping to better his circumstances. If he is poor, he hopes by diligence to extricate himself from poverty. If he is rich, he hopes by prudence to increase his riches. If he is sick, he hopes by the use of medicine, to recover his health. If he is weak, he hopes by exercise to grow strong. The artist toils at his chisel or his pencil, in the hope of acquiring celebrity in his profession. The merchant embarks in great speculations, in the hope of their successful issue. The mariner sets out on a long voyage, in the hope of a safe return. The soldier exposes his life on the battlefield, in the hope of defeating the enemy. The patriot shrinks from no fatigue or privation, in the hope of securing the safety, or advancing the glory of his country. And so on, with men in all the varied occupations and pursuits of life.

They are full of hopes; and all their hopes are uncertain, and most of them are resting on a bad foundation, and many of them have no foundation at all. But these hopes, such as they are, exercise a potent, and, on the whole, in regard to temporal things, a beneficial influence. They act as a spur to human enterprise; they throw animation into human character; they diffuse cheerfulness through human society. And when such hopes decline,—when men give way to doubt and despondency, all their activities are paralyzed; their spirits flag; their wonted sagacity forsakes them; their strength is enfeebled; their enterprises fail; and nothing awaits them but discomfiture and disgrace.

Assuredly, my friend, this is no overdrawn picture. And from it we may learn how great is the injury which the Christian must suffer, when, through the influence of doubt, he loses his firm reliance on that heavenly hope which is the only, but the sure and stedfast anchor of his soul. Whether the Christian is called to act in the way of personal sacrifice and self-denial, or of strenuous and devoted service, or of patient and continuous suffering, the influence of doubts in damping his hopes beyond the grave, must sadly interfere with the faithful discharge of present duty. The doubting and dejected Christian, who does not realize his own interest in the promised rewards of the world that is to come, can scarcely be expected to forsake all in the world that now is, should that be required of him, and to take up his cross, and to follow the Saviour into prison and to death. None can endure hardness as good soldiers of Jesus Christ, who have not strong confidence in the Captain of their salvation, and in his promise to make them more than conquerors. And those whose hopes are not bright for the heavenly kingdom, and the crown of glory that fadeth not away, will tremble to enter into the dark valley, because they know not whether the rod and staff of Omnipotence will be their comfort; neither is it their happy lot to encounter the last enemy with that song of triumph which an inspired apostle puts into the lips of true believers: "O death! where is thy sting? O grave! where is thy victory? The sting of death is sin; and the strength of sin is the law; but thanks be to God which giveth us the victory through Jesus Christ our Lord," 1 Cor 15:55-57.

In the ancient Grecian games, to which there are frequent allusions in the writings of St. Paul, it was the practice publicly to exhibit the prizes, that by the sight of them the combatants might be roused to the utmost exertions for success. And thus the Christian, who earnestly desires so to run that he may obtain the prize, and to fight not as one that beateth the air, behoves to have Christ in his heart the hope of glory, and heaven in his eye as the conqueror's resting place.

He who made us, and who knows our mental constitution, employs the most effectual method to secure our diligent and persevering obedience, when he reveals the rewards of faithfulness as the objects of our faith and hope. And it is worthy of our continual remembrance that, whilst Jesus Christ, God manifest in the flesh, sojourned on earth, he was himself acted upon in a similar manner. Of God's incarnate Son it is written, that *"for the joy set before him* he endured the cross, despising the shame, and is set down at the right hand of the throne of God," Heb 12:2. "The joy that was set before" our Lord when he was in a suffering and conflicting condition, could only have been the sure and certain hope of success in delivering man from the power of the devil, and of death, and of sin. This hope filled him with holy joy; and under its animating influence he endured the agonies, and despised the shame, of an accursed crucifixion. He was faithful, and he was successful. And by way of encouragement to us, we are enjoined to "run with patience the race that is set before us, *looking unto Jesus*, the author and finisher of our faith," "who is set down at the right hand of the throne of God." And Jesus, from his seat of glorious exaltation, knowing well the temptations to unbelief, or doubt, or fear, which beset his people still on earth, and knowing also what is best fitted to promote their constancy and their comfort, and to secure their final and eternal safety, addresses himself to their hopes. "Be thou faithful unto death, and I will give thee a crown of life:"—"to him that overcometh will I grant to sit with me in my throne, even as I also overcame, and am set down with my Father in his throne," Rev 2:10 and Rev 3:21. These are great promises; and so firmly were they believed, and so elevating were the hopes which they inspired, that the primitive Christians "took joyfully the spoiling of their goods, knowing in themselves that they had in heaven a better and an enduring substance," Heb 10:34. The crown of life, and a place on the Saviour's throne, were so clearly realized, and so certainly expected, that neither bonds, nor imprisonments, nor the gibbet, nor the stake, shook the stedfastness of their adherence to Christ, or interrupted their joy and peace in believing. Multitudes rushed to martyrdom, regardless of all tortures, and of life itself, because they rejoiced in the assured hope of living and reigning with Christ in glory everlasting.

And now, my friend, I have only, in conclusion, to add, that as doubts obscure the Christian's prospects for eternity, and deprive him of the strength for combat, and of the consolation under trial, which the hope of glory imparts, let us be anxious to keep our faith in lively exercise, always "looking unto Jesus" as our Pattern, as our Guide, as our Encourager, as our bleeding Sacrifice for sin, as our triumphant Forerunner, and as our glorious High-Priest who intercedes for us within the veil. This is our duty. This is our privilege. And should times of persecution for righteousness's sake ever again arrive, and there are even now portentous signs of their approach, it will then be more fully experienced and manifested than can be done at present, that doubts are most pernicious in their influence, in tarnishing the lustre of the Christian's character, and in excluding him from the enjoyment of that strength and comfort which he is warranted to draw, in the hour of danger, from the sure word of promise.

May God, of his mercy, keep us in the possession of an assured faith, and of a joyful hope, which is a treasure of inestimable worth!

Believe me, yours, etc.

LETTER 9

THE PERNICIOUS INFLUENCE OF DOUBTS

III. THEY EXHIBIT THE RELIGION OF CHRIST TO THE WORLD IN A FALSE AND FORBIDDING POINT OF VIEW

The previous illustrations recapitulated.—Proposition III. considered.—Doubts give to the world a false and forbidding view of the religion of Christ.—1st. Doubts occasionally produce *inconsistencies of conduct*, which bring reproach upon our holy religion.—2nd. The *gloomy looks* and *desponding sentiments* of doubters make religion repulsive.—The happy service of God is unjustly associated with ideas of moroseness and melancholy.—Christians abstain from the sinful pleasures of the world, because they possess purer sources of joy.—The want of cheerfulness in doubting Christians drives unbelievers from the Saviour.—God desires to make his creatures happy.—The Gospel eminently fitted to accomplish this desire.—Every believer should enjoy happiness.—Doubts make sad, those whom God would make glad.—Concluding remarks.—The *occasional* doubter is less injured, and does less injury, than the *permanent*.—Distinction between the effects of *real* and *speculative* doubts.—All doubts are hurtful; but not in the same degree.

My dear Friend,

As the remarks I am now to offer will close our illustrations of the pernicious influence of doubts, it may be of some use, at the commencement of this Letter, to present you with a brief summary of what has been stated in the preceding five Letters.

You may remember that the plan I proposed for illustrating this important branch of the general subject was to show, That doubts are dishonouring to God: that they are injurious to the doubting Christian himself: and that they also injure the cause of true religion in the eyes of the world.

On the *first* of these three particulars I deemed one Letter sufficient for the observations I had to make, as it is abundantly obvious that to doubt the word or promise of God, in any degree, is doing him such a dishonour as would be deeply felt, and highly resented, between man and man. The apostle John speaks strongly on this very point—"If we receive the witness of men," he says, "the witness of God is greater; for this is the witness of God which he hath testified of his Son. He that believeth on the Son of God hath the witness in himself: he that believeth not God, hath made him a liar; because he believeth not the record that God gave of his Son. And this is the record, that God hath given to us eternal life, and this life is in his Son," 1 John 5:9-11. To doubt the testimony of a fellow-creature is by no means the same thing as to deny it. For as the best of men are liable to err, there may often be good and great cause for doubting the *correctness* of their testimony, even whilst we have the most perfect confidence in their *intentions* of stating only what is true. *But God cannot err*. With him there is neither want of truth, nor want of accuracy in its statement. And therefore to doubt his word must be nearly as offensive to him as it would be to deny it. To doubt his word is at least to withhold our belief: and "he *that believeth not God hath made him a liar*." This is a fearful result; and nothing can more forcibly set before us the pernicious influence of doubts.

The *second* particular specified was, the injury which doubts occasion to the doubting Christian himself. And this point has been considered as all the more entitled to a lengthened elucidation, as it is decidedly of the greatest practical importance.

I have endeavoured to explain the nature and extent of that injury which doubts inflict upon the character and comfort of a Christian, by adverting—

1st. To *the anxieties and fears* to which they give rise, and which necessarily interfere with that cheerful, and confiding, and courageous obedience to God, which the Christian should ever feel it his privilege, as well as his duty, to render. This is a positive injury, and its influence is most extensive. But in order fully to estimate how very hurtful doubts are to the Christian, in regard both to the consistency of his conduct, and to his enjoyment of spiritual comfort, it is needful also to look at them in a negative point of view, that he may understand the magnitude of the privations to which they subject him: and therefore I have shown,

2nd. How the doubting Christian is excluded from that soul-satisfying *peace with God and peace of mind* which flows from a firm faith in the meritorious obedience, in our stead, of the Lord Jesus Christ.

3rd. How his doubts disqualify him from *rejoicing in the Lord*, and *rejoicing evermore*, even with a joy that is unspeakable and full of glory, which is one of the most exalted of those gospel blessings, in which the true believer participates, amidst the changes and conflicts of his earthly pilgrimage.

4th. How a doubt of ourselves being the objects of God's forgiving love, naturally *cools and represses the ardour of our love to God and man*; and in this way retards our progress in holiness, by weakening the strongest incentive to obedience.

5th. How that *spirituality and heavenly-mindedness*, which we ought earnestly to cultivate, and which are of great efficacy in raising us above the world and the things of the world, are checked in their proper exercise through the influence of doubt; and thus our spiritual prosperity is seriously hindered.

6th. How *the hope of a resurrection to life and glory*, to which we are begotten again by the resurrection of our Lord himself from the dead, is damped and restrained in the natural outgoings of its animating and sanctifying tendencies, by doubts respecting either the reality of such a hope, or our own warrant to entertain it.

We have viewed the subject in all these several aspects. Some of them have received a very full examination. And I trust it has been made manifest to your satisfaction, that doubts are indeed not merely injurious, but exceedingly injurious, to the doubting Christian himself.

But, to complete the plan laid down at the outset, there yet remains to be considered the *third* of those propositions in which we behold the evil influence of doubts. They not only dishonour God, and injure the spiritual prosperity of those who indulge them; but they are also most pernicious *in giving to the world a false and forbidding view of true religion.*

On this last particular, I do not mean to trouble you with many remarks. It will be sufficient briefly to advert, 1st, to the inconsistencies of conduct from which the doubting Christian can hardly escape; and 2nd, to the gloom and despondency which are too generally the accompaniments of doubts. These two points do not embrace the whole of the subject. But I have selected them as being in strict harmony with the illustrations already adduced; and there is advantage in preserving continuity of thought.

Well, then, my friend, I request you to recollect that my one aim and desire has been to convince you how injurious are doubts to the Christian, in regard both to *his character* and to *his comfort*. These are two distinct things, and doubts have a baneful influence on each of them. Doubts tarnish the bright lustre of that holiness in which the Christian ought to shine as a light in the world; and they rob him, at least to a certain extent, of that peace, and joy, and love, and heavenly-mindedness, and hope for eternity, which a strong and stedfast faith in Christ Jesus would yield. And is it not precisely in these two respects, that a stumblingblock is thrown in the way of ungodly men, who are sharp-sighted enough to perceive the inconsistencies of some believers, and the gloomy dispositions of others? From these circumstances erroneous and unfavourable impressions are made on their minds. They thus take occasion to justify themselves in a continued life of carelessness or gaiety, or vice. Their natural aversion to the gospel scheme of salvation is increased. And it must be acknowledged that this is a most deplorable proof of the evil tendencies of doubts.

In the first place, I remark, that *the inconsistencies of Christians*, in whatever manner they are manifested, and by whatever cause they are produced, do bring a reproach on the holy religion which they profess. I am far from affirming that all these inconsistencies ought to be laid to the charge of doubts; yet certain it is, that, to this one fruitful source, very many of them may most fairly be ascribed. For instance, wherever there is any hesitancy in bowing to the divine authority of gospel truth, the heart is hindered from receiving the fulness of its sanctifying power, and of course there is a corresponding deficiency of influence over the outward conduct. The portion of divine truth which is not fully believed cannot be expected to operate, as it otherwise would do, either on the heart, or on the life. And so likewise, whenever a man is distressed with doubts respecting the genuineness of his own Christianity, it would be unreasonable to expect from him, a ready and uniform compliance with those holy precepts and practices which are enjoined on believers. For these reasons whether a man's doubts respect Christianity itself, as a system of divinely revealed truth, or merely his own participation in its inestimable blessings, he cannot, while he is in a state of doubt, take the decided ground which is incumbent on him as a Christian; nor can he stand forth to the gaze of the world, bearing the lovely image, and breathing the loving spirit of *him*, by whose name he is called. I am not supposing that the doubting Christian allows himself to live in open or avowed neglect of duty. But he is satisfied with a low standard, and with low attainments. There is about him an indecision of principle and of action, which justly exposes him to the disgrace of having his sincerity suspected. He is afraid to take his stand on the Lord's side. Thus, as it respects these waverers and doubters, the world is not furnished with a proper opportunity to take "knowledge of them, that they have been with Jesus." Such cases are numerous, I fear; and we cannot think of them without grief and sorrow of heart.

I am sure you will admit that every Christian should be set for the defence of the Gospel when its truths are attacked, and eager to spread the Gospel wherever its truths are unknown. Every Christian, indeed, should be ready and willing, like the apostle Paul, "to spend and be spent" in advancing the knowledge of Christ among men. It cannot be denied that we all come far short of what we ought to be and to do. But doubters *necessarily* halt and hesitate. Sometimes they are ashamed to speak as it becomes the Lord's redeemed. At other times they are afraid to act in the cause of Christ against his enemies. And their indecision cannot remain concealed from observation. It quenches the Spirit's light and heat within themselves. It discourages the sweet and constraining impulses of redeeming love. Thus their strength fails; and they shrink from boldly ranking themselves under the banners of the cross. They are not prepared to part with all for Christ's sake. They are unwilling to subject themselves to reproach or persecution. They are not fortified against the allurements of the world, and the devices of Satan. They do not fight the good fight of faith "like good soldiers of the Lord Jesus Christ;" and hence the world does not recognise them as "living epistles of Christ," which ought to be known and read of all men. In them the beauty of holiness is too dimly discerned to attract notice. And altogether their light fails to shine so as to benefit their fellow-creatures, and to glorify their Father which is in heaven. This is a sore evil: for, by a want of consistency between their professed principles and actual practices, these timorous and doubting Christians dishonour the great Redeemer, and retard the progress of his gospel within the limits of their own social circle; whilst, at the same time, they furnish ungodly men with a plausible excuse for declining the service of Christ, or the profession of Christianity.

But, in the second place, doubting Christians, instead of winning souls to the Saviour by the attractive power of a godly example, too commonly give a repulsive character to religion, by *their gloomy looks and desponding sentiments*. This is another sore evil, for it is quite undeniable, that from this very circumstance, multitudes of the gay and the godless studiously avoid the society of those whom they consider to be religious. And they dislike the very name of religion, because in their minds it is associated with moroseness and melancholy. Is it not deeply to be regretted that we have such a state of things amongst us?

It is indeed true that the men of the world have ideas of happiness totally different from those of the people of God, and there cannot be, and there ought not to be, any compromise between them. The decided Christian neither seeks nor finds his happiness in those pursuits and pleasures to which the worldling exclusively looks. But in condemning what are usually called worldly amusements, as unworthy of intelligent and immortal creatures, and too often as positively dangerous and sinful, it is injudicious to affirm that these vanities can yield no happiness to their votaries. The Bible itself speaks of "the pleasures of sin." And it is confirmed by daily observation, that worldly people do gather a certain kind and measure of happiness, from sources which those who know better have abandoned as polluted and poisonous. It is, however, very desirable that we, who will not mingle in their amusements, or share their mirth, should give evidence from the cheerful tone of our own conversation, and even by the joyous expression of our countenances, that we have other sources of enjoyment within our reach,—sources of a purer and nobler and more satisfying kind than the world can either understand or appreciate.

I do regard it as a great injury to the cause of Christ in the world, when his followers become marked for the austerity of their looks and manners. And on the other hand, we can scarcely estimate what great benefits might result from a more general exhibition of "the fruits of the Spirit," in the conduct and conversation of Christians. Surely we ought to be mild, and gentle, and loving, and happy. The reign of Jesus Christ in the heart, should be productive of "righteousness, and peace, and joy in the Holy Ghost." The whole design and tendency of the Gospel is to deliver us from the miseries of sin, and from the terrors of a guilty conscience, and from the wrath of an offended God. And the only man on earth who experiences, or is entitled to experience, solid and substantial happiness, is he who lives by the faith of the Son of God.

The true Christian, who inwardly enjoys the sense of sin forgiven, and who believes that God is reconciled to him, and who entertains the well-grounded hope of life eternal, is richly compensated for his self-denial in renouncing what the world can offer in the way of pleasure. Oh yes; the Christian alone is in possession of the elements of *true* happiness. And were it not that doubts and fears hinder Christians from acting out their holy principles, and living up to their high privileges, as the redeemed of the Lord, and as his adopted children, and as joint-heirs with Christ of the glory in which he is ere long to appear, their opponents would have less reason to complain, that the religion of Jesus makes men sad and sorrowful. Were their faith strong and always in exercise, then their meekness under injuries, their patience under sufferings, their contentment under privations, their thankfulness, not only for the blessings poured into their cup, but even for the afflictions laid upon them; in short, their general cheerfulness in whatever circumstances placed, and their manifest delight in the service of God, might go far to convince even the giddy and the dissipated, that, in genuine godliness, there is something divine; and that the people who are most religious, are also the most happy. This would be gaining a point of great practical importance. It would be foolish to expect that any human heart would, by this means alone, be disarmed of its enmity to God and to godliness; or, that Christians would cease to smart under the hatred and persecution of the world, merely because their principles kept them always buoyant and happy. But it is indeed a great point gained when stumbling-blocks are removed out of the way; and when the service of God is exhibited to the world as affording a rational and elevated enjoyment, notwithstanding all the restraints it imposes; and when the false accusations of ignorant and ungodly men are put to shame and silenced, by the holiness and happiness of believers.

How well-pleasing would it be unto God, how honouring to the name of Christ, and how serviceable to his cause in the world, if all Christians presented to the admiration of their fellowmen, the noble spectacle of a people separated from whatever is evil, and united in the observance of all that is "lovely and of good report," and rejoicing before the Lord continually in the experience and acknowledgment of his grace! But what is so desirable in regard to the whole body of believers, is only exemplified in the case of a few individuals, scattered here and there, who, Abraham-like, are strong in faith, giving glory to God. And it is for a lamentation, that, in consequence of the doubts and the misgivings and the spiritual darkness and distress, which are so prevalent, our holy religion is too often exhibited in a false and forbidding aspect. I say, in a most false and forbidding aspect, because it will be found, that persons who are not themselves religious, when they see professing Christians avoid what would yield them "the pleasures of sin," and at the same time remain destitute of "the joys of salvation," will eagerly, although falsely, ascribe this want of cheerfulness to the tendency of religion. Under such mistaken impressions, we need not wonder that an increased dislike to religion is engendered. And thus poor thoughtless sinners, instead of being drawn to the Saviour, are driven farther and farther from him, by those very persons who know how precious are immortal souls, and whose duty it is, perhaps I might say, whose desire it is, to honour Christ, and to do good to all men as they have opportunity. This is, I do believe, a frequent, as it also is, a melancholy result. It teaches us how ineffectual the best precept is without a corresponding example. And it furnishes another painful illustration of the pernicious influence of doubts. For inasmuch as the gloom and despondency which they generate, deter many sinners from taking upon them the yoke of Christ which is easy, and his burden which is light, it is obvious that such doubts not only dishonour the God of our salvation, and injure the spiritual peace and prosperity of those who are enslaved by them; but they impede the progress of the Gospel among men, and truly, although unintentionally, lend a helping hand to the power of Satan, and to the continuation of sin, and to the propagation of error.

    I cannot dismiss these brief remarks without expressing a hope of your hearty concurrence in condemning doubts, as one of those powerful instruments by which Satan contrives to cheat Christians out of that happiness which our gracious God designs they should enjoy. I feel assured, that, in your meditative hours, you must have reflected often, and with delight on the multiform arrangements of God for the happiness of his creatures. Notwithstanding the curse which rests upon man and upon the earth which he inhabits, it gives us a most attractive and endearing conception of the Divine character, when we read in Scripture that "the earth is full of the goodness of the Lord;"—that "his tender mercies are over all his works;"—that "he maketh his sun to rise on the evil and on the good, and sendeth rain on the just and on the unjust;"—and that he never leaves himself without a witness, in that "he does us good, and gives us fruitful seasons, filling our hearts with food and gladness."

But the goodness of the Lord towards fallen men is chiefly conspicuous in the efficacious scheme which the Gospel unveils, for the immediate counteraction of moral evil, and for its ultimate removal from the universe. Debased as we naturally are by sin, and separated in affection from the God of holiness, we are slow to discover the tokens of his bounty and lovingkindness by which we are surrounded, or to feel their subduing and sanctifying influence. Neither the grandeur of the works of Creation, nor the beneficent provisions of an all-pervading and overruling Providence, give us any intimation of *God's forgiving love*; whereas, to guilty creatures, this one attribute in the Godhead is of supreme and indispensable importance. For this reason, so long as conscious guilt fills the minds of men with the dread and dislike of "the unknown God" whom they ignorantly worship, the richest profusion of temporal blessings fails to afford that satisfying and enduring happiness after which all are panting, and over their want of which God himself is represented as tenderly lamenting: "O that thou hadst hearkened unto my commandments! then had thy peace been as a river, and thy righteousness as the waves of the sea," Isa 48:18. Until God himself is sought after and trusted in as our chief good, and until the advancement of his glory is seen and acknowledged to be our chief end, we shall never enjoy exemption from discontent and disappointment. Until we love God himself better than his gifts, we shall never experience the happiness which his gifts are designed and fitted to convey to us. Oh! then, how greatly should we prize, and how thankfully should we embrace, that blessed Gospel, which gives to sinners the assurance that *God is love*! This is indeed "good tidings:" and in the belief of it we shall find an antidote to all the varied forms of misery with which our sinfulness makes us conversant. Oh yes, my friend, the Gospel does with no uncertain sound proclaim the forgiving love of God; and the belief of it carries home to our hearts the delightful conviction that Jesus Christ is his best, his greatest, yea, his "unspeakable gift." The belief of this precious Gospel makes us experimentally to know, that Jesus Christ is the true and only resting place for poor souls, who are heavy laden with a sense of sin, and wearied with the fruitlessness of their own endeavours to obtain rest and peace. This Gospel is the opened door for man's return to God; and faith enables us to enter in, assured that we shall find a welcome. Thus, whilst all classes of unbelievers are looking around them on every created object, and saying, "Who will show us any good?" the prayer of the psalmist flows fresh from the hearts and lips of true believers, "Lord, lift *thou* up the light of thy countenance upon us!" The prayer of faith will certainly be answered. And when God does shine forth upon us with the beams of reconciliation and of love, then we too shall thankfully acknowledge, as the psalmist did, "Thou hast put gladness into my heart, more than in the time that their corn and their wine increased," Ps 4:6-7.

As substantial and abiding happiness is only to be found in God, and as the faith of Jesus Christ is the only way of access to God, it is reasonable to expect that those who do believe, should be continually rejoicing in the God of their salvation. But is this the case? Alas! neither you nor I have our hearts so much or so often expanded as they always ought to be, with that holy gladness of which the psalmist tells us he was a partaker. And it is seldom that we meet with fellow-pilgrims resembling the Ethiopian eunuch, of whom it is recorded "he went on his way rejoicing," Acts 8:39. It is painfully manifest that even believers come far short of that strength for serving God, and of that happiness in his service, which are their undoubted privileges. Too many are living inconsistently with their privileges and their principles. And many more, instead of singing to the Lord with joyful voice, are heard to utter the most desponding sentiments, whilst gloom and sadness are depicted in the expression of their countenance. Thus it is that the merciful designs of God for the happiness of men are, at least to a certain extent, frustrated by men themselves. God is at the same time dishonoured. The devil triumphs. And the world will not believe that the only way to be happy, is to be religious.

I speak of things as they actually exist throughout the length and breadth of our land; and my object in doing so is not to act as an accuser of the brethren, nor to censure any individual Christian. Far from it. But I do wish fully to expose the pernicious influence of doubts, and to deepen the impression, which I trust is already made on your mind, that the extensive prevalence of doubts is the cause to which we must ascribe the lamentable deficiency of religious peace and joy, and love and hope, and of all the purest and most pleasurable emotions that can animate the human breast, amongst professedly Christian people.

Throughout the several Letters addressed to you on the pernicious influence of doubts, I have not attempted to maintain any distinction betwixt such as are systematic and permanent, and such as are only occasional and temporary. To have done so would have caused continual embarrassment, and introduced many repetitions into my remarks. Now, however, when we are come to the winding up of this department of our subject, it would be wrong not to advert to this distinction, because there is in reality a marked line of demarcation between the one class of doubters and the other. At the same time I shall feel disappointed if there is not, on your part, a willingness to admit the general applicability of my remarks and illustrations even to the least objectionable kind of doubts. And I assure you of a perfect readiness, on my part, to own that the Christian whose faith is shaken only during seasons of sudden and peculiar temptation, and whose doubts are of short continuance, dishonours God in a much smaller degree, and does far less injury to the cause of Christ in the world, than he does who doubts always, or, what is still worse, who intentionally remains in a doubting state. Besides, it is undeniable that *the occasional doubter*, however trying are the fears, and anxieties, and discomfort into which he may be plunged,—and however humiliating his aberrations and declensions may be,—sustains little damage in his spiritual interests, compared with *the permanent doubter*. This is a point of comparison, you will observe. For all doubts are hurtful, and all doubters suffer from their influence. And you and I, my friend, have merely to examine our own experience in order to ascertain, what we ought never to lose sight of, that, as the vigorous exercise of faith in Christ Jesus keeps the soul in a healthy and happy condition; so the indulgence of doubt of any kind, and to any extent, and for any length of time, deranges our whole spiritual system, and deprives us at once of spiritual health, and of spiritual enjoyment too, just as certainly as the introduction of some poisonous matter into our bodily frame causes disorder and pain through all the members.

I have purposely specified *the indulgence* of doubt, because I suppose every Christian, even the most settled and stablished in the faith, is subject to the intrusion of involuntary and unwelcome doubts, which stagger him for a moment, and shock his feelings, and disturb his usual tranquillity of mind. These very transient doubts get no encouragement. They are exceedingly troublesome, and we are anxious to be quit of them. But, for the most part, as they come seldom, so they flit fast away, and their evil consequences are scarcely felt. On the other hand, it is no more than justice to acknowledge, that these flying doubts may have a beneficial tendency in exciting us to vigilance and humility, and in increasing our thankfulness for exemption from doubts of a more fixed and determined character. And if we cannot altogether escape from doubts whilst our present Christian warfare continues, truly we should be very thankful, when the unpleasant assaults of these disturbers of our peace are neither lengthened nor frequent. But there are pious people, and I apprehend their number is not small, who never attain to great stedfastness in the faith; and when doubts assail them, their power of resistance is not sufficient to repel the enemy. In such cases doubts make a lodgment in the mind, and are too often treated with a dangerous indulgence. Then their baneful influence is bitterly felt; and the lives of those Christians who thus give way to doubts are marked by ceaseless alternations. When faith maintains its rightful ascendency, light and gladness are experienced. But doubts sometimes prevail, and bring with them darkness and sorrow.

> There is a midnight of the mind,
> A darkness deep and undefined,
> Which e'en o'er pious souls will steal,
> And heaven's resplendent beams conceal.

This is not all. A midnight of the mind is bad enough. A winter of the mind is still worse. And such a winter is sure to come whenever doubts predominate. The doubting Christian has his seasons of coldness and barrenness, as well as of gloom and despondency. Such seasons are indeed only *occasional*, being intermingled, in the cases of different individuals, with longer or shorter intervals of sunshine; and they are only *temporary*, being sometimes of longer and sometimes of shorter duration. But come when they may, and last while they may, they are always prejudicial to the Christian's spiritual progress and comfort, and likewise to his usefulness amongst his fellowmen. The kind of doubts, however, which are most to be dreaded, and chiefly to be denounced, are those that are *systematically* encouraged, and allowed to become *permanent*, under a mistaken plea of checking presumption, and with the deluded expectation of promoting spiritual safety. These are dangerous doubts,—dangerous to the Christian who cherishes them, and dangerous to the men of the world who observe them. Alas! my dear friend, how miserable it must be, when the darkness of midnight is never relieved by the morning dawn, nor irradiated with the meridian sunbeams! And how cheerless, and how fruitless must that life be, which passes away amidst the dreariness of a spiritual winter, which terminates only in death! Let us hope that doubts of this description are not very prevalent; for they cannot exist without causing incalculable mischief.

Another distinction in the nature of doubts requires some notice. The assertion may be made that many doubting Christians do practically live near to God in the observance of his ordinances and commandments, and are ready to every good word and work. Now, I think it must be conceded that this assertion is not groundless. We do meet with pious and excellent persons who profess to be in doubt, not so much in respect of the truth of any part of God's word, as of their own interest in the Saviour's work; and the only rational way in which this can be explained is, to distinguish *between real and speculative doubts*.

Is it not true, my friend, that we meet with people who boldly profess to have an assurance of salvation, and yet they give us no evidence of having faith in Jesus Christ at all? Their assurance has no solid or scriptural foundation. Their profession is without principle. Their religion is nothing more than a dry and uninfluential speculative theory. It possesses no spiritual vitality. It is destitute of love either to God or to man. It is utterly worthless. But is it not also true that the notorious worthlessness of this speculative assurance is the very thing that brings contempt and disgrace on that real assurance of salvation, which flows from a strong faith in the Saviour—that assurance which the word of God warrants, and which is most sanctifying in all its tendencies, and which every Christian should endeavour to attain? So, in like manner, we meet with Christians who entertain doubts that are merely speculative, and do not essentially interfere either with their enjoyment of inward comfort, or with the consistency of their ordinary walk and conversation. When we interrogate these professed doubters about their state of mind, we generally have the satisfaction to learn that they would not part with Christ for all the world. They *feel* him to be their Saviour, although they hesitate to *say* so. And because he is *their Saviour*, they cheerfully acknowledge their obligations to love and serve him with all their heart, and soul, and strength. In fact it is chiefly in words that their doubts have any existence at all: and so far as it concerns themselves, this is a cause of congratulation. But as it concerns other people, it is much to be lamented. For inasmuch as these speculative doubters exercise a real faith in the Son of God, and in their lives deny all ungodliness, and participate in the consolations of the Gospel, they give a very dangerous encouragement to real doubters, who deceive themselves with the vain hope of being equally holy and happy. But it is of the highest importance clearly to understand, and constantly to remember, that it is not the doubts which are merely speculative, but the faith in Christ Jesus which is a living principle, that brings forth in any man the fruits of righteousness, which are to the glory and praise of God.

There is yet another distinction which ought not to be overlooked. As there are different degrees of faith,—weak and strong faith; little and great faith,—so we may be certain that, betwixt the highest and the lowest points, *there are many gradations of doubt*. For this reason it would be unjust to expect that all doubts should be equally hurtful. But where doubts do really exist, the amount of evil which they occasion will be in proportion to their strength, or to their frequency, or to their duration.

In finishing this Letter, I also finish the subject which has occupied so much of our time. And, now, my friend, I shall be glad if anything I have said has strengthened your convictions of the pernicious influence of doubts, as they respect God, and Christians themselves, and also the men of the world. It is a great advantage to know who our enemies are, and from whence they come. It will therefore be our wisdom to give no quarter to doubts, whenever they assail us; but ever to stand fast in the faith, and to quit us like men.

Yours, etc.

LETTER 10

THE CAUSES AND THE CURES OF DOUBTS

I. PHYSICAL OR NATURAL CAUSES

A desire to ascertain *the causes of doubts* naturally springs from the observation or experience of their pernicious influences.—The causes are diversified.—I. Physical or natural: subdivided into, 1st. *A constitutional tendency* to doubt.—This not uncommon.—Grace does not eradicate those propensities and dispositions which constitute individual character.—Enlarged supplies of the Spirit of all grace, the only cure for doubts arising from this cause.—2nd. *A disordered state of mind* is productive of doubts.—Melancholia.—Cases described.—In such cases the removal of the malady is necessary to the removal of the doubts.—3rd. *Bodily disease* affecting the mind.—Hypochondriasis.—Childish imbecility.—Interesting anecdote of Luther.—His despair in a time of sickness.—His strong faith in health.—Case of an eminent clergyman.—Excessive grief, causing the loss of health.—Doubts and spiritual darkness resulting from the reciprocal action of the mind and the body on each other.—Moral causes operating along with natural, to produce a state of doubt.—The cases adduced may be called extreme.—But they show the more clearly in what manner doubts sometimes arise.—We should guard against harsh judgments of doubters.—And judiciously apply remedies suited to the causes in which their doubts originate.

My dear Friend,

In proportion as the pernicious influence of doubts is observed in other people, or felt and acknowledged in ourselves, there will be a desire to ascertain, as far as possible, to what sources their origin and continuance may be legitimately traced, and by what method their rise and growth may be most speedily and effectually counteracted. In other words, we have now to consider *the causes and the cures* of this great evil, which it must be admitted prevails so extensively throughout the professedly Christian community.

This distinct branch of our general subject is equally interesting with that to which I felt warranted in devoting no less than six long Letters. I must therefore again bespeak your patient attention; and should my observations be somewhat full and minute, I shall do my utmost to avoid tediousness.

The sources in which doubts originate,—the causes to which they may be ascribed, are numerous, and of very diversified character. This is no more than might reasonably be expected, since the doubts which assail Christians are also very various, accommodating many of their peculiarities to the variety of character, and attainments, and external advantages or disadvantages, which are manifested among Christians themselves. You will be satisfied if I select some of the most prominent and influential of these causes. And in adverting to each of them separately, I shall likewise take occasion, in passing, to hint briefly at the different remedial measures that may be resorted to, with the best promise of success. It is unquestionable that different cases of doubt will require different kinds of treatment. And as the causes vary, so must the cures. But at the same time, it is of importance to remember, that, excepting where the doubts arise from disease of mind or of body, there is only one grand remedy, although the modes of its application may be varied to suit existing circumstances; and that the one sovereign cure for every kind of doubt, is a strong and unwavering faith in the pure and unadulterated Gospel of our salvation. All doubts, with the exception already stated, are the effects of some imperfection

PHYSICAL OR NATURAL CAUSES OF DOUBTS 195

either in our knowledge of Gospel truth, or in our belief of what we know. At the outset, therefore, of our present inquiry, I deem it proper to apprise you of my intention, in the concluding Letters of the series, to expose those *inaccurate* and *defective* views of the Gospel, with which many Christians rest contented, and which I do regard as the most fruitful source of the doubts that are prevalent. And in doing this, favourable opportunities will occur for exhibiting those *comprehensive* and *correct* views of Gospel truth, which, when understood and embraced with a lively faith, are most admirably calculated, either to prevent the existence of doubts, or to remove them where they already exist.

We have then, in the first instance, to dispose of certain less common and more subordinate causes of doubt which are peculiar to Christians of a certain temperament, or to the particular circumstances in which Christians of all temperaments occasionally may be placed.

Of these subordinate causes, I place foremost on the list such as may be designated *physical* or *natural*. I use the word in opposition to spiritual, moral, or religious. And you know very well that the doubts under which some people labour may be fairly attributed, 1st, to a constitutional tendency; 2nd, to a disordered state of mind; and 3rd, to bodily disease. Here are three distinct causes of that kind to which I have given the designation of *natural*. And now let us take a glance at the operations of each of them.

1. There is *a constitutional tendency to doubt* in certain individuals. Their mental temperament is cautious and incredulous. They are "slow of heart to believe," not only events that are anywise extraordinary, but even the statements of their own friends and acquaintances about the commonest transactions of life. They are generally of a very argumentative turn of mind; and whatever proposition is submitted to them, they

are always ready to start a long train of objections, or to imagine insurmountable difficulties. Although what is reported to them has actually happened, they hesitate to receive it as a fact; and their usual expressions are, how can *that* be? or, *this* is very unlikely; or, *something* else cannot be true. They are besides of a timorous disposition. They shrink from coming to a determined and immediate conclusion in regard to anything, however trifling in itself; and if you ask their opinion on a matter of importance, their answers are generally evasive, and at best they are couched in the language of uncertainty and indecision. Speak to them about their own personal concerns—touch upon a subject in which their health, or their success, or their safety is involved; and you are instantly repulsed with a look of anxiety, or a shrug of the shoulder, or a shake of the head. These are very intelligible signs. It is scarcely possible to mistake their meaning. They are plain indications of the suspense and doubt which hold an unhappy mastery over this class of persons.

The character I have thus hastily sketched is to be found almost in every place, and in all the different circles of society, from the lowest to the highest. Perhaps you have in your eye, at this moment, some one or other of your friends and companions who answers exactly to the description given. And I can honestly declare that my sketch is not imaginary. It is a copy taken from real life. But it will be said that divine grace effects so great a change on those to whom it is imparted as to make them "new creatures." And true it is that through this transforming energy, sinners become saints, and they who were the enemies of God are converted into his loving friends and obedient children. Still it is also true that the natural propensities and dispositions which constitute individual character, and distinguish between one man and another, are not eradicated. Grace does much to subdue and control what is evil and unholy; and to purify and direct what is right and amiable. Grace renovates and ennobles and beautifies our sinful humanity. But it neither makes anyone of us at present perfect in holiness, nor does it make all of us alike. The broad lineaments of every Christian's natural character remain nearly as they were previous to his being "born again." And hence it is that when persons, with a strong constitutional tendency to doubt, undergo this blessed change, and become obedient to the faith of Christ Jesus, the exercise of their faith is continually impeded by the natural bias of their minds. And as they are doubters on every other subject, and especially on subjects of importance, we should be prepared to find them full of doubts respecting their own salvation, which they cannot fail to regard as the most important of all subjects to themselves. Indeed it would be quite a moral phenomenon were these constitutional doubters to express such an assurance of their pardon and acceptance with God, and of their entrance into his heavenly and eternal kingdom, as many Christians, even of a sanguine temperament, never attain.

And does not the actual state of the case precisely harmonise with all the calculations and conjectures respecting this class of doubters, in which we feel warranted to indulge? Amongst my own Christian friends I know more than one or two, who manifest a strong natural tendency to doubt; but who nevertheless are eminent for piety and devotedness to the service of God, and whose views of the Gospel seem to be sufficiently clear and comprehensive. Much of their conversation is spiritual and edifying, and conducted with animation too, so long as it is confined to religious topics of a general character, or of peculiar adaptation to the circumstances of other people. Should an experimental turn however be given to the conversation, it is marvellous how quickly the holy pleasure which had been beaming in their countenances gives way to an expression of uneasiness, if not of pain; and at the same time there is a palpable sinking in the very tone of their voice. If you bring them to close quarters, and address them directly on the privileges which belong to believers, and on the hope of glory to which they are begotten again by the resurrection of Jesus Christ our Lord, then you hear of nothing but doubts and fears; and their natural temperament shows itself without disguise.

The doubts of these good people have a resemblance to hereditary disease, which nobody expects to be cured. But, you ask, are these constitutional doubts really incurable?—do they baffle the application of every remedy? No, my friend: they are indeed deeply seated; they are difficult of removal; but they are not incurable. I do believe, however, that their removal will never be accomplished by any ordinary methods. It is not human teaching that doubters of this description need; nor can the affectionate counsels, or urgent exhortations of a Christian brother, bring them deliverance. It is power from on high that alone can silence their reasonings against themselves, and subdue their timidity, and overcome their cautiousness. *Their* cure depends on a large supply of the Spirit of all grace to strengthen the principle of faith, and to keep it in active and constant exercise. To obtain this divinely provided and efficacious antidote to doubt, nothing is necessary but daily and importunate prayer. And although the constitutional tendency to doubt may continue, just as Paul's "thorn in the flesh" did not depart from him in answer to his beseeching requests, yet to every Christian labouring under natural infirmities or physical impediments, which he brought not upon himself, and which he cannot remove, the gracious declaration which the Lord made to his tried apostle, is equally applicable and encouraging,—"My grace is sufficient for thee; for my strength is made perfect in weakness," 2 Cor 12:9.

2. *A disordered state of mind*, is another of those less common and more subordinate causes of doubt which we denominate natural: and it is certain that interesting cases do occur, in which the deep depression of spirits and the great spiritual distress that are endured, can be decidedly ascribed to mental disease, without reference to any other cause whatever.

PHYSICAL OR NATURAL CAUSES OF DOUBTS 199

In our ordinary discourse, it is customary to apply the term *melancholy* to any individual who appears to be cast down and out of spirits. But strictly speaking *melancholia* is a kind of partial insanity. Medical men tell us that it is characterised by sadness and despondency, the mind being overwhelmed with fears and anticipations of evil, in consequence of an erroneous belief or impression concerning one subject, or a particular series of subjects. It is in fact a diseased state of mind, to which the most religious people are liable as well as other men. Nor is it necessary for me to say one word as to the causes of this sad disease. It is sufficient for the object we have in hand to point attention to cases where the disease is developed; and if the unhappy individuals who are afflicted with melancholia happen, while in health, to have been of a devout and pious disposition, it will be something singular if their fears and anticipations of evil have not an exclusive or an almost exclusive reference to their everlasting salvation. This one subject is in their estimation of the highest importance, and naturally occupies much of their thoughts. And if on this subject their conversation betrays a belief or impression which we cannot hesitate to pronounce erroneous; then, whatever doubts they harbour respecting their spiritual condition and prospects, and whatever depression or despondency they manifest in connexion with their doubts, must, in fairness, be ascribed to the mental disease under which they are suffering.

I recollect the cases of two gentlemen of my own acquaintance, both of whom were wealthy, and both of them, when first taken ill, gave proofs of their minds being partially deranged, by the distress into which they were thrown, in consequence of the same kind of erroneous impression. The one of them was haunted with the idea that he was to die a beggar. This false but fearful anticipation was the one subject of which he talked, and over which he mournfully brooded. He was a very worldly man; and the ideal loss of his riches made him truly wretched. The other gentleman, with a constitutional predisposition to melancholy, had his mind thrown off the balance by a domestic bereavement. The disease manifested its presence, however, not so much by an excessive and unnatural sadness for the loss of a beloved child, as by an erroneous belief that he was ruined in his worldly circumstances—that he had lost all his property. Besides having much money in the public funds, he possessed large landed estates, entirely unencumbered with mortgages; and yet so deep was the mistaken impression on his mind, that he gravely told his wife one night, how sorry he was on her account, as he feared it would be necessary to sell the bed on which she was lying. But he was a man of decidedly religious principle; and, as might have been expected, he fancied that he had suffered loss in his religion as in other things. Kind friends, not knowing the nature of the malady under which he laboured, endeavoured to direct his thoughts to the privileges of believers in Christ Jesus, and to the consolations of the Gospel. Their labours were all in vain. Indeed they were worse than useless. Because, as he felt himself incapable of being consoled, or of enjoying these privileges, he doubted his own Christianity, and this gave a new direction to his sadness and despondency. In a short time he ceased to speak about the child whose death was at first the ostensible cause of all his dejection; and by degrees he was relieved, in a great measure, from the notion of having lost his property. At least he seldom mentioned it. But he was as much depressed in spirits as ever. He feared that his own soul was lost. He feared that he was not, and never had been, a true believer in the Saviour; and thus his dejection assumed a religious character. He was tormented with doubts about his own salvation, and it is evident that these doubts were the effects of the mental disease with which he was afflicted.

I should think that when religious people are attacked with melancholia, their imagined causes of fear and of sadness may frequently, at the outset, be something widely remote from religion, as in the case to which I have just alluded: and yet it is quite natural that religion itself should ultimately acquire the ascendency. But we know also that in other cases, the deep dejection is altogether of a religious nature from first to last; and religion is the one solitary subject on which an erroneous belief or impression is ever expressed. You have surely come in contact with melancholy persons, whose only ground of complaint and disquietude was an unconquerable persuasion that God had cast them off, and that there was no salvation for them. You must at all events have heard of persons, who, out of the depths of their painful depression of spirits, write and speak bitter things against themselves, as having committed the sin which is unto death, and for which no prayer is to be made, or as being guilty of the sin against the Holy Ghost, for which no pardon can be granted. And sometimes the impression on their minds is so very erroneous, that, with a comprehensive knowledge of scriptural truths, and a correct application of them to other people, they aggravate their own distress, by saying, like Cowper, the poet, that the declarations and promises of God's mercy are true to all sinners, except themselves.

The men of the world eagerly seize on every instance of religious melancholy that comes under their cognizance, as an excuse for their own irreligious practices, and for their condemnation of that serious deportment, and devotedness to the service of God, which is incompatible with worldly amusements. But it is a great mistake to blame the cheerful and happy service of our redeeming God, as if it either generated or nourished the melancholy which occasionally manifests itself in religious people. The truth of the matter is, that a diseased state of mind has perverted their views of Scripture in reference to themselves, and caused the dejection, as well as the doubts, which make them so miserable.

And now the question presents itself—how is it that these painful doubts, and this sad dejection, are to be removed?— by what methods are these downcast and miserable Christians to be restored to the calm serenity or heavenly joys which formerly sweetened their existence? I feel confident that this desirable object is not to be attained in the way of argument or remonstrance. You may remonstrate against their dejection as causeless and absurd; and you may argue against the inconsistency and unreasonableness of their doubts. But you will not move them one inch from their false impression by the most powerful arguments; nor will your strongest remonstrances produce any salutary effect. All such moral appliances will be found utterly unavailing, so long as the mental malady continues. On this account every expedient that human skill and science can devise should be tried, to bring back the mind from its aberrations. The blow must be struck at the root. The seat of the disease must be assailed. And if God is pleased to crown our exertions with success, the doubts and dejection will disappear of their own accord when the mind is restored to a healthy condition, just as the darkness of midnight, with all its terrifying dreams and visions, gives way to the returning light of the sun. In decided cases of this sort, as it is the disease that causes the doubts, and not the doubts that cause the melancholy, the removal of the disease itself is the only cure on which we can depend, and for which we ought to labour and pray.

3. *Bodily disease* is the last of the three natural causes of doubt which I specified as deserving of notice. And although it may not be of very frequent occurrence, yet we know that sometimes even Christians of established character and of large growth, have their mental faculties so sadly impaired during seasons of sickness, that, in many respects, they become like children.

It falls not within the scope of my present remarks to advert to the delirium or incoherency attendant on various kinds of fever. But cases of *hypochondriasis* are directly in point. The hypochondriac labours under real bodily disease; but it is of the very nature of his disease to disturb the usual exercise of the mind; and, in inveterate cases, the mental derangement almost amounts to insanity. The poor patient is full of the most extravagant whims. He magnifies beyond measure his own ailments, and is so wholly engrossed by them, as to render it nearly impossible to fix his attention on any other topic. Of course, his spirits sink into extreme depression; and his case borders on melancholia, inasmuch as there is no *adequate cause* for the deep despondency in which he indulges.

Have you, my friend, ever seen any of the true children of God smarting under the lash of this dreadful disorder? I have: and it is a most afflicting spectacle. To a great extent they lose their self-command. They cannot read. They cannot rest. Their sensations are more uncomfortable than they can describe. Wretchedness and agony are often depicted on their countenances. And in such circumstances, it would be unreasonable to look for a manifestation of that "joy and peace in believing," which was wont to be manifested by the same individuals, when they were blessed with health of body. They fancy themselves to be spiritually shipwrecked, and sinking into a fathomless gulf. They feel as if they were abandoned by God and man. And as they are lost to every kind of personal and social and intellectual enjoyment, it would be marvellous indeed if they escaped from distressing doubts about their interest in spiritual blessings. Those Christian men whom I have seen struggling for months together under the galling yoke of hypochondriasis were never free from doubts. They doubted whether God the Father still regarded them with love; and whether Christ retained the character of their Saviour; and whether the Holy Ghost was such a Comforter as he was promised to be. They were overborne with doubts. But all their doubts proceeded from disease. As health returned to them, their fears vanished; their doubts departed; their mind recovered its proper tone; and, in the faith of Jesus Christ, they again served God with peace of conscience, and joy in the Holy Ghost.

I have entered into a detail of the peculiar symptoms and

aspects of hypochondriasis, and assigned to it the first place under the present division of our subject, because it is a kind of connecting link between the melancholia, which is a purely mental malady, and those bodily diseases which occasionally and partially impair the mind, and depress the spirits. In these respects, hypochondriasis has a bad preeminence; for it always, and often very seriously, interferes with the rightful exercise of the mental faculties. And in addition to the magnified and mistaken estimate which the poor hypochondriac forms of his own case, you must have observed how dependent and helpless he becomes. He is afraid to act on his own judgment. He even dislikes to be left alone, as if he were afraid of his own company. He leans on some friend or another for direction in everything, and needs to be led like a child.

But childishness is by no means peculiar to hypochondriasis. It is at least a common *result* of other diseases, such as paralysis and epilepsy. And when Christians do lapse into this weakened state of mind through the loss of bodily health, their childishness will be exhibited in very various ways. I fondly hope that most of them are patient, and contented, and happy. This is the actual condition of some dear afflicted children of God, with whom I am personally acquainted. Others I have seen reduced to great mental imbecility, who were continually recounting their mercies, and expressing their gratitude to God and man. They could not speak on any solemn or sacred subject without weeping. These afflicted saints have not the capacity for holding communion with God, or rejoicing in Christ Jesus as their righteousness and strength. But they suffer no distress of mind. They are not harassed with doubts respecting their own interest in the great salvation. They are strangers to that fear which hath torment, 1 John 4:18. It is not so, however, with all the children of God, when they are reduced to this extremity. Some of them grow peevish, and irritable, and discontented. Nothing pleases them. Others again, with a better command of reason, are more resigned and submissive, but nevertheless they are destitute of true peace. Their recollection of Scripture precepts and promises is too inaccurate to yield them the comfort which they need. The Gospel presents itself to their minds like a broken vessel, or a disjointed piece of mechanism. There is a want of something to lay hold of, and with which to be satisfied. They do not see Christ in the all-sufficiency of his mediatory work. Nor can they discern in themselves any evidences of their faith in him. And thus doubts of their own spiritual and eternal safety arise from every point to which they look, and overwhelm them in sadness and dismay. But it is probable that such doubts used not to trouble them in the days of health, when body and mind were alike vigorous and active. And were health again restored, we should find that these doubts, and the distress which accompanied them, had simultaneously vanished.

The truth of these general statements may be best illustrated by a specific case of the power of bodily disease to unstring the bow of a holy man's mind, and leave him a defenceless prey to harassing doubts and fears.

Have you read Merle D'Aubigne's *History of the Reformation*? It is a captivating book. The Author favours us with a full-length portrait of Luther; and one is constrained to believe that it is drawn to the life. Nobody with even an imperfect knowledge either of Luther's character, or of Luther's conduct, would for a moment suspect that the intrepid German Reformer was ever chargeable with want of boldness in the faith of Christ, or likely to sink into a state of childishness. He who defied the threats of popes and of princes, and who so often endangered his life from love to Christ, and to his cause, must have been as far remote from doubting, or from giving indulgence to doubts, as any human being well could be. But towards the close of his extraordinary life, so marked by relentless opposition to all that he regarded as error, and by undaunted perseverance in the maintenance of evangelical truth, it is recorded by the historian of the Reformation, that "Luther's health suffered. One day he fainted in the arms of his wife and friends; and for a whole week he was as if 'in death and hell.' He had lost Jesus Christ, he said; and was driven hither and thither by tempests of despair. The world was about to pass away; and prodigies announced that the last day was at hand."*

This quotation certainly supplies us with a very animated representation of the violence of the Reformer's inward conflicts when the strength and soundness of his judgment were overpowered through his bodily exhaustion. For many years he had lived in the midst of stormy debates and discussions, which convulsed all Christendom. Nothing upheld him holy in his conversation, happy in his mind, and stedfast in the prosecution of the great object which he had in view, but his having found Jesus Christ, and his holding fast by him, and his being strong in his imparted strength. It was his life of faith on the Son of God that kept him buoyant amidst the raging waves which dashed around him. And however black the clouds that hovered over him, it was his unshaken confidence in Jesus that cheered his spirits with an assured hope, not merely of his own everlasting salvation, but of the approach of brighter and more peaceful times to the church of Christ, and to the world. But now, when his health suffered, his giant mind became enfeebled, and he was incapacitated for the exercise of that faith in the truth of divine revelation which had hitherto carried him triumphant through all opposition. A disordered imagination usurped the throne of reason; and he complained that "he had lost Jesus Christ." How emphatic was this complaint! But still fancying himself to be in the storm, and left alone, without his unerring Guide and almighty Helper, he fancied that all was lost. How natural this appears in the circumstances of the case!

---

*D'Aubigne, vol. iii, p. 413.

Nor can we wonder at the good man being "driven hither and thither." And, considering the vehemence of his natural temperament, and the singularly uncompromising energy that characterised his lengthened exertions to defend and propagate the pure doctrines of the Gospel, neither need we wonder that his fancied failure raised within him "tempests of despair." This is a strong expression. But we must remember that Luther did nothing by halves. As an enlightened and devout Christian, Christ was everything to him. He had renounced the idolatrous, and superstitious, and self-righteous observances of Romanism; and as a sinner seeking to be justified, and sanctified, and saved, he rested all his hopes on Christ, and on him alone. And thus, whenever he lost his hold of the Saviour, and his sense of his gracious presence, through the sympathy of his mind with his diseased body, instead of sinking merely into a state of perplexity and doubt, as might have happened to other Christians whose previous faith had been less full and firm, the noble-minded Reformer was doomed to encounter "tempests of despair."

I trust, my friend, you will not fail to draw the conclusion, that if bodily disease can produce such an effect on the mind of such a man as Martin Luther, how much more easily and certainly will it cause *doubts* in men of weaker minds and of weaker faith! And that Luther was reduced to a state of *despair*, altogether in consequence of the prostration of his mind along with his body, by the illness under which he laboured at the time, is quite apparent from the narrative. Such a distressing state of mind he never experienced whilst he enjoyed health. And now it lasted only for a week. As his bodily health improved, his reason resumed its wonted authority. His faith in Christ Jesus was again active, and his devoted services were recommenced. The inward storm subsided, and once more he was bold as a lion to face the enemies of his heavenly Master, and "earnestly to contend for the faith which was once delivered to the saints," Jude 3.

To Erasmus, who was of a timid and vacillating temperament, which sometimes gave his conduct too much the appearance of trimming, Luther expressed himself strongly against doubts, in a letter written not many months before the illness which threw him into so great distress of mind; and from this letter D'Aubigne has favoured us with the following extract:—"We Christians ought to be well persuaded of what we teach, and to be able to say *yes* or *no*. To object to our affirming, with full conviction, what we believe, is to strip us of our faith itself. The Holy Spirit is no spirit of doubt. And he has written in our hearts a firm and peaceful assurance, which makes us as sure of the objects of faith, as we are of our existence."*

It gives me a sincere satisfaction to be able to place this quotation in contrast with the former. Here, in a few brief sentences, but with great force of language, the Reformer states his opinion with that decision which belongs only to a man who is "strong in faith," as Abraham was, Rom 4:20; and who, like the Thessalonians, "knowing his election of God," 1 Thess 1:4, knew also that he had "received the Spirit of adoption, whereby we cry, Abba, Father," Rom 8:15. *The Holy Spirit*, he nobly and justly declares, *is no spirit of doubt*. This was his belief; this was his experience, until his mental faculties were impeded in their natural exercise by the pressure of bodily disease. And then he stopped not short at *doubts* respecting either God or himself, but he became frantic with *despair*. He despaired of his own salvation, and of the reformation of the church, and even of the preservation of the world.

Perhaps you are thinking that I have dwelt at unnecessary length on the case of Luther. But to me it seems so strikingly illustrative of the subject we are explaining, and in other respects is so interesting and instructive, that I could still expatiate upon it with delight. This much I shall grant you, that it is not an ordinary case we have been considering; and simply

---

*D'Aubigne, vol. iii, p. 374.

for this good reason, that Luther was not an ordinary man. Let us, however, proceed to a new illustration of a milder and more mixed character. I say *more mixed*, because it cannot have escaped your notice, that the deep distress under which Luther suffered for a whole week, is attributed purely and solely to the influence of bodily disease upon his mind. And whilst it is very true that many other Christians experience a similar loss of mental power from the same cause, although not to the same extent; yet I do apprehend that in cases of this kind it will most generally be found that other causes of a moral or religious nature, operate in conjunction with want of bodily health to occasion a state of doubt and dejection.

Well then, I shall tell you of a clergyman, whose private life was much adorned with "the fruits of the Spirit," which are enumerated by St. Paul in Gal 5:22-23; and whose public ministrations had been extensively owned of God with a blessing. He was indeed a very lovely character, both as a domestic man, and as a parochial minister. But all the spiritual children of God are partakers of chastisement; "for what son is he whom the father chasteneth not?" Heb 12:7. So this eminent servant of the Lord was visited with a heavy trial in the long illness and early death of a favourite son. This youth was sufficiently advanced in years to have become a kind of companion; and, by his natural intelligence and literary attainments, by his amiable dispositions, by the gracious principles which had latterly been developed in the most satisfactory manner, and by the constant and anxious watchings which the state of his health elicited, he had entwined himself so fast around the father's heart, that the bare idea of separation could hardly be endured: and when the dreaded separation did take place, the same stroke which numbered the hopeful youth with the dead who have died in the Lord, numbered the sorrowing parent among the diseased in the land of the living. In silent grief he mourned the loss of his darling boy. Not one word of murmur or complaint against God was ever heard to escape from his lips. He was outwardly resigned: but there was a want of resignation within. And he never again exhibited that placid and pious cheerfulness which used to distinguish all his intercourse with his own family, and with his Christian friends. The continued indulgence of unexpressed grief made him an easy prey to disease of body; and bodily disease in its turn reacted on his mind. He gradually pined away,—losing flesh, and strength, and the enjoyment of life, and all his wonted energies. The lively interest which he had been accustomed to take in the concerns of his parish and his parishioners was past and gone; so was the holy delight he had experienced during many years in the discharge of ministerial duty. To preach the glad tidings of salvation to others, ceased to make his own heart glad. Although he had been remarkably social, he now shunned society. And I fear, although I cannot say positively, that he lost his relish for communion with God, as well as for conversation with men. And having lost so much, it will not surprise you to hear, that, as his weakness of body and mind increased, he sunk into a state of spiritual darkness, accompanied with doubts respecting his spiritual safety.

The man who had so often refreshed the weary and the fainthearted of his flock with rich supplies of the water of life, and comforted the sorrowful with the abundant consolations that are in Christ Jesus, now himself stood much in need of consolation and refreshment. But, alas! he felt unable to receive either the one or the other, although many kind friends were ready and eager to administer both. It ought, however, to be mentioned, that, during the progress of his physical and religious declension, which continued for upwards of a year, he was meek and gentle and uncomplaining as ever he had been, and very grateful for the smallest services rendered him. Neither irritation nor sourness of temper was at any time manifested. And even when reduced to the lowest extremity, I never understood that he suffered *much* of what we call spiritual distress. The degree of imbecility that had crept upon him, blunted his feelings, at the same time that it impaired his judgment. And as he was precluded from enjoying the high and holy privileges which appertain to a state of faith in the Lord Jesus Christ, so was he also exempted from a great deal of the anxiety and anguish which often are attendant on a state of doubt. His distress was negative rather than positive. He was deprived of the cheering light of life which beams from the Sun of Righteousness, and therefore he was in darkness. And he had ceased to experience the comforting assurance of God's love, as a sin-pardoning God in Christ, and in that respect he was in doubt. But as he was unable to estimate the full extent of his privations, his doubts did not excite great alarm or dismay. And the darkness in which he groped was widely removed from the blackness of despair.

I had an opportunity of visiting this stricken man of God before he was entirely confined to his bed, or even to the house; and before his faith in Christ Jesus had well-nigh failed, and his hopes of glory been shorn of their heavenly brightness. But I shall never forget his wan and wasted aspect, even on that occasion when not a word was uttered about doubts or fears. He was seated in his study, all alone; and on observing how his once intelligent and happy countenance was now disfigured with a settled expression of melancholy vacancy, my own heart became oppressed with sadness, and we wept together, while he touched the only string of his harp that seemed to be in tune. He spoke with tender and mournful affection of his departed boy—his bud of promise; and evidently wished him back, or rather wished he had not been taken away. But his state of mind was disconsolate rather than rebellious. He did not fret against the dispensations of the Almighty; but he would not, or could not be comforted.

I left the sick man's chamber deeply impressed with the conviction that he was an irreparable wreck in mind and body. And, months afterwards, when tidings reached me of his death, and of the cloud which overhung his deathbed, I could not participate in the astonishment which was felt by many good people, however sincerely I joined in their regrets. Those who had seen and heard and known this gifted minister of Christ, only in his best days, when blessed with health of body and of soul; and when his own rejoicing in the service of the Lord, and in the experience of his grace, stimulated others to imitate his example, expected that so happy a Christian—so honoured a servant of God, would leave the world in heavenly peace, if not in holy triumph. Nor was their expectation unreasonable. But I had no hesitation in tracing much of his doubts and depression to a *natural* cause. For, from what my own eyes had witnessed, I was sure that his mind had decayed along with his body. Both of them had simultaneously lost their wonted powers of action. Thus the man became as unfit for profitable meditation or for religious converse, as he was for the public ministrations of the sanctuary. Nor was he capable of exercising that faith which is "the substance of things hoped for; and the evidence of things not seen," Heb 11:1. And for these reasons the channels were shut up, through which, in other circumstances, he would have received "grace to help in time of need."

But it is not to be denied that bodily disease, impairing the mental faculties, does not altogether account for the doubts and darkness which prevailed in this case. How different in all its features from the case of Luther! Here the commencement of the mischief must be traced backwards to an inordinate affection on the part of the father towards his son while yet alive; and afterwards to an excessive and sinful indulgence of sorrow when God removed him hence. This conduct, however amiable it appears to be, was an unbecoming selfishness on the part of a Christian, who ought to know that God is love, and that whom he loves, he chastens. In this way, the fond parent, if I may so speak, hindered God from binding up the wounds he had been pleased to inflict, and excluded himself from the consolations which are so richly provided in Christ Jesus for all mourners in Zion. There was, therefore, a powerful *moral* cause for the doubts that arose in his mind, and for the darkness which enveloped his prospects.

But to this moral cause we must not attach more weight than it merits. Had not this good man sunk under the power of disease, we are entitled to believe that with him, as with multitudes besides whose keenest sensibilities are sorely lacerated by domestic bereavements, his bereaved feelings would have soon lost their improper ascendency, and submitted to the dictates of reason, and to the soothing and sanctifying influence of Gospel faith. And none can tell what struggles he had with himself, to control the intensity of his sorrow, which brought upon him the loss of health. Let us judge charitably. Let us give him credit for real and earnest desires not only to be resigned, but to make his resignation manifest to others. And then we shall be warranted to conclude, that, in the commendable attempt to suppress any violent or unbecoming ebullition of his heartfelt grief, he cast continual fuel on that inward fire, which, in fact, consumed his very vitals. Thus, from the acknowledged existence of a moral cause, we come back to the acknowledgment of the natural cause also. In this case we see how the natural and the moral were interwoven, and how they reciprocally aided each other. And in this, and similarly complicated cases, it may be difficult to determine which of the two causes operate with the greatest efficiency. A point so nice as this, and necessarily dependent on many contingencies, we are not at present required to decide. But it does seem clear and certain, that wherever doubts of personal salvation, accompanied with spiritual darkness and distress, coexist with any kind of bodily disease that enfeebles the mental faculties, the removal of the doubts can scarcely be expected, until bodily health is restored. In such cases, the removal of disease is the thing to be chiefly aimed at. And yet moral and religious remedies must be prayerfully applied, especially where *moral causes are conjoined with natural* in producing a state of doubt.

Under the head of bodily disease, I have now placed before you three different illustrations, all of which you probably regard as descriptive of extreme cases in different departments of illness. This is just what I intended. Extreme cases have been selected on purpose, as showing most distinctly, in what manner, and to what extent, doubts may be raised and continued, through the natural operations of some bodily distemper. It is indeed very painful, and likewise very humbling, to see great and good men enveloped in spiritual darkness, or oppressed with doubts and fears, or, it may be, driven hither and thither amidst tempests of despair. But their condition ceases to be a stumblingblock when we can trace it to a natural cause. And all that I have written in this Letter under the various heads of constitutional temperament, and mental disease, as well as of bodily disease affecting the mind, may be of use in modifying the harsh judgments concerning doubters which we are too ready to pronounce, and in regulating our treatment of those cases of doubt which fall within our own notice, and claim our particular care and sympathy.

Wishing you may long enjoy health of body, and soundness of mind, and spiritual peace and prosperity, I remain yours, etc.

LETTER 11

II. SPIRITUAL CAUSES OF DOUBTS AND THEIR CURES FIRST, THE HIDINGS OF GOD'S FACE

Spiritual influences are next in order to physical, in causing doubts.—Deemed subordinate only on account of their comparative infrequency.—Classified into, *First*, the hidings of God's face: *Second*, the temptations of the devil.—In this Letter we are to examine the first of these.—The fact stated that *God does hide himself*, Isa 45:15.—The scriptural origin and import of the expression explained.—References to Israelitish history.—Application to gospel times.—The Saviour's promise to manifest himself to his disciples, John 14.—Under the Law the hiding of God's face was specially outward and visible.—Under the Gospel it is chiefly inward and spiritual.—The Gospel is a dispensation of light.—But believers are sometimes involved in spiritual darkness.—To be forsaken of God is synonymous with the hiding of his face.—Christ himself was thus forsaken.—In general God only hides himself from those who forsake him.—When in darkness, Christians are apt to fall into doubts.—The prescribed remedy is revealed in Isa 50:10.—The general principle illustrated by particular examples.—God appears to hide his face, *First*, when he appoints some one trial of extraordinary severity, as in the case of Abraham when called to offer up Isaac; or, when he appoints a succession of trials, as in the case of Job when bereft of his family, his property, and his health.—Second, When *He* declines to hear, or delays to answer, the prayers of his people.—Trust in the unchangeableness of God is the grand security against doubt in all such cases.

My dear Friend,

Of the various causes of doubts to which I adverted at the commencement of the preceding Letter as being less common, and more subordinate, and peculiar only to Christians of a certain temperament, or to those who are thrown into peculiar external circumstances, we have as yet considered none but such as may be designated *physical* or *natural*. And I think you must be fully aware how proper it was,—I might say, how necessary it was, in the first instance, to fix attention on causes of this class, which are so frequently altogether overlooked. These physical or natural causes of doubt claim our first consideration, not simply on account of the deep interest they are calculated to excite when their operations are understood and watched, and of the very powerful and depressing influence which they exert wherever they do exist; but because they tend so much to give strength and energy to causes of a *spiritual, or moral, or religious* kind, when they happen to be combined. These latter classes of causes are quite distinct from the former. But many of them, as we shall have occasion to notice, are likewise exceedingly influential; although in estimating their productiveness of doubts, we should be careful to ascertain whether they are acting alone, or in conjunction with causes that are physical or natural.

We are now, then, to advance to the consideration of some of those causes of doubts, to which belongs the designation of *spiritual*. And all of those which particularly deserve attention may in one sense be regarded as only subordinate, because, their operation is limited to a comparatively small number of Christians, and to comparatively rare occasions even in the experience of these few. But, in another sense, it would be quite unseemly and unsuitable to speak of such causes as of subordinate importance; because the mysteriousness in which some of them are wrapped up, and the feelings of solemnity and of awe to which others give rise, and the distressing perturbations and perplexities which are the sure accompaniments of them all, invest them with a very high degree of interest.

Whilst attempting to make a judicious selection from amongst the *spiritual causes* of doubt that might be mentioned, it occurred to my own mind, as a matter of convenience, that it might be well to classify them. And the classification which most strongly commended itself was, first, the trials that come directly from the appointment or with the permission of God; Second, the temptations of the devil.

Each of these classes presents an interesting field for research, and, by the guidance and blessing of God, I trust we may glean a sufficiency of useful information from each of them, to occupy two separate Letters.

At present I shall adduce a few of the *special trials* with which God is pleased, at times, to visit his own peculiar people, not with the intention of leading them to doubt, either his love to them, or their own relationship to him; but of bringing their faith to the test, that it may be purified and strengthened, and that God may thus be glorified in them and by them. But this good and gracious design of God may be, and sometimes actually is frustrated, at least for a time, in consequence of the faith of his people being too weak to stand the trial to which it has been subjected; and whenever this happens to be the case, it is to be expected that doubts, with spiritual darkness and distress, will take possession of the Christian's mind. I must therefore request of you never to forget that the latent and real cause of doubts resolves itself into a deficiency in the measure, or in the exercise of faith; and that the divinely appointed trials, of which we are about to treat, are only a superinducing or ostensible cause.

The hiding of his face from his people, is one of those painful trials to which God at times subjects them. We have Scripture testimony to the fact that such a trial was not unfrequent under the old dispensation; and there need be no hesitation in ascribing to the same cause, some of the most distressing doubts with which Christians, even in our own more favoured circumstances, are occasionally afflicted.

It is recorded in Isa 45:15, "Verily thou art a God that hidest thyself, O God of Israel, the Saviour." I look upon this as a very remarkable text, especially when viewed in its connection with the context. By referring to the Bible, you will perceive that this inspired declaration stands isolated in the midst of a memorable prophecy respecting Cyrus the Persian king, and respecting his deliverance of God's people from the Babylonish captivity, for the accomplishment of which, as God's anointed servant, Cyrus was to be raised up. The prophecy, be it remembered, was uttered more than 150 years before Cyrus was born, and a long time previous to the capture of Jerusalem, and the removal of the princes and people of Judah into Babylon. But *he* who is omniscient inspired his prophet Isaiah to uplift the curtain, and to disclose to view, both the scenes and the actors in times yet future, and in events involving judgments and mercies of awful magnitude. And thus, amidst the wondrous prophetic detail of great temporal deliverance out of great temporal calamity, combined with rich promises of spiritual blessings, the verse which I have quoted proclaims the mysterious truth, that the covenanted God of Israel, notwithstanding the immutability of his love towards his own chosen people, is a God who verily "hideth himself," and that *he* who brings them low under the weight of his own chastening hand, is nevertheless "the Saviour."

> "God moves in a mysterious way,
> His wonders to perform."

And this is especially true as it respects his providential dispensations towards individuals, and towards the church at large. For he often hides himself for a time behind the thick darkness in which he permits those to be enveloped, for whom he is nevertheless secretly carrying forward plans of great mercy, and of whom his thoughts have been thoughts of love, even from everlasting.

But when we read of God *hiding his face*, the language is to be understood in a figurative sense. Indeed it is beautifully figurative; and at the same time so expressive that nobody can miss its meaning. Not that every reader will recollect its strictly scriptural meaning, or comprehend the depths and fulness of it. But even persons who read and reflect superficially can scarcely err in the correct interpretation of this phraseology. We all understand it to signify, not merely the withdrawal of those manifestations of his gracious presence which God is wont to vouchsafe unto his people, but likewise some real, or at least some apparent expression of his displeasure. Just as when a friend, on whose protection and counsel we much depend, neither smiles upon us, nor admits us to his presence, as he used to do, we should be constrained to fear that in our exclusion from the enjoyment of his society, we had also forfeited the advantages of his friendship. I confess, however, that to me it appears unwise, if not unwarrantable, to make use of scriptural phrases, unless we give to them their scriptural acceptation. And I am persuaded that in investigating the scriptural origin and import of God's hiding his face, we shall find a profitable employment; and, at the same time, prepare ourselves in the best way for estimating the severity of those trials to which Christians are exposed from this particular procedure on the part of God, and the consequent likelihood of such trials giving rise to anxious doubts.

The first mention we meet with of this expression, is from God himself, and that under circumstances of peculiar solemnity. Towards the close of the life of Moses, after he had rehearsed all the commandments of the Lord in the hearing of the people, and revealed the blessing and the curse connected with their obedience or disobedience, "the Lord said unto Moses, Behold, the days approach that thou must die: call Joshua, and present yourselves in the tabernacle of the congregation, that I may give him a charge." "*And the Lord appeared in the tabernacle in a pillar of a cloud.*" On this occasion the Lord announced unto Moses how sadly the people would backslide and transgress after his decease. He said, "They will forsake me, and break my covenant which I have made with them. Then my anger shall be kindled against them in that day, and *I will forsake them, and I will hide my face from them*, and they shall be devoured, and many evils and troubles shall befall them, so that they will say in that day, Are not these evils come upon us, because our God is not among us? And *I will surely hide my face in that day*, for all the evils which they have wrought, in that they are turned unto other gods. Now, therefore, write ye this song for you, and teach it the children of Israel: put it in their mouths, that this song may be a witness for me against the children of Israel," Deut 31:14-19. The following chapter contains the song of Moses, which is certainly one of the richest and loftiest portions of ancient Scripture—magnifying the name of the Lord, who is "the Rock," and whose "work is perfect;" and recounting what he had already done for the redemption of his chosen Israel, and the base returns they had made, and would continue to make; and what were to be his dealings with them in the way both of terrible judgments and of wondrous lovingkindness, even unto the latter days which have not yet arrived, but are evidently nigh at hand. Now, in this song, which was indited as a perpetual witness for God against the children of Israel, it is written, "Of the Rock that begat thee thou art unmindful, and hast forgotten God that formed thee. And when the Lord saw it, he abhorred them, because of the provoking of his sons and of his daughters. And he said, *I will hide my face from them*. I will see what their end shall be; for they are a very froward generation, children in whom is no faith," Deut 32:18-20.

These quotations, in which we hear the voice of Jehovah himself again and again giving utterance to a threatening of punishment, furnish us with *the origin* of the expression, "I will hide my face from them." I mean the scriptural origin. And you will remark that the persons who are thus threatened are spoken of as "his sons and his daughters"—the people whom he had graciously brought into covenant relation with himself, but who proved to be "children in whom is no faith." It is, then, in reference to this original threatening that the inspired psalmists and prophets so frequently made it the burden of their complaints or lamentations, that God *had hid his face* from his people, and therefore they were in trouble; or the subject of their prayers, that he *might not hide his face* from them, which they regarded as their best security for preservation from dreaded calamities; and in confirmation of what I have stated, you will find an interesting selection of passages at the bottom of the page.*

But having ascertained the origin of the expression, we must proceed in search of *its scriptural import*. And I do conceive that an important light is thrown upon it, in the first of the quotations from the book of Deuteronomy. There we read that when Moses and Joshua had presented themselves in the tabernacle of the congregation, according to divine command, "the Lord *appeared* in the tabernacle in a pillar of a cloud." The tabernacle was the appointed place of meeting: see Exod 29:42-43; "the door of the tabernacle of the congregation before the Lord, where I will meet thee, to speak there unto thee. And there I will meet with the children of Israel, and the tabernacle shall be sanctified by my glory." So, in like manner, the cloudy pillar was the promised emblem of God's favourable presence. When the Israelites commenced their

---

*Job 13:20-24; Job 23:3-10; Job 34:29; Ps 10:1; Ps 13:1-2; Ps 30:7; Ps 44:24; Ps 55:1; Ps 88:14; Ps 89:46; Ps 104:29; Isa 8:17; Hos 5:6; Mic 3:4. See also Jer 29:10-14, and Ezek 39:29, where the promise of God not to hide his face or conceal himself from his people is expressive of the highest degree of blessedness.

journey through the wilderness, "the Lord went before them by day in a pillar of a cloud, to lead them the way; and by night in a pillar of fire, to give them light; to go by day and night," Exod 13:21. And afterwards "on the day that the tabernacle was reared up, the cloud covered the tabernacle, namely, the tent of the testimony; and at even there was upon the tabernacle as it were the appearance of fire, until the morning," Num 9:15. But when the journeyings were completed, the mercyseat, in the holy place within the veil, was the special place of divine manifestation. "I will appear in the cloud on the mercyseat," said Jehovah: and this cloud by day and fire by night were what he calls his "glory." "The tabernacle shall be sanctified by my glory." And in reference to its first erection we read, "So Moses finished the work. Then *a cloud* covered the tent of the congregation, and *the glory of the Lord* filled the tabernacle," Exod 40:34.

Thus it was that God, who, as a Spirit, is invisible, showed himself to be amongst his chosen people, and shone upon them in a manner which plainly intimated his intentions to protect and prosper them above all that they could ask or think. And as the expressions of his face or countenance often indicate the thoughts and feelings of an earthly friend towards us, so these visible and glorious displays of God's presence with them, very naturally came to be interpreted by the Israelites as strong and decided proofs of his favour and friendship; or, in figurative language, as the shinings of his face, and as the light of his countenance. Indeed, we are justified in saying that God himself taught them this interpretation. For in the official benediction which he instructed Aaron, the priest, to pronounce, there seems to be a pointed and intentional allusion to those tokens of the divine presence with which the Israelites were honoured, and which were the pledges of grace, and peace, and every blessing. "The Lord bless thee, and keep thee; the Lord make his face shine upon thee, and be gracious unto thee: the Lord lift up his countenance upon thee, and give thee peace," Num 6:24-26. In this way the people were led to value, and to desire, the gracious and glorious manifestations of the presence of their covenanted God, as that one thing which distinguished them from all other people on the face of the earth, and which embodied within it the very life and soul of their whole temporal and spiritual prosperity. Hence we learn the true meaning and the unspeakable importance of the petitions which are preserved in various Psalms—"Lord, lift thou up *the light of thy countenance* upon us," Ps 4:6. "Make *thy face to shine* upon thy servant," Ps 119:135. And in the 80th, a psalm evidently composed when the church and kingdom of Israel were brought very low, we find the prayer three times repeated, "Turn us again, O God, and *cause thy face to shine*; and *we shall be saved.*" Ps 80:3,7,19 And here I ought to add, it is only in the peculiar language which God himself prescribed for the form of blessing which Aaron was to use, that we find the key which opens up to us the right interpretation of many other passages of Scripture, in which mention is made of the face of the Lord, and of seeking his face. For instance, "Glory ye in his holy name: let the heart of them rejoice that seek the Lord. Seek the Lord, and his strength; *seek his face evermore,*" Ps 105:3-4. And again, "Blessed is the people that know the joyful sound: they shall walk, O Lord, *in the light of thy countenance. In thy name shall they rejoice all the day; and in thy righteousness shall they be exalted. For thou art the glory of their strength; and in thy favour our horn shall be exalted,*" Ps 89:15-17. I would also refer you to several portions of Ps 27, were it not for the fear of being tedious. But enough has been said to guide us to the real meaning of God's *hiding* his face, which is placed in direct opposition to his *showing* his face. And as exceeding great and precious blessings were dependent on his causing his face to shine, and on the lifting up of the light of his countenance upon the people; so when that glorious shining ceased,—when that light from heaven was withdrawn, there could be no mistake as to the result. The hiding of God's face could only be interpreted by them, as a signal that he was withholding the blessings which they ought so highly to prize, as it would also be the proof of his own visible departure from them. And it is easy to conceive how forcibly this interpretation must have been impressed on their minds, from the fact, that the glory of God was covering the tabernacle at the very moment, when his audible voice, out of the midst of the pillar of a cloud, uttered the awful words, "I will forsake them, and I will hide my face from them, and they shall be devoured, and many evils and troubles shall befall them, so that they will say in that day, Are not these evils come upon us, *because our God is not among us?*"

I formerly made the remark that it is only in a figurative sense that God is said to hide his face from any of his creatures. It will, no doubt, however, occur to you, that to the Israelites there was much less of figure in this expression than there is to Christians. For although God, having no material form, can neither hide nor reveal a real face or countenance, yet he did literally and actually manifest his presence with that favoured people by visible symbols; and therefore it was possible for him literally and actually also to hide himself from them by removing the visible symbols. But we are not so highly favoured in that respect. We have neither the pillar of cloud by day, nor the pillar of fire by night, to teach us that the Lord is with us of a truth. Our religion is of a more spiritual character than theirs. Still it is true, even under the Christian dispensation, that we are fully warranted in this instance to adopt the language which was so peculiarly appropriate to the circumstances of the ancient Israelites, and to speak of God as either manifesting himself unto us, or hiding his face, because his people can testify from their own experience, how truly God continues to act in this manner towards them. And, therefore, these expressions, however figurative, are perfectly intelligible to all the spiritual seed of Israel,—to all the sons and the daughters of God, who are born again of the Spirit,— to all his adopted children in the faith of Jesus Christ, his only begotten and well-beloved Son.

I dare say, my dear friend, you are thinking I have taken a very circuitous road to reach this conclusion. Do forgive the discursiveness of my scriptural explanations: for I am not without hope that the references to Old Testament times and events with which we have been occupied, must shed some useful light on the subject of our present inquiries. And my hopes are all the more sanguine, because, whilst it is consistent with Christian experience, and with the language of spiritually-exercised Christians, to speak of the hidings of God's face, as alike descriptive of certain severe dispensations of Providence, and of a peculiarly painful state of mind, we do not meet with this phraseology in any part of the New Testament Scriptures. But we do meet with its counterpart. And as the Divine Saviour gave a positive promise to his disciples before he left them, that, notwithstanding his corporeal absence, he would manifest himself to them, and that both the Father and he would come to them, and make their abode with them; so it is in the forfeiture of this blessed manifestation that we learn in what the hiding of his face really consists. And still farther, I am humbly of the opinion, that the inward and spiritual manifestation which the Saviour promised, and which is accompanied with an abiding in our hearts, on the part of God,—the Father, and the Son, and the Holy Ghost, can only be rightly understood by a consideration of that outward and glorious manifestation of the divine presence, which the Israelites enjoyed in the tabernacle and the temple.

Open your Bible to the 14th chapter of St. John's Gospel; and as you read John 14:15-23, keep in remembrance that the disciples whom our Lord was addressing were a company of Jews, whose religious notions and feelings were all in unison with the historical records of Moses and the prophets. This was the standard by which his discourse would be interpreted.

And when Jesus tells them of the mission of the Comforter, who was to abide with them for ever, and of his own coming to them, and of their seeing him although the world was to see him no more, and of his manifesting himself unto them, it is worthy of notice that they never questioned *the truth* of these gracious promises; but they could not comprehend *in what way* they were to be accomplished. They evidently had their thoughts directed backwards to those palmy days in Israel's history, when the Almighty "spake unto Moses face to face, as a man speaketh unto his friend," and when the whole people beheld the visible emblems of his presence and his glory. "And therefore Judas saith unto him, (not Iscariot,) Lord, *how is it* that thou wilt manifest thyself unto us, and not unto the world?" As if he had asked, What will be the manner of this special manifestation? How can you show yourself in the sight of your few disciples, to the exclusion of all other men? "Jesus answered and said unto him, If a man love me he will keep my words; and my Father will love him, and we will come unto him, and make our abode with him." This answer of our Lord, which speaks of an inward and secret communion, was fitted to dispel the erroneous idea of an open and public manifestation; but in explaining the spiritual nature of his promised and permanent presence, he still employs language which might well remind his disciples of the oft-repeated promise of God to their fathers—"We will come unto him, and make our abode with him."* And certain it is that although *the modes* of divine manifestation under the Old Testament, and under the New, are essentially different; yet there is great similarity in *the purposes* for which it is made.

---

*Out of the burning bush the Lord said unto Moses, "I am come down to deliver my people." And previous to the delivery of the law from Sinai, "the Lord said unto Moses, Lo, I come unto thee in a thick cloud," etc. And again, when Moses complained of his inability to manage the people alone, the Lord commanded him to gather the elders to the door of the tabernacle, and said, "I will come down to talk with thee there."

After the tabernacle had been set up in the wilderness, and the Lord had appeared at the door in the pillar of a cloud, Moses was emboldened to ask divine guidance, and he received for answer, "My presence" (or, according to the literal Hebrew, "my face,") "shall go with thee, and I will give thee rest." To this encouraging assurance Moses replied, "If thy presence go not with us, carry us not up hence. For wherein shall it be known here that I and thy people have found grace in thy sight? *Is it not in that thou goest with us*? So shall we be separated, I and thy people, from all the people that are upon the face of the earth."

Thus it is obvious that *God's manifested presence* was regarded as a distinguishing act of grace, whereby the Israelites were marked out as a peculiar people whom God had chosen for himself. But Moses was not yet satisfied. He became more importunate in his requests. "I beseech thee show me thy glory." He was instantly answered, "I will make all my goodness pass before thee, and I will proclaim the name of the Lord before thee; and I will be gracious unto whom I will be gracious, and will show mercy on whom I will show mercy," Exod 33 *passim*. The next day, from Mount Sinai, the promised proclamation was made—"The Lord, the Lord God, merciful and gracious," etc. In this most marvellous way, God taught the people that the exercise of mercy and grace and goodness is his glory. And therefore, when their eyes beheld what he himself selected as the material emblems of his glory, then it was that they realized the forgiveness of their transgressions; and in the light of his countenance they experienced peace, and were exalted in his righteousness, and rejoiced in his salvation.

Surely these manifestations of the divine presence, which enlightened and cheered the Israelites of old, were to them, "the gospel of the grace of God." This was the grand purpose which they subserved. But on us a clearer light shines. To us a fuller and brighter manifestation is given. *God has mani-*

fested himself in our humanity. The eternal *Word* has been made flesh, and dwelt, or tabernacled, amongst us, "full of grace and truth;" on which account the evangelist observes, "And we beheld his glory, the glory as of the only begotten of the Father," John 1:14. And with this agrees the declaration of St. Paul to the Corinthians, "For God, who commanded the light to shine out of darkness, hath shined in our hearts, to give us the light of the knowledge of the glory of God in the face of Jesus Christ," 2 Cor 4:6. And in the context he speaks of "the light of the glorious gospel of Christ, who is the image of God." Your own memory will supply many other similar passages, where the use of the words "light" and "glory," in their application to gospel times, and truths, and privileges, is apparently designed to connect the two dispensations, as having the same merciful objects; and likewise to establish the superiority of the Gospel to the Law, as a revelation of God's forgiving love to sinners. "For," as the apostle argues, "if the ministration of condemnation be glory, much more doth the ministration of righteousness exceed in glory. For even that which was made glorious had no glory in this respect, by reason of the glory that excelleth. For if that which was done away was glorious, much more that which remaineth is glorious," 2 Cor 3:9-11.

But although God has been pleased to manifest his grace and goodness under both the Mosaic and the Christian dispensations, yet he has chosen very different methods of doing it. *Of old* his manifestations were of an external character, addressed to the senses of sight and hearing. The people heard his voice, and they saw the cloud and the fire, out of which he spake to them. His manifestations *now* are of an internal and spiritual character, addressed to our faith. Even during the short period when the Son of God in human flesh sojourned on the earth, the men amongst whom he lived knew him not. As St. John says, "The Light shineth in darkness; and the darkness comprehended it not." They had no ears to hear his gracious words; nor had they eyes to see in him "the brightness of his Father's glory, and the express image of his person." The record of what he said and did, is to us the gospel of our salvation. But it is only by faith that we realize and enjoy it. To us the manifestations of the exceeding riches of God's grace are not outward and visible. We only see them mentally, when it is given unto us to know the things of God. We experience the reality and blessedness of them in our hearts, only when the Holy Spirit enlightens our natural darkness, and removes our sinful aversion to God, and brings us into fellowship with the Father and the Son. Faith is a most powerful principle in its varied operations; and in regard to what is spiritual and out of sight and hearing, it serves us in the stead of ears and of eyes. And thus it is true of the believer, that he lives as seeing *him* who is invisible; he walks with God; he dwells in God, and God in him. All these are strong expressions; but they are scriptural, and they teach us the blessed truth, that God in Christ does manifest himself unto his people; and also in what way it is that they realize his gracious presence, and enjoy the sweet shinings of his face, and are comforted by the lifting up of the light of his countenance upon them.

The Gospel is emphatically a dispensation of *light*. It emanates from him of whom it is written, "that God is light, and in him is no darkness at all," 1 John 1:5. And Jesus Christ, the manifested God, said, "I am the light of the world; he that followeth me shall not walk in darkness, but shall have the light of life," John 8:12. He was "the true light," which was only adumbrated by the shekinah which illuminated the tabernacle and the temple. And it is "in the face of Jesus Christ" that the glory of the invisible Father is revealed in all the fulness of pardon and of peace and of reconciliation. Hence the Gospel itself, as unfolding "the mystery of God and of Christ," is called "marvellous light;" whilst those who believe its truths are called "the children of light," because they have the Spirit of truth dwelling in them, and abiding with them. And their own joyful experience testifies to the reality of that internal manifestation of himself, which our Lord and Saviour promised to his disciples.

Let us thankfully remember that the same Jesus who has already appeared in our world, in humiliation, as the man of sorrows and of sufferings, and who, after his resurrection, ascended into heaven, has assured us of his personal return in glory. And to that great event in the history of redemption, our faith and hopes are continually directed, by the Lord himself, and by his holy prophets and apostles, as the period of the church's triumph, and of the earth's renovation and blessedness. And as a beautiful illustration of the harmony of Scripture in its descriptions of the work of Christ, in the age which is to come, as well as in the present, I wish you to notice how frequently the inspired penmen introduce the emblem of bright and unfading light in their predictions of Messiah's reign. The narrative of the transfiguration furnishes us with some idea of what may be our Lord's own appearance when he comes in his glory. "His face did shine as the sun, and his raiment was white as the light." Of the heavenly Jerusalem, which is the church of the firstborn redeemed from amongst men, and redeemed from the grave,—the arisen and glorified saints, we read, "And the city had no need of the sun, neither of the moon to shine in it; for the glory of God did lighten it, and the Lamb is the light thereof. And the nations of them which are saved shall walk in the light of it." Again, "The throne of God and of the Lamb shall be in it and his servants shall serve him; and they shall see his face, and his name shall be on their foreheads; and there shall be no night there; and they need no candle, neither light of the sun: for the Lord God giveth them light," Rev 21-22. These are striking passages, to which I shall add one more from Isaiah, and it respects the state of things on the earth, "when the Son of man shall come in his glory, and sit on the throne of his father David." "Moreover the light of the moon shall be as the light of the sun, and the light of the sun shall be sevenfold, as the light of seven days, in the day that the Lord bindeth up the breach of his people, and healeth the stroke of their wound," Isa 30:26.

On this grand and animating theme, however, I must not enlarge, feeling that even in these passing remarks, I justly expose myself to the charge of digressing. It more immediately belongs to the subject of our inquiries to know, that, during our Lord's personal absence—for he has ascended to his Father and our Father, and the heavens must retain him "until the times of restitution of all things, which God hath spoken by the mouth of all his holy prophets since the world began,"— I say, during the period of his personal absence, he favours his people with a spiritual presence. Those, in an especial manner, who are commissioned to preach the gospel, are encouraged to faithfulness and zeal with the assurance, "Lo, I am with you alway, even unto the end of the world," or "age." And to every individual Christian, who loves his Saviour, and keeps his commandments, he gives the mysterious but delightful promises, "I will love him, and will manifest myself unto him;" "and my Father will love him; and we will come unto him, and make our abode with him."

These are the promises and assurances of "the Amen, the faithful and true Witness." Multitudes of Christians, during the past eighteen centuries, have rejoiced in the experience of their truth. And I trust both you and I, my friend, have by divine grace been made to know somewhat of that light and peace and gladness, which fill the heart, when God visits us with the smiles of a reconciled countenance; and when the Spirit, the promised Comforter, witnesses with our spirits that we are cleansed from our sins; and when our faith responds to the apostolic testimony, that we have "Christ in us the hope of glory." Oh! it is true indeed that those who are experimentally strangers to the power of God's grace, cannot intermeddle with the heavenly joys of God's children! And it is no easy matter to explain to other people, how pure, how satisfying, how elevating, how overflowing is that happiness which is transmitted from the face of our redeeming God, when he shines upon us as with the refreshing beams of a summer sun. But nevertheless a happiness from this wondrous source, although not always—perhaps not often enjoyed in its noontide effulgence, is the privilege, the possession of all genuine Christians, even now, amidst the tribulations which they must expect from the world, so long as they are in it. Nor do many of them know how truly they have possessed this happiness, or how much of it has been their portion, until the hidings of God's face have involved them in spiritual darkness and distress—just as a solar eclipse, whilst it enwraps creation in its mantle of cold and cheerless gloom, reminds us of the sweet sunshine which we have lost for a time, and which we valued too little when we enjoyed it.

The Bible is a book of wonders. It reveals to us many things of which we could otherwise never have formed a conception; and many things too, which we would never have believed, had not our faith the firm foundation of divine authority to rest upon. Now, I rank it among the wonderful things which the Bible reveals, that God, who has manifested his transcendent love to sinful men, in sending his Son to suffer and to die for their salvation, and who causes the hearts of those who believe in the provided Saviour to rejoice in the light of his reconciled countenance, should be pleased at times, in the exercise of his infinite wisdom, to hide his gracious face from any of the objects of his redeeming love, and thus to turn their joy into mourning. And that the God of love and wisdom, of rectitude and faithfulness, should deal after this fashion even with his own incarnate and beloved Son, is a truth most deeply mysterious; but at the same time, a truth rich in mercy and consolation to us, on whose account the guiltless, the holy Jesus was forsaken of his Father at the awfully trying crisis, when obedience to that Father's will placed him as a malefactor on the ignominious cross,—deserted by his friends, and derided by his foes, and inwardly enveloped in a darkness far more dense and horrible than that which outwardly overspread the land, in consequence of the sun having veiled its face, as if in sympathy with him who made it.

I advert thus prominently to the experience of Christ on the cross, because he was there as our representative and surety. As the Lamb of God, without spot or blemish in himself, our transgressions were laid to his charge, and he endured the penalty. The justice of a sin-hating God wreaked its vengeance on the voluntary and innocent substitute of sinners. And whilst the wrath of a holy God raged like a consuming fire against the sins which were imputed to him, the bleeding anguish of his soul extorted the bitter cry, "My God, my God, why hast thou forsaken me!" Then it was that in the estimation of man, he was "stricken, smitten of God, and afflicted." And his own sensible loss of the loving and approving smiles of his Father, overwhelmed the Saviour himself in darkness and dismay. Surely this is the most remarkable instance which it is possible to adduce of the spiritual distress which is occasioned by the withdrawing of the light of God's countenance, and the cessation of the shinings of his face.

To be forsaken of God is the same thing as to be subjected to the hiding of his face. Of this you may find many illustrations in Scripture; but it will be sufficient to remember that, in the original threatening of God against the Israelites, his own words were, "And I will forsake them, and I will hide my face from them," as if the latter expression were added to explain the former; for God never in reality forsakes his people. He always loves themselves, although he may abhor their practices: and he is always near to them, although he may not always show himself. But God pronounced this threatening, because he knew that the people would forsake him; and we may lay it down as a general principle in the moral government of God, that, when he forsakes, or hides his face from any of his called and chosen ones, it is done in the way of penal infliction. That it was so in the case of our suffering Saviour is undoubted. We know that he was subjected to the desertion of his loving Father, because he was at the time suffering the curse due to sin, in order to its removal; because he was suffering the punishment which we deserved, that he might deliver us from the wrath to come, and open up the way for our return to God with acceptance. As a Son he had on no occasion forfeited his Father's favour. But we whose humanity he took into union with his divinity, that, as our kinsman, he might interpose for our redemption, had forsaken God. We had withdrawn from him the affections of our heart, and had followed after idols. We had broken his laws, and neglected his ordinances. And for these offences of ours, the Lord Jesus Christ was forsaken of God. He who is the light of the world, and the brightness of his Father's glory, was nailed to the accursed tree, and doomed to undergo the awful hiding of his Father's face, because he was the substitute and surety of guilty men. Nor should we forget to look to him, amidst the thick darkness of the cross, as the firstborn among many brethren;—not only as our representative and Redeemer, but as our elder brother, with whom it becomes us to have fellowship in his sufferings, and from whose example we are encouraged to hold fast our faith in God, even when he hides his face from us. Jesus, when plunged into darkness, sank not into despondency. He gave no place to doubts. He still trusted in the Father as *his* God. And he only gives vent to the pressure of his unutterable inward agony, when with a loud voice he makes the doleful complaint or lamentation, "My God, my God, why hast thou forsaken me? why art thou so far from helping me? and from the words of my roaring," Ps 22:1.

I believe it would be found, on examination, that, with few exceptions, the people of God are never subjected to the withdrawal of his gracious presence, without some great dereliction of duty towards him on their part. My object, however, is rather to direct your attention to the fact that God does sometimes hide his face, than to investigate the causes of it. And as it has probably happened through a defect of faith that the Christian has exposed himself to this severe trial, so it can hardly be expected that he will either endure the trial, or escape from it, without undergoing the additional distress and agitation of harassing doubts. Like the Saviour, he may feel that he is forsaken of God. But unlike the Saviour, he may fear that God, in ceasing to shine upon him with the gladdening light of his countenance, has likewise ceased to be his God. This is doubt. It is a doubt of such a nature, and arising at such a time, as must necessarily debar the tried Christian from the consolation he so much needs. It is a doubt dangerous for the Christian himself, as it drives him farther away from God, and cherishes feelings of despair. And it is a doubt most dishonouring to God; for it impugns the unchangeableness of his love, and the riches of his grace, and the faithfulness of his promises, and that whole revelation of gospel truth on which he would have us to rest as on a rock which cannot be shaken.

When a Christian basks in the beams of divine favour, he feels himself strong, and he feels himself happy. God says to him, "Seek ye my face," and the delighted response of his heart is, "Thy face, Lord, will I seek;" and this blissful communion with Heaven enables him with the psalmist to sing, "The Lord is my light and my salvation; whom shall I fear? the Lord is the strength of my life; of whom shall I be afraid?" Ps 27:1,8. But when this light is exchanged for darkness, the confidence of safety also gives way: and he who was so fearless before, because the Lord was his strength, becomes a terror to himself. Again he finds his own experience expressed in the language of inspiration: "Lord, by thy favour, thou hast made my mountain to stand strong: thou didst hide thy face, and I was troubled," Ps 30:7. Thus, as the light of God's countenance, the manifestation of his favour, has imparted stability to the Christian, and opened up to him a source of highest and purest joy; so it should not surprise us that the hiding of God's face, not only turns his joy into mourning, and his light into darkness, but causes to spring up in his mind a succession of painful doubts, which affect the foundation of all his hopes towards God, and strike a blow at the very root of his own Christianity.

Now then if you inquire what a Christian is to do in such distressing circumstances? How is it that he may expect to obtain relief, and once more feel himself strong and safe and happy? I refer you to the best of all authorities: I refer you to the unerring word of God. There, as if in anticipation of such circumstances of trial, and with a view to meet the exigencies of such a case of spiritual distress, God himself has in great mercy issued his own prescription. "Who is among you that feareth the Lord, that obeyeth the voice of his servant, that walketh in darkness, and hath no light? *let him trust in the name of the Lord, and stay upon his God,*" Isa 50:10.

Disconsolate believers, from whom God is hiding his face, are here counselled and comforted by God himself. He encourages them to cherish the assurance, that, notwithstanding the darkness in which they walk, he is still *their* God. And on Him who is almighty they are to stay themselves, and in that name of his which has been proclaimed, "the Lord, the Lord God, merciful and gracious," they are still to trust. The darkness in which they walk must indeed disturb their present peace and enjoyment, but they are required to believe, not only that in God there is no darkness at all, but that the light which is in him will again shine forth upon themselves. Instead of yielding to the depressing and desponding influence of doubt, they are called to the strongest exercise of faith. In the faith of his being their God, it is their privilege to pray for the returning light of his countenance; and for this desirable result it is their duty patiently to wait. In the hope of finding him who has in the meantime withdrawn his presence, although his love remains unaltered, they will seek after him with the greater importunity, and wrestle on during the dark night of desertion, until the dawn of day begins to break upon them.

> Our hearts, if God we seek to know,
> Shall know him, and rejoice;
> His coming like the morn shall be;
> Like morning songs his voice.
>
> As dew upon the tender herb,
> Diffusing fragrance round;
> As showers that usher in the spring,
> And cheer the thirsty ground:
>
> So shall his presence bless our souls,
> And shed a joyful light:
> That hallow'd morn shall chase away
> The sorrows of the night.

This subject seems to require some farther elucidation, and I must request you to keep in mind that the hidings of God's face were specially outward and sensible under the Mosaic dispensation; whereas, under the Gospel, they are specially inward and spiritual. But as the saints of old did also use the expression to describe their distressed state of mind when they lost the sensible enjoyment of God's favour, so believers in Christ apply the same phraseology to those events in their history which wear a peculiarly adverse and calamitous aspect. Indeed, we may safely assert that the hidings of God's face are indicated to us, not only *inwardly*, by that overwhelming feeling of desertion,—that fearful spiritual darkness, which sometimes does involve believers in unutterable anguish of soul; but likewise *outwardly,* by some unusually afflictive dispensations of providence. I dare not attempt to dwell on the horrors of a case of pure desertion. Having never experienced it, I could not describe it. And if such cases do occur as acts of divine discipline, we may be sure they are very uncommon. I shall therefore advert to two of the more customary methods which God appears to employ, when he hides his face from those who are, nevertheless, the objects of his everlasting love.

Of these the first in point of frequency is in apparently declining to hear, or, at least, in delaying to answer, their persevering and importunate prayers. The other is, in visiting them with some one trial of extraordinary severity; or; in heaping upon them in succession an overwhelming accumulation of trials of a more ordinary character. On each of these particulars my observations shall be brief; and it may be most convenient to begin with the last mentioned of the two.

I cannot do better than refer you to the cases of Abraham and of Job, as furnishing exact types of those peculiar trials which *seem* to indicate on the part of God the withdrawment of the light of his countenance, and which *really* exhibit such an unfavourable change in his procedure towards them, as to raise doubts in the minds of his people, whether God has utterly cast them off, or whether they have not deceived themselves in ever thinking that they were the objects of his love and favour.

In regard to Abraham, the affecting narrative of his behaviour, when required to offer up Isaac, has this striking commencement: "And it came to pass after these things *that God did tempt Abraham*, and said unto him, Abraham: and he said, Behold, here I am. And he said, Take now thy son, thine only son Isaac, whom thou lovest, and get thee into the land of Moriah, and offer him there for a burnt offering upon one of the mountains which I will tell thee of," Gen 22:1-2. It would be difficult to imagine a trial of greater severity than this; and you will observe that it was expressly of divine appointment. But when we read "that God did tempt Abraham," we must free our minds from all those ideas of something designedly evil, or morally injurious, which we are accustomed to associate with temptation; "for God cannot be tempted with evil, neither tempteth he any man," James 1:13. The obvious meaning of the passage is, that God made an experiment on the faith and piety of the patriarch, with a view to try their sincerity and strength.* We hear of nothing irregular or offensive in the immediately previous conduct of Abraham with which God had occasion to express his righteous displeasure. We therefore conclude that the requirement which was laid upon him was not punitive, however painful it must have been to his paternal feelings; and we may rest assured that it could not be the design of God, in this extraordinary transaction, to tempt his servant, yea, his friend, to cherish hard thoughts against him, or to doubt his faithfulness, or to renounce his service, although he was pleased to subject him to such a severe ordeal of moral discipline. It was, in fact, merely an experimental trial how truly the patriarch feared the Lord, and how far his principles of obedience would carry him. But what a trial! and how nobly was it sustained! Under any circumstances, the threatened bereavement of a son, an only son, and a beloved son, would be keenly felt by any parent. But before we can enter into the feelings of Abraham on this occasion, it behoves us to call to remembrance the very peculiar circumstances connected with the birth of Isaac; for he had been, in the strictest sense, a gift from God. He was truly the child of divine promise, and he was the one child on whose life depended the fulfilment of numerous and most important promised blessings, not only to Abraham and his seed, but to all the nations of the earth. All the many blessings which God had promised to Abraham, and all the great hopes he had taught him to entertain, were bound up in Isaac, the one son whom Sarah his wife bare unto him, and of whom God speaks so justly and so pathetically when he says, "thy son, thine only son Isaac, whom thou lovest." And therefore,

---

*St. Paul, in referring to this event, says, "By faith Abraham, when he was tried," etc. See Heb 11:17-19.

considering that Isaac was the acknowledged darling of his old age, and that Abraham himself had been so signally favoured of God with many tokens of his lovingkindness on former occasions, it must indeed have been a trial of extraordinary severity when he was now unexpectedly required, not to stand by and witness his beloved Isaac prematurely cut off by some dire disease, but with his own hands to lay him on the altar and offer him up as a sacrifice to the God who gave him,—"Get thee into the land of Moriah, and offer him there for a burnt offering." These words must have caused inexpressible anguish of soul, as well as great astonishment, to the venerable patriarch. But it probably strikes you, as it does myself, that Abraham must have felt it as a painful aggravation of this most painful trial, that he was commanded to leave his own home, where he might at least have enjoyed the fellowship of grief, and the sympathy of friends. I have often thought that those three days which were spent on the road to Moriah must have appeared of interminable length, and surely never did an affectionate parent perform so sad a journey. To have travelled alone would have been comparative bliss; but to see his Isaac, whom he loved, ever at his side, and to have none other companion, and to be obliged to conceal from him the agonized feelings of his heart, and likewise the real purpose for which the journey was undertaken,—all this must have been a continual crucifixion of his tenderest sensibilities. But on reaching the appointed place, when the devoted son climbs the mount with the wood on his shoulder, and when the afflicted father carries in his hands the fire and the knife, the scene becomes too affecting even to be read. And when we hear Isaac, in the simplicity of youth and of ignorance, say to Abraham, "Behold the fire and the wood, but where is the lamb for a burnt offering?" we are lost in wonder at the composure and self-command with which the good old man was able to reply, "My son, God will provide himself a lamb for a burnt offering."

This, then, was a trial of no ordinary kind to which Abraham was subjected, and it came direct from the Almighty God who had established his covenant with him. Severe, however, and extraordinary as this trial was, the faith of the patriarch did not fail. Although God shrouded himself in a cloud of such awful blackness, and ceased, for the time, outwardly to shine upon his servant with the light of a gracious countenance, as he had been wont to do, yet Abraham held fast by the covenant, and neither doubted the faithfulness of God, nor dreaded the consequences of the unheard-of deed which was required at his hand. How prompt, how unwavering his obedience! He uttered no word of murmur. He attempted no evasion. He presented no entreaties to God for the preservation of his guiltless boy, as he had formerly done in behalf of guilty Sodom. Without hesitancy, without delay, he obeyed the divine command. Nor did the angel of the Lord interpose for his deliverance until the dreadful moment when his arm was uplifted to strike the fatal blow.

Abraham was sorely tried, and stood the trial. His trial may be regarded as unparalleled. But amidst the many sore trials with which the people of God are occasionally visited, how often does it happen that their faith gives way! I allude to such trials as get the name of dark dispensations of providence, in consequence of their severity, or their magnitude, or of something uncommon in their character and aspects. And is it not true, that these dark dispensations seldom come or go without having given rise to discouraging fears and distressing doubts? We meet with few Christians who have strength of principle to follow in the footsteps of faithful Abraham. His faith upheld him stedfast in the dark and cloudy day of trial. Even when enveloped in the thickest darkness, he believed that light would arise. Thus God was honoured, and he himself was comforted. But, in our times, instances are frequent in which the desponding language of the psalmist harmonizes too well with the experience of many suffering and fainthearted believers, who under the pressure of their trials exclaim, "Will the Lord cast off for ever? and will he be favourable no more? Is his mercy clean gone for ever? doth his promise fail for evermore? Hath God forgotten to be gracious? hath he in anger shut up his tender mercies?" Ps 77:7-9. They do not realize the unchangeableness of God's character; they cannot stay themselves on the faithfulness of his word; and thus, when *he* smites them they become discontented and clamorous; when *he* ceases to smile upon them, they cease to believe and to rejoice in the God of their salvation; when *he* hides his face, they begin to doubt the existence or the immutability of his love; and thus they are thrown into perplexity and spiritual distress.

The case of Job differs from that of Abraham. It represents God as still hiding his face from a man whom he loved, but doing it in a manner essentially different from that which we have just been considering. Instead of one solitary trial of surpassing severity, the history of Job details a succession of calamitous events rapidly following one after another, and producing, by their accumulated influence, those unhappy results which were not produced by any single trial.

A high character is given of Job as a perfect and upright man, who feared God, and eschewed evil. He was also blessed with great prosperity. There were born unto him seven sons and three daughters, and, in point of worldly substance, he was, in his day, the greatest of all the men in the east. But he, too, as well as Abraham, had his religious principles brought to the test; and Satan is introduced to our notice as a principal actor in the trials which plunged Job into darkness and doubt. "Then Satan answered the Lord, and said, Doth Job fear God for nought? Hast thou not made a hedge about him, and about his house, and about all that he hath on every side? Thou hast blessed the work of his hands, and his substance is increased in the land; but put forth thine hand now, and touch all that he hath, and he will curse thee to thy face," Job 1:9-11. I stop not at present to offer any remarks on the reality of satanic agency and satanic interference in human affairs. Let us take the narrative simply as it stands in the sacred page. And, humbling as it is to human nature, we must admit that our grand adversary is too near the truth when he insinuates how easy it is to bless God when he blesses us, and how prone are the best of men, when stript of their blessings, to give utterance to their natural enmity to God, and to betray their faithless distrust of the wisdom and rectitude which pervade all his providential arrangements.

God gave Satan power to do as he pleased with all that belonged to Job, only upon himself he was not to lay his hand. But whilst it is most consoling to know that Satan cannot injure us without divine permission, it is very alarming to learn, from this portion of Scripture, with what eagerness, and to what extent, he exercises power for evil whenever he can. In one short day what a change was effected in the circumstances of the wealthiest and most prosperous man in the east! One messenger announces the loss of his five hundred yoke of oxen, and five hundred she-asses by the Sabeans. Another comes to say that fire had fallen from heaven and consumed his seven thousand sheep with the servants who attended them. A third follows with the tidings that the Chaldeans had carried away the camels and slain the servants. And, to crown this series of ruinous disasters, a fourth messenger entered with the mournful intimation to Job, that his sons and his daughters had all perished in their eldest brother's house, as a great wind from the desert had smitten its four corners, and the whole assembled family were buried in the fallen ruins. All these unexpected and heavy losses were endured with meekness and submission. We cannot but admire the man, who, under such grievous bereavements, made no complaint against God, but fell down upon the ground and worshipped, and said, "Naked came I out of my mother's womb, and naked shall I return thither: the Lord gave, and the Lord hath taken away; blessed be the name of the Lord."

Thus Job held fast his integrity, and still showed himself to be a perfect and an upright man, although his trials had been so aggravated. Satan had utterly failed in his hellish design of causing the much injured patriarch to "curse God to his face." But he was ready for another onset; and God now gave him permission to afflict the person of his servant, with an injunction to save his life. "So Satan went forth from the presence of the Lord, and smote Job with sore boils, from the sole of his foot unto his crown." The good man became loathsome to himself and to all around him. And in this miserable condition, his own wife, who ought to have been his nurse and his comforter, tempted him to "curse God, and die." Here were new trials, and painful ones. But Job patiently bowed to the will of Heaven, and firmly rebuked his faithless spouse, to whom he said, "Thou speakest as one of the foolish women speaketh. What! shall we receive good at the hand of God, and shall we not receive evil?" And in the winding up of this sad catalogue of afflictions, it is added, "In all this did not Job sin with his lips," Job 2:10.

This submissive silence, however, was not of long continuance; for, in the contemplation of his trials in the aggregate, or in their accumulated amount, the spirit of Job was overwhelmed within him; and he lost the meekness, and patience, and resignation, which he had so beautifully expressed from time to time, as he was successively deprived of his immense property, and of his numerous family, and of his health and personal comfort. It is nowhere recorded that he ever "cursed God to his face," as Satan expected and desired. But with a lamentable spirit of discontent and peevishness, he did curse the day wherein he was born. And in "the bitterness of his soul" he gave unblushing utterance to many angry and complaintive remarks, and to many cheerless and doleful forebodings, which proved how sadly he had declined in the fear, and in the love, and in the obedience of his God.

I must not lengthen my already too long Letter by inserting the quotations I had selected. A glance over the various speeches which Job addressed to the three friends who came to mourn with him, and to comfort him, will furnish you with frequent indications of the darkness, and distraction, and discontent under which he laboured. And he himself emphatically describes the deplorable condition into which the providence of God had brought him, when he so anxiously inquires, *"Wherefore hidest thou thy face, and holdest me for thine enemy?"* Job 13:24. These interrogations may be interpreted as evidence that the faith and patience of Job were overpowered, and that he attributed all the calamities in which he was involved to the withdrawal of God's favour from him; and that he tormented himself with the false and faithless notion, that God, because he thus dealt with him, looked upon him as an enemy. In other words, he was in doubt whether God was now, or ever had been, his friend. His doubts, with all their attendant distress, arose out of the continued and accumulated trials with which he had been visited. And it is remarkable that he ascribes the existence of his trials to the hiding of God's face. Perhaps it might be more correct to say that he considered the loss of visible tokens of divine favour as synonymous with a state of actual and severe affliction.

It was not on account of some flagrant transgression, nor was it at all in the way of punishment, that God permitted his servant to be brought so low. Like that of Abraham, the trials of Job were experimental. And do we not, my dear friend, now and then see or hear of something resembling the case of Job, among those who fear God, and eschew evil? Nobody can detect any gross or open sin in their conduct, and their own consciences, which accuse them of great and continual shortcomings, acquit them of any increased or intentional neglect of duty. But God is pleased, in the exercise of his own sovereignty, to single them out for trial, and he visits them with one hard stroke, and follows it up with another, and another still. Each stroke as it falls upon the sufferer may be endured without a murmur; but the rapid repetitions of such fatherly chastisements stun and overcome him. And it may be that the man, whose faith enabled him to recognise a father's love in the blow which snatched from his fond embrace some beloved member of his family, nor repined when a second, and even a third or a fourth was attacked with disease, and soon numbered with the dying or the dead,—when he begins to survey the sad blanks in the domestic circle, and to brood over the extreme severity of his chastisements, will first secretly harbour a suspicion that trials such as he has undergone cannot be the pledges of divine love; and ere long he may advance another step in the downward career of unbelief, and avow his doubts of being a child of God, or having warrant to appropriate the consolations which God provides for his afflicted children.

I have alluded to family bereavements; but the principle is the same, whatever is the peculiar character or aspect of the trials appointed. All I mean is simply this, that the Christian to whom God sends great and sore troubles, one on the back of another, like the frequent and mountainous waves of a tempestuous sea, and can discover no reason why God should thus contend with him, is apt to fall away from the wonted stedfastness of his faith, and to yield improperly to the enervating influence of discouragement. He too hastily concludes that his afflictions are tokens of divine wrath rather than of divine love. He mourns and refuses to be comforted. He finds himself enveloped in spiritual darkness; and out of the darkness there springs no immediate light, because faith has given place to doubt. Perhaps, in the very language of Job, he indulges in similar complaints against God. "I was at ease, but he hath broken me asunder: he hath also taken me by my neck, and shaken me to pieces, and set me up for his mark."—"He breaketh me with breach upon breach: he runneth upon me like a giant," Job 16:12,14. And this hiding of the face of God, which used to shine upon him sweetly and favourably, may be assigned as the immediate cause of this afflicted Christian's doubts and disquietude.

Our limited knowledge of God's dealings with his differently situated and widely scattered people, precludes us from speaking with certainty on the subject; but it is not probable that the instances are numerous, in which trials resembling those of Abraham and Job are experienced. When God, however, does hide his face *externally* by means of a frowning providence, we may hope, that, if some of the severely tried ones lapse for a time into a state of doubt as Job did, others like Abraham are nobly carried through by the exercise of a strong and stedfast faith.

But I believe it is more common for God, in an *internal* way, to hide his face from his own people. He declines to hear, or, at all events, he delays to answer, their earnest and persevering prayers. And this is another cause of the doubts that are prevalent.

You well know that much of the Christian's safety amidst surrounding dangers,—much of his strength for duty and for trial,—and much, too, of his spiritual prosperity and happiness, is suspended on his right use of the privilege he enjoys of making all his requests known unto God. Indeed a true Christian will always be a man of prayer. From a feeling of manifold necessities, and from a sense of duty, and from his experience of a holy satisfaction and delight in holding communion with his reconciled and loving Father in heaven, he is constrained to pray. Under the influence of the strongest motives, he prays much and often; and he is encouraged from Scripture, not only to believe that his prayers are heard with acceptance through the continual intercession of our great High Priest, but to expect that he will receive the blessings which he has asked.

Now, it is my conviction that very many of us who are most regular in presenting our supplications at the footstool of the throne of grace, are extremely remiss in noticing the answers which God is pleased to send us. We regard it as a sacred duty, at stated times, to make certain confessions of guilt and of helplessness, and to entreat God to grant us forgiveness of sin, with all the blessings of grace and goodness that our present circumstances require. But it is notorious how great is the lack of watchfulness for the receipt of what we ask. And where there is a becoming measure of watchfulness, I fear there frequently is a very unbecoming spirit of impatience,—a want of waiting in faith until the Lord's own time comes, for bestowing what his own good Spirit has taught us to request of him. This impatience naturally enough engenders doubts. For if our requests are not granted instantly, or within the period which we have taken it upon us to prescribe, we begin to suspect either that God has closed his ears against our importunate cries, or has failed in his promise to answer his people when they call upon him, or that we are not numbered among his people, as he appears neither to hear nor to answer us.

There certainly are not wanting many instances of immediate answers to prayers. I should think that almost every Christian, from the treasury of his own experience, will be furnished with the remembrance of occasions on which the desired blessing was shed upon him abundantly, for his spiritual refreshment, before he had risen from his knees. It was so with Daniel of old, to whom, "while he was yet speaking" in prayer, the angel Gabriel was sent to give him skill and understanding, Dan 9:20-22. And it was so likewise with the many believers in the house of Mary, who were gathered together praying for Peter, when, lo! at the dead hour of the night, he knocked at the door, having been miraculously rescued from his imprisonment, Acts 12:1-12. But we ought not to forget that although a great encouragement lies in the unconditional declaration of our Lord, "Ask, and it shall be given you; seek, and ye shall find; knock, and it shall be opened unto you," Matt 7:7; still it is implied in this and other similar declarations, not merely that our petitions must be restricted to things agreeable to the will of God; but that his time and mode of giving must be left to his own unfettered choice. In truth one of the most important benefits we derive from prayer is the continual acknowledgment of our dependence on God, and the cultivation of an humble and habitual spirit of trust in him for all things. And we may rest assured it is from no unwillingness on his part to enrich us with spiritual blessings above what we can ask or think, that God sometimes seems to withdraw himself, and to hide his face from us, when we pour out our hearts before him. His designs are always full of wisdom and goodness. The whole paths of the Lord are mercy and truth towards them that fear him. But if our faith and patience cannot stand the trial, then we become disheartened; and the first indulgence of a doubt, or the least suspicion of God's faithfulness and love, is like the outbreaking of waters, which increaseth more and more, and cannot easily be stopped.

I am well aware that the selfishness of our nature operates, to an extent of which we may at the time be unconscious, in regulating the tenor of our addresses to God. We pray for many things because they are agreeable to our own feelings or fancies, and without stopping to inquire how far they are consistent with the revealed word and will of God. And, besides, it is too often the case, that we pray with much greater earnestness and perseverance for things which are comparatively of small moment, than we do for the infinite and everlasting blessings of redemption. On these accounts we meet with many disappointments. We ask, and receive nothing. We seek, and are sent away empty. We knock, and there is no opening to us. And we may complain that God has hid his face from us; whereas the fault lies all with ourselves. But at present I refer not to such cases, because the darkness and doubts into which we may thus be brought, ought to be ascribed to our own injudicious and selfish conduct. My object is to speak of trials appointed by God. And I do consider it a great trial when he appears to disregard our prayers for things which directly concern the advancement of his own glory in ourselves, or in others. It may be that we supplicate him even with tears of earnestness, for those spiritual blessings which he has expressly promised to those who ask in faith:—it may be that we wrestle with him in the most importunate manner, and continue to do so for a great length of time; and still the answer is delayed. This is intended for a trial. God has hid his face from us, not because we have forsaken him, and he will therefore forsake us,—not because we are asking what is sinful, or asking in a sinful way, and must be punished for our presumption; but in order either to teach us the weakness of our faith, that we may be humbled, or to give additional strength to our faith by this extraordinary exercise of it. And it need not surprise us if the first result should be more general than the second. A Christian who loves his God, and who takes pleasure in the privilege of prayer, is cast down and distressed when he has long persevered in asking, and seeking, and knocking, and all as he imagines to no purpose. Then his patience is worn out. His faith diminishes. And consequently the continued hiding of God's face gives rise to many painful doubts respecting his own acceptance and safety, as well as the truth and preciousness of the promises of God.

In regard to the varied causes of doubt, to which I have referred in the latter part of this Letter, I have only to add, in conclusion, that the one prescribed remedy applies to them all. Whosoever among the people of God is oppressed with doubts, and walks in darkness, having no light, because of the hidings of God's face, let him still trust in that *name* which is "merciful and gracious." Let him still stay himself upon *his God*,—his covenanted God in Christ Jesus. Let him calmly meditate on the parable which our Lord and Saviour spake unto his disciples for the avowed purpose of teaching them "that men ought always to pray, and not to faint," Luke 18:1-

8. Let him also remember the former days of light and joy which cheered his heart, and pray for their return. And let him employ the little faith that remains, in appropriating to himself the sentiments and the language of an afflicted saint of old, "Why art thou cast down, O my soul? and why art thou disquieted within me? Hope thou in God: for I shall yet praise him, who is the health of my countenance, and my God," Ps 42:11.

The exercise of trust in God, and the attitude of waiting on him, are most becoming and salutary, especially under circumstances of trial. They that trust in the Lord, shall be like mount Zion, which cannot be removed. They that wait on the Lord shall renew their strength, and rise heavenwards as on eagle's wings. However great our present depression, "there is an expected end." The God of Abraham and of Job is also our God. And if he hides his face from us as he did from them, it is our duty and our privilege to repose in his unchangeableness; and to believe that as he again lifted up the light of a favourable countenance upon these two sorely tried patriarchs, so likewise he will dispel our darkness, and overcome our doubts, and cause his gracious face to shine upon us, that in him we may have peace, and that we may again with joy draw water out of the wells of salvation.

I remain, yours, etc.

LETTER 12

SPIRITUAL CAUSES OF DOUBTS—*Concluded*

II. THE TEMPTATIONS OF THE DEVIL

Opposite causes often produce similar results.—Extremes meet.—Trials from God, and temptations of Satan, may plunge the same Christian into doubts.—Satan an active and constant enemy of man; but his voluntary machinations must be distinguished from his acts as a commissioned servant of God.—The injuries Satan inflicted on Job considered.—God may use any of his creatures as instruments for effecting his own designs.—When God authorizes Satan to afflict men, it is not strictly speaking Satan who tempts, but God who tries them.—In his ordinary temptations Satan does not himself act against believers; but induces them to think, or speak, or act against God.—He often tempts them to doubt the truth of God's word, or the certainty of their own salvation.—The Son of God was manifested to destroy the works of the devil, 1 John 3:8.—St. Paul's fear lest Satan should beguile the Corinthians from the simplicity of Christ, 2 Cor 11:2-3.—The temptation under which our first parents fell explained.—The Tempter insinuates doubts before he proposes disobedience.—He still goes about like a roaring lion.—Many of the sudden and hateful doubts which distress even strong believers, must be ascribed to "our adversary."—The temptation of our Lord in the wilderness.—Satan's grand object with us also is to infuse doubts of our adoption.—The remedies.—St. Paul's negative precept, Eph 4:27.—St. James's positive precept, James 4:7.—The use our Lord made of the written word when he was tempted.—Knowledge.—Faith.—Watchfulness.—Prayer.

My dear Friend,

In prosecuting our inquiry into *the causes of doubts* which are so prevalent among Christian people, and which are so prejudicial to their own spiritual prosperity and comfort, there is a satisfaction in finding that there are causes in operation almost as varied and numerous as are the doubts themselves.

We have already seen how doubts of the darkest and most distressing kind are occasionally to be traced to causes that are either altogether, or in a great degree, of a *physical or natural* character. And you will recollect that in my last Letter, when entering upon the consideration of the causes which must be denominated *spiritual*, I proposed to classify them under two heads:—*First*, the hidings of God's face, and *second*, the temptations of the devil. On the first of these particulars I troubled you with a Letter of unwonted length; and on the second, I fear the present Letter cannot be much shorter.

The classification which was adopted shows not merely how varied, but how opposite one to another, are those circumstances in the experience of a believer which exert a powerful influence in raising doubts in his mind, and in subjecting him to their hard bondage. At first sight it may appear an unlikely, if not an impossible thing, that the dealings of an infinitely wise and gracious God towards those whom he dearly loves, sometimes involve them in as much perplexity and distress in regard to their personal and eternal salvation, as do the crafts and assaults of the devil. Yet a little reflection convinces us of its truth.

We often say that extremes meet. It is so in the natural world. For instance, the most intense cold produces a sensation of burning heat. But in the experience of a Christian there is occasionally a meeting of the uttermost extremities of the spiritual world. For where in all the universe can two beings be found so immeasurably remote from each other in character as are God and Satan? And what two objects can possibly be more dissimilar than perdition and salvation? And what two motives of action so thoroughly antagonistic as are love and hatred? And it is not only true that the Christian's heart is the place where these greatest of all extremes meet; but that there also these greatest of all extremes produce the same effects. The trials which come from the love of the holy God, and which are designed to carry forward and secure our salvation; and the temptations of the wicked one, whose hatred of man prompts him ever to plot our destruction; when they are experienced by the same individual, may alike envelope his mind in the gloom of spiritual darkness, and overwhelm him with doubts of the worst and most dangerous kind. I do not say that either God's loving trials, or Satan's wicked temptations *always* produce such effects. On the contrary, the one are sometimes endured with faith and patience, and the other resisted with firmness and success. But, alas! faith often fails. And whenever this is the case, then whether it be that the tried Christian ceases to discern the wisdom and love of his heavenly Father in the trials with which he is visited; or, that the tempted Christian yields to the suggestions of the tempter, the result is the same. Unworthy suspicions and unwarrantable fears take possession of the mind. And thus causes, which, in their origin and tendency, are diametrically opposite one to the other, may even cooperate in leading the Christian to entertain very painful and injurious doubts respecting God's relation to him as a forgiving and loving Father in Christ Jesus, or his own relation to God as one of his pardoned and adopted children.

In the preceding Letter, in which I had occasion to advert to the fact that God really does at times "hide his face" from his people, I furnished you with a scriptural explanation of the origin and import of this peculiar and very emphatic expression, and with some illustrations of those trials, connected with the withdrawal of God's favourable countenance, which give rise to a doubting state of mind. And now, before attempting more particularly to illustrate *the reality and power of satanic agency*, as a cause of doubt, I would remind you that, in the arrangements of Providence, some things are merely *permitted of God*, whilst other things are *his own special appointment*. The severe trial that Abraham underwent when called to offer up his son, his only son, his beloved Isaac, *came direct from God*. The heavy calamities which left Job naked and desolate, were *the doings of Satan, by the permission of God*. We do not read that Job was molested or injured by Satan until God himself commissioned him, as his agent, to bring to the test the strength and soundness of the patriarch's principles. We must therefore rank all that befell him among the trials which come from God, and not among the temptations of the devil. And I conceive that the two distinct cases of Abraham and of Job are conspicuous and intelligible examples to us, of *divinely appointed trials*, such as the people of God have been subjected to in all ages, and such as are continually taking place among ourselves, although on a smaller scale, and in a less apparent manner.

Truly God is wonderful in working, whether it be by direct or indirect instrumentality; and whether the agents employed are angels, or devils, or human beings. And although there are deep and inscrutable mysteries in Providence, as well as in all the other works and ways of *him* who is infinite, yet it is the duty of the Christian to acknowledge the sovereign hand of God in every event, and to rest in the happy assurance, that whatsoever concerns himself as an individual, or the Church of Christ collectively, or the kingdoms of the world at large, is all ordered in wisdom, and will be overruled for good. This is our obvious and bounden duty. No Christian can calmly dare to deny it. And, in general, all Christians find a sweet consolation in this constant recognition of God. It is a satisfying relief to their mind amidst the crosses and disappointments from which there is no other escape. It is a peaceful refuge to which they may ever resort when the sky begins to frown, and when the waves lift up their heads and make a noise. But if the storm rages with unusual violence, and should the aspect of Providence be peculiarly threatening in reference to our own circumstances, then the very darkness in which we are encompassed renders it difficult for us to discern the divine *wisdom* which appoints or permits such trying dispensations; and the shaking of our faith which they occasion, renders it still more difficult to say, "*Good* is the will of the Lord." These are the elements out of which doubts may be expected to arise. Nevertheless it remains as true as ever, that either in the appointment or in the permission of such special trials as Abraham and Job were doomed to endure, God is influenced by unerring wisdom and abounding goodness.

It is of vast importance, whilst yet we are exempted from trials of extraordinary severity, to have our minds strongly fortified in the belief that it is the undeviating design of God, never to crush, but always to confirm, the faith of his chosen ones; and that even when he hides his face from them, it is for the purpose of bringing their Christian graces into brighter exercise, that their unwavering trust, and patient submission, and indomitable hope, may shine forth for the encouragement and comfort of all the afflicted, and for the honour and glory of the God of all grace.

Why God permits Satan to buffet his people as he did Paul; or to inflict disease, and to stir up enemies, and to raise storms, as in the case of Job; or *why* God permits his existence at all, are curious questions with which I desire not to meddle. These are deep things, into which we cannot dive. They are secret things, which belong unto the Lord our God. But, believing what is revealed unto us, we cannot deny that this wicked spirit is not only allowed to live, but allowed to injure the people of God in their persons, in their property, in their domestic relationships, and in their social enjoyments. To imagine that Satan has power of himself to inflict such injuries would be to impeach the sovereignty of God, and, therefore, in all trials of this kind, it behoves us to acknowledge the hand of our heavenly Father, even where the instrumentality of Satan is discerned. Nor should we forget, that, so far as these trials lead to a state of doubt and of spiritual distress, this result does not harmonize with the gracious intentions of God.

Now, however, when we are to make *the temptations of the devil* the subject of our consideration, inasmuch as they are a fruitful cause of doubt in believers, it is necessary, at the very outset, to remember that he is influenced by hatred as strongly and constantly, as God is by love towards them that fear him. We are taught to look to God as a kind Friend—as a loving Father, even when he most severely chastens us; but Satan must be regarded as a bitter enemy at all times, and never more so than when he puts on the garb of an angel of light. It is needful still further to remember, that, although God employs this wicked spirit on some occasions as the author of the temporal calamities, by means of which the Christian principles of his people are brought to the test, yet there is no evidence, nor the least ground to suppose, that he ever authorizes him to tempt them to doubt the sure word of promise, or to commit any other species of moral evil. I wish you clearly to understand that there is an important line of distinction between those acts of the devil which *God commissions him to execute*, and in the execution of which he is acting in subordination to the Almighty; and those other acts in which he gratifies *his own* malicious desires to withdraw men from their dutiful dependence on God, or from their belief of his revealed word, or from a ready submission to his providential arrangements. We ought, indeed, to be fully convinced that our "adversary the devil, who, as a roaring lion, walketh about seeking whom he may devour," 1 Pet 5:8, is always under the impulse of bad motives; for by nature he is emphatically *"the tempter,"* 1 Thess 3:5; and our Lord says respecting him, "He was a murderer from the beginning, and abode not in the truth, because there is no truth in him. When he speaketh a lie, he speaketh of his own; for he is a liar, and the father of it," St. John 8:44. But, admitting him to be ceaselessly actuated by deadly hostility to man, my aim in these preliminary remarks is to point out with precision the difference between what he does from his own free and deliberate choice, and for which he is solely responsible; and what he does as a servant or instrument under the direction and control of God himself.

In a certain sense it may be said with truth, that as God permits the devil to exist, he also permits his evil deeds of every kind to be perpetrated; just as it may be said, that, as he permits wicked men to live, so he gives his permission to the wickedness of which they are the authors and abettors. Some people will think that I am now treading on the borders of what may be called dangerous ground; but we need not dread the danger of running into error so long as we tread *within* the limits of Divine revelation; and I feel warranted to advance a step farther than God's permission of evil to which I have just adverted, for Scripture teaches us to acknowledge his own hand in the evil that exists,—"I form the light, and create darkness: I make peace, and create evil. I, the Lord, do all these things," Isa 45:7. "Shall there be evil in a city, and the Lord hath not done it?" Amos 3:6: and the narrative contained in 1 Kings 22:1-38, deserves especial attention: at present I have room only to quote 1 Kings 22:23, "Now, therefore, *the Lord hath put a lying spirit in the mouth of all these thy prophets*, and the Lord hath spoken evil concerning thee." These are the words of Micaiah, a true prophet of Jehovah, to Ahab, the wicked king of Israel; and, looking to the truth which they unfold, we need not shrink from admitting it as another Scripture fact, that the God of all holiness sometimes even employs Satan himself as his hired servant.

On this most marvellous topic, Job 1-2 supply us with minute information, and unfold a state of things, which, without so distinct a record, would be altogether inconceivable. Let me request you to read these chapters with renewed attention. Read them not as a mere detailed account of the sudden and desolating afflictions by which this "perfect and upright man" was almost overpowered, but as a development of *the hidden causes* in which these afflictions originated, as well as of *the hidden machinery* by which they were accomplished. The description given is very scenic; and you will observe that Job and his family are not the only, nor the principal characters that are brought upon the stage. The Great Jehovah and the great *adversary* of God and man, although as spirits they are invisible to the eye, are represented as meeting together in the same place, and holding converse one with another respecting the venerable patriarch. It is thus written: "Now there was a day when the sons of God came to present themselves before the Lord, and Satan came also among them. And the Lord said unto Satan, Whence comest thou? Then Satan answered the Lord, and said, From going to and fro in the earth, and from walking up and down in it. And the Lord said unto Satan, Hast thou considered my servant Job, that there is none like him in the earth, a perfect and upright man, one that feareth God, and escheweth evil? Then Satan answered the Lord and said, Doth Job fear God for nought? Hast not thou made a hedge about him, and about his house, and about all that he hath on every side? Thou hast blessed the work of his hands, and his substance is increased in the land: but put forth thine hand now, and touch all that he hath, and he will curse thee to thy face. And the Lord said unto Satan, Behold, all that he hath is in thy power, only upon himself put not forth thine hand. So Satan went from the presence of the Lord," Job 1:6-12. I insert this remarkable passage entire, and it requires no comment. There is another equally copious, and of a similar nature, at the beginning of Job 2; and I am sure that did we not read it in the Bible, we could not and would not believe it possible that God and Satan ever met in mutual conference, or ever conferred about the particular circumstances of any of the human race.

From the recorded history of Job we unequivocally learn, that his amazing prosperity was the consequence of God's special blessing; and that, so long as God made a hedge about him, Satan, however great his power, and however strong his inclination to mischief, did not, and could not injure him. There is much consolation to us all in this portion of the narrative. But it is awful to contemplate to what extent Satan did indulge his wicked inclinations and exert his hellish power against Job, so soon as he was permitted. He set about his work instantly, and with alarming success. And it is to us most deeply mysterious that this permission to afflict the man whose moral excellence was unrivalled was given to him by God himself. This is what I mean by Satan sometimes occupying the place, and doing the work of an engaged servant of the God of holiness. The bare mention of such a thing is not a little startling; and although it is a scriptural truth, still I grant that we should be cautious how we think and talk of the acts of that *Holy One* who is of purer eyes than to behold evil, and who cannot look on iniquity, Hab 1:12-13.

The sinfulness of our nature incapacitates us for cherishing sufficiently exalted views of God's infinite wisdom and spotless holiness. It therefore behoves us to repress every rising thought and opinion that might tend to lower our conceptions of the Almighty. From the consciousness, however, of our own liability to be influenced for good or for evil by the persons with whom we associate, and because we are ever prone to regard God as such an one as ourselves, our finest and holiest feelings may be shocked at the very thought of the holy God entering into conversation with the arch-enemy of all holiness, and employing Satan himself to fulfil any of his holy and merciful plans. But this kind of pious sentimentalism ought not to be encouraged, nor should *our* feelings and propensities at any time constitute a standard by which to estimate the doings of the Lord. His own declaration, in reference to the exercise of pardoning mercy, is equally applicable to the greater part of his providential administrations. "For my thoughts are not your thoughts, neither are your ways my ways, saith the Lord. For as the heavens are higher than the earth, so are my ways higher than your ways and my thoughts than your thoughts," Isa 55:8-9. And, after all, why should not God hold intercourse with *all* his creatures, and what should hinder him from calling *any* of them into his own service? Or wherefore should he not use them all as *agents* or *instruments* for the accomplishment of his own designs? To imagine that *he* is capable of contamination as *we* are is a grievous mistake; and so likewise would it be highly derogatory to his supreme authority over universal nature, if any one of all his creatures, from any cause whatever, were shut out from his absolute control. God is the sovereign Lord of heaven and earth and all their hosts, and it seems right and needful that his sovereignty should be manifested in the subjection to his will of devils, as well as of holy angels, and of fallen men.

Nobody doubts the legitimacy of that service which God exacts from the heavenly hosts, and which they render with untiring delight. Is it not also true, and a truth which is nowise offensive to us, that God is continually making use of men as instruments in his own hand for conferring benefits, or for inflicting judgments, on some of their fellow-creatures? This is an undeniable fact. Even heathens, who knew him not as the only living and true God, and who gave their worship to dumb idols, were nevertheless selected and named by himself as his honoured servants. You will recollect what is written in the prophets respecting Nebuchadnezzar and Cyrus. And in modern times, and amongst those who have a Christian name, it is notorious that we often speak of the very worst of men as scourges whom God has raised up for special purposes. These men, who either know not God, or who love him not, are, according to the language of Scripture, "children of disobedience," because they have no fear of God before their eyes, nor do they profess or pretend to live conformably to his laws; and they are "children of wrath," because the wrath of God is revealed against all unrighteousness of man, and because they who continue impenitent cannot escape from his threatened condemnation. Nay, more, ungodly men are by our Saviour called "children of the wicked one;" and the apostle John says, that, with the exception of true Christians, "who are of God," the whole world lieth in wickedness, or rather in the wicked one. Since this, then, is the condition of mankind in general,—since all are by nature estranged from God and subject to the devil, who is the god of the world in its present state, it need not be a matter of greater astonishment that God should call into his service the devil himself, than that he should so constantly and so extensively employ sinful men as his subservient agents in conducting the moral government of the world.

So far as I understand the subject, nothing ever takes place in heaven or earth,—in the material or moral universe, but either by the appointment or by the permission of *him* who made all, and who presides over all. Whatsoever God does not expressly appoint, he tacitly permits, and wisely overrules for the development of his own plans and purposes. Thus we perceive how God gives a *general* permission to the acts as well as to the existence of the devil and his numerous associates. But the Bible teaches us that this wicked spirit has also a *special* permission to afflict particular persons at particular times; and I have stated it as my opinion that in every case in which Satan brings distress upon good men, under the authority or with the sanction of God, such trials ought not to be ranked amongst the temptations of the devil. They really are trials appointed by God, and therefore they ought to be acknowledged as coming from him.

There can be no doubt, however, that although all the creatures of God are necessarily, as creatures, under a certain restraint and control, each of them has also a certain measure of liberty to act in accordance with natural tendencies and inclinations. It must be so in regard to rational beings, otherwise they could not be addressed as responsible to God for their conduct. Thus wicked men, abusing the liberty they possess, go onwards in their iniquity, waxing worse and worse, and enticing others by their precept and example, to accompany them in the broad road that terminates in everlasting perdition. Thus, likewise, it is with Satan and his emissaries. Gifted as they seem to be with intellectual faculties of a very high order, and with vast stores of knowledge, and with powers of motion almost investing them with ubiquity, and with facilities of access to our minds, such as belong only to spirits, and which surpass our comprehension, they systematically pervert their natural gifts and their moral liberty, and endeavour with continual and unrelenting assiduity to make men as much the enemies of God, and of truth, and of righteousness, as they are themselves. To devise evil devices is what best accords with the tendencies of their evil nature; and, in acting out such devices, they experience a miserable delight. To counteract to the utmost of their power the just commands of Heaven, and to maintain their usurped dominion over man, and to hinder our participation in the blessings of the Gospel, is the work in which they spontaneously labour; and in the prosecution of this work they exercise the full amount of that freedom which belongs to them as intelligent and accountable creatures. And if it happens only occasionally, perhaps very rarely, that God does give Satan an express and special permission, or commission, to afflict any of his peculiar people, we ought to know that Satan is always, and of his own accord, watching for opportunities to do us whatever injury he can. It does not follow, however, that all his machinations against us should indiscriminately get the name of *temptations*. I think, on the contrary, that this term should be exclusively applied to those insinuations and suggestions and allurements which are artfully addressed to our minds, with the intention and desire of leading us to think, or speak, or act sinfully. We have reason to believe that Satan still exerts his unhallowed power in many different ways to disturb our peace, to blast our prosperity, and to darken our prospects. And in all these acts of his, he proves himself to be our ceaseless enemy. But in his temptations his object is not so much to act himself directly to our hurt, as to induce *ourselves to act* against the warnings or the injunctions of God. In his temptations his object is to conceal his hostility to us, and under the guise of friendship, with all the blandishments of flattering speeches, and of fair but false promises, to beguile us from the duty which we owe to our great Creator and gracious Redeemer, that by *our own disobedience* we may forfeit his life-giving favour, and subject ourselves to his righteous displeasure. And whilst his temptations are manifold and multiform, and all skilfully accommodated to our peculiar characters, or to some existing peculiarities in our circumstances, it is not needful at present to advert to any of them, excepting those which are designed to sap the foundations of our confidence in God, and to fill our minds with suspicions and doubts of the truth of his word, or of our own interest in his grace and goodness. This you may think is reducing a large and interesting subject to a very narrow point. But recollect, my dear friend, that it is the one and only point which now claims our attention, and, besides, it is a point of sufficient importance to be distinctly, and even conspicuously, revealed in the holy Scriptures.

In one short sentence of God's word, what an immensity of truth is often wrapt up, like the germ of a small seed which in due time is to expand into a wide-spreading tree! Within the compass of a few words we find ideas so vast and so valuable as to require a whole volume to unfold and express them! Of this character what the apostle John affirms in reference to the incarnation of the Son of God may be adduced as an illustrious example: "For this purpose the Son of God was manifested, *that he might destroy the works of the devil*," 1 John 3:8. And with this agree the first words of mercy and of hope with which God cheered the hearts of Adam and Eve after their fall, and previous to their expulsion from Paradise. In their hearing he addressed the serpent, "And I will put enmity between thee and the woman, and between thy seed and her seed; *it shall bruise thy head*, and thou shalt bruise his heel," Gen 3:15. These two brief quotations contain the elements out of which may be drawn not only the whole details of man's redemption, but also the most precious hints respecting the character of God himself, and the overflowings of his wondrous love to fallen man. They give us at the same time a plain intimation of that mysterious warfare which the devil had waged against God, and which still continues;—that warfare of which man, newly fashioned in the image of his Maker, and this lovely earth, which God made for man and gave to man, were the objects. And they farther assure us, that, whatever success during a protracted struggle may attend the wily and malicious stratagems of our great enemy, still the struggle is destined to terminate in the total and eternal overthrow of "that old serpent, which is the devil and Satan," Rev 20:2; and in the triumph of the glorified Redeemer and his saints.

The enmity which we are informed God has put between the woman and her seed, and the serpent and his seed, is a part of the curse our first parents brought upon themselves and their posterity, first, by doubting the truth of what God had threatened, and then by disobeying his command. This enmity is something in which the whole family of man participate; but we may safely say that none have such a bitter experience of it, as those whom the grace of God has "turned from darkness to light, and from the power of Satan unto God," Acts 26:18. The enemy keeps quiet possession of all such as are still in the darkness of their sinful nature, and over the children of disobedience he rules with undisputed sway. They are his willing servants: yea, they are his bonded slaves, although they know it not. But against those who have been rescued from his thraldom by a mightier than himself, he plots with deadly malignity, and rages as for a prey snatched from his possession, which he eagerly desires to regain. On this account true believers in the Lord Jesus Christ are continually exposed to "the fiery darts of the wicked one," Eph 6:16. But so far from being surprised by these assaults of our great adversary, a knowledge of the word of God prepares us to expect them; and on the same divine authority we are encouraged to stand fast in the faith, and to quit us like men valiant for their Lord, instead of yielding to his artful solicitations to rejoin his deserted standard, or of listening to his treacherous enticements to doubt the reality of that final and glorious victory which is promised to Emmanuel.

Here, then, is solid ground for our faith to rest upon. The promised seed of the woman,—the incarnate God, the great Deliverer of man from sin and death and Satan, has been manifested. And, during his short sojourn on this earth in humiliation, we know that he was doomed to endure the fiercest onsets of the enemy, who, although unable to shake his allegiance to God, succeeded nevertheless in bruising *his heel*, when he brought the Prince of life within the precincts of the tomb. So far, the original prediction is fulfilled. But it is our blessed privilege to know farther that *he* who died bearing our sins and in order to make an end of sin, in dying and in rising again, destroyed death and "him that had the power of death, that is the devil," Heb 2:14. And now we are required in faith to expect his appearing the second time without sin unto salvation:—to wait for his manifestation in glory, when he will bruise the serpent's *head*, and be acknowledged by men and angels as the destroyer of the works of the devil.

These are great leading truths which the Gospel reveals to our faith. But, alas! my friend, it is not always that our faith holds them fast. Were the apostle Paul yet alive, he would find ample cause to repeat to us, and to multitudes of Christians of all denominations, the words of affectionate concern which he addressed of old to the church of God which was at Corinth. "I am jealous over you with godly jealousy; for I have espoused you to one husband, that I may present you as a chaste virgin to Christ. But I fear, lest by any means, as the serpent beguiled Eve through his subtilty, so your minds should be corrupted from the simplicity that is in Christ," 2 Cor 11:2-3.

I would have you to notice here, my dear friend, how expressly St. Paul couples together, as proceeding from the same source, and having the same end in view, that first temptation before which Eve, the mother of all living, fell, and those temptations with which believers in the Lord Jesus Christ are still assailed. This quotation from the epistle to the Corinthians is of particular value, not so much on account of the intimation which it gives us, that Satan continues to work upon the minds of men under the gospel dispensation with the same subtilty as he did from the beginning, as because it so plainly teaches us that, in the case of believers, his grand object is to seduce them from what the apostle calls "the simplicity that is in Christ." This expression, when examined in connection with the context, where mention is made of "another Jesus," and "another Spirit," and "another Gospel," cannot easily be misunderstood. St. Paul had fears lest these Corinthian Christians should abandon that simple and entire reliance for salvation on the Lord Jesus Christ, in which he had laboured to instruct them. And he was led to entertain these apprehensions in consequence of the insidious teaching of certain individuals among them, whom he hesitates not to designate "deceitful workers, transforming themselves into the apostles of Christ. And no marvel," he says, "for Satan himself is transformed into an angel of light. Therefore it is no great thing if his ministers also be transformed as the ministers of righteousness." Thus it appears to be the doctrine of Scripture that Satan has a power of tempting us by subtilty to abandon our confidence in Christ as a complete Saviour; or, in other words, of exciting doubts within us respecting the sufficiency and trustworthiness of his meritorious righteousness and atoning death; and that he puts forth this power either in the way of some direct influence on our minds, or through the public instructions of men who are his ministers, under the pretence of being the servants of Christ.

But the apostle makes special reference to the case of our first parents in Paradise, as illustrative of the kind of temptation to which Christians are still liable, and also of the mode in which they are tempted. "As the serpent beguiled Eve through subtilty," so, in like manner, the Corinthians might be drawn away by the craftiness and cunning of Satan or his ministers, from the purity of gospel truth which they had received, or from the assured faith in which they had hitherto been upheld. And what was possible among the members of that particular community of Christians is just as likely to happen anywhere else. Indeed, we ought to be without ceasing on our guard, lest we ourselves should become the unhappy dupes of Satan's devices. We may, therefore, find it useful to look back to that early period of human history, when man, bearing the image of his Maker, held uninterrupted communion with him, and enjoyed the sovereign dominion of all the earth, with the exception of one solitary tree in the midst of Eden, which God reserved in token of his own superiority, and as the test of obedience to him on the part of his creatures.

Well, then, if we turn to the book of Genesis, we find it thus written: "Now the serpent was more subtile than any beast of the field which the Lord God had made. And he said unto the woman, Yea, hath God said ye shall not eat of every tree of the garden?" Gen 3:1.

We know that the serpent, on this occasion, was merely the visible organ through which the devil spake; and the question with which he addressed the woman was artfully designed to shake her confidence in the words which God had so solemnly uttered in the hearing of her husband and herself. The tempter does not boldly and at once attempt to undermine her belief in the truth of God's own words, or to invite her totally to disregard the divine prohibition. He sets about his mischievous work with "subtilty;" and, therefore, whilst seeming only to inquire, for his own information, whether God had said, "Ye shall not eat of every tree of the garden," his real intention was to raise a doubt in her mind in regard either to the meaning, or to the justice, or to the kindness, of the command which God had issued. For he was well aware, that could he succeed in inducing her to take this first dangerous step, he might anticipate with certainty its being followed by another and a farther declension from implicit faith in God's word, and from unquestioning compliance with his will. And, alas! it is too true that "the serpent did beguile Eve through his subtilty." She was caught in the snare that was laid for her. Instead of sternly resisting his first advances, she listened to the enticing question of her beguiler, and she answered him, "We may eat of the fruit of the trees of the garden; but of the fruit of the tree which is in the midst of the garden, God hath said, Ye shall not eat of it, neither shall ye touch it, lest ye die." There is some truth in this answer; but there is a withholding of the whole truth, which proves that already the poison had been infused, and was beginning to take effect. She candidly acknowledges they were not to eat of *every* tree; for there was *one* in the midst of the garden which God had forbidden them to eat, or even to touch. But there is an evident evasion of the truth when she alludes to the threatened penalty of disobedience. With determinate and awful peremptoriness, God had said to Adam, "*In the day that thou eatest thereof thou shalt surely die*;" or, according to the marginal reading, "*dying thou shalt die.*" No threatening could have been less equivocal. No sentence could have more precisely and emphatically expressed the full amount of the punishment which God had affixed to transgression; and no language could have been better selected to produce the conviction, that, in the event of the forbidden fruit being eaten, the sentence would certainly be carried into execution, and the threatened punishment instantly inflicted. But in her reply to the serpent, the expression which Eve employs is altogether different, and conveys the idea of doubt and uncertainty as to the execution of the sentence. She says, "God hath said, Ye shall not eat of it, neither shall ye touch it, *lest ye die*." This was a sad departure from the simplicity of truth. "*Lest ye die:*" this is a most unwarrantable restriction, or rather perversion of the "*surely thou shalt die*," which the voice of the Almighty had uttered. She does admit that death was the sentence passed on disobedience; but she fritters away the execution of the sentence to a perchance—to a mere probability—"Lest thou die!" And Satan catches the expression as a proof of her having swerved from a firm faith in the truth of God's word, and in the rectitude of his moral government. He could have desired no more. He perceived that his first question, which covertly impugned the character of God in unjustly prohibiting the fruit of even one tree, had led Eve to suspect the sincerity of God in pronouncing such an awful sentence, and to doubt his faithfulness in adhering to it. He had the fiendish satisfaction of discovering that the threatened punishment was not so stedfastly believed or dreaded as to secure the integrity of her obedience. And regarding her now as standing on the very brink of ruin, he does not hesitate to submit to her consideration his own lie, in unblushing opposition to the assurances of the God of truth. "And the serpent said unto the woman, Ye shall not surely die; for God doth know, that in the day ye eat thereof, then your eyes shall be opened; and ye shall be as gods, knowing good and evil." "*Ye shall be as gods, knowing good and evil,*" was a tempting bait; but it would not have caught the prey, had not Eve's previous doubts and suspicions prepared her to believe the fatal lie, "*Ye shall not surely die.*"

It is unnecessary for present purposes to follow out the

melancholy narrative of that first act of human transgression which brought death into the world, and all our woes. Some attention to the recorded facts of its commencement has taught us how the devil, at the very outset of his assaults on mankind, tempted them to *doubt* what God had threatened, before he ventured to tempt them to *disobey* what God had commanded. And is not this an instructive warning to us? And does it not also abundantly authorize the assertion, that *satanic temptations* are entitled to a prominent place among the causes which create doubts in the minds of believers?

We have no reason to imagine that "the cunning craftiness" of Satan's nature has abated by the lapse of time, or that he has ceased to exercise it in the methods which promise to be most effectual for weakening the faith of Christians, and thereby withdrawing them "from the simplicity that is in Christ." St. Paul exhorts us to buckle on the whole armour of God—the coat of mail and weapons of defence which the God of our salvation has provided for us—that we may be able to withstand the wiles of the devil. "For we wrestle not against flesh and blood, but against principalities, against powers, against the rulers of the darkness of this world, against spiritual wickedness in high places," Eph 6:11-12. And St. Peter says in his first epistle, "Be sober, be vigilant, because your adversary the devil, as a roaring lion, walketh about, seeking whom he may devour; whom resist stedfast in the faith, knowing that the same afflictions are accomplished in your brethren that are in the world," 1 Pet 5:8-9. Our ascended Lord himself in his epistles, addressed, through his servant St. John, to the seven churches in Asia, makes frequent allusions to the presence and power of Satan among them, as the instigator of all sorts of defections from Christian doctrine and from holy practice. And as these epistles are exceedingly short, it is the more remarkable that in so many of them the tempter should have been mentioned at all.

The collective testimony of Scripture represents the

church of Christ, and the individual members thereof, as enjoying no respite from a militant state, until that predicated period arrives, when an angel from heaven, having the key of the bottomless pit, and a great chain in his hand, shall lay hold on the dragon, that old serpent, which is the devil and Satan, and bind him a thousand years, Rev 20:1-2. Then the church will be triumphant in kingly glory with her glorified Head. But it is vain to expect any cessation of his assaults during the existing era. For my own part, I am persuaded that the roaring adversary of whom St. Peter speaks, and all his subordinate principalities, and powers, and rulers, of whom St. Paul speaks, were never more ingenious in their devices, or more successful in their exertions, to beguile Christians, and to injure Christianity, than they are in these eventful days in which we live. And if the portions of God's holy and unerring word which I have quoted to you inform us, in a general way, of the danger to which our spiritual interests are exposed from satanic agency of a ceaseless and most inveterate kind; we are warranted, from other scriptural statements, to conclude, that, although the machinations and wiles of the wicked one are very various, as well as very numerous, yet, in his attempts upon believers, he still pursues his original and successful plan of insinuating doubts, before he dares to propose either unbelief or disobedience.

We cannot be sufficiently thankful when such a measure of grace is vouchsafed as to lift us up above the cloudy and cheerless region of doubts, into the bright sunshine of an assured faith. But even those Christians whose ordinary condition may be described as that of enjoying a peaceful assurance of salvation, are by no means exempt from occasional doubts. Indeed, I believe there are moments in the experience of all Christians when they are constrained, in defiance of their most matured and deliberate convictions, to question the truth of almost every peculiar doctrine of the Gospel, and even to stagger at the bare idea of having been redeemed by the blood of God's Son, or sanctified by God's Spirit, or admitted by adoption into God's family. Such doubts have many times passed through my own mind, and produced that kind of uneasiness and alarm, which we cannot overcome when a flash of lightning takes us by surprise. With such doubts, you, too, have probably been teased and wounded, and by experience you can testify how painful they are. Have you ever endeavoured to discover how or whence they originate? This subject has cost me a good deal of thought; and I know not really in what way to account for these sharp and sudden doubts, except we trace them to the great enemy, who watches every opportunity to pounce upon his prey, and who, when he can throw us off our guard by his "fiery darts," expects to gain some after-advantage: and I incline to the opinion, that, especially among Christians who are well enlightened and established in the faith, a great proportion of that class of doubts which are called *occasional and temporary*, may be correctly attributed to this one secret cause of *satanic temptation*.

In treating of this subject, I am sure you would blame me were no mention made of the temptation of our Lord, the particulars of which mysterious incident in his earthly sojourn are recorded by St. Matt 4:1-11, and St. Luke 4:1-13. I feel, however, that I need only hint at the "subtlety" with which Satan attempted to beguile even the Son of God. He came to him "in the wilderness," when removed from the endearments of human society, and from the activities of human life; thus teaching us that solitude has its snares, as well as its sweets. And he came to him when he was "an hungered," after having fasted forty days and forty nights; teaching us, that if fasting is sometimes profitable for the subjugation of the flesh, it also renders us vulnerable through faintness. Whilst our Saviour was alone and hungry in the dreary wilderness, apparently an outcast from men and from God, then and there it was that the devil assailed him. And mark how he did it! It was not by directly suggesting how easily he might extricate himself by the exercise of his divine power from the hardships under which he was suffering, but by insinuating a doubt whether such power belonged to him; or, in other words, whether he truly was a divine person.

The tempter's first address to our Lord displays great craftiness: "If thou be the Son of God, command that these stones be made bread." How suitable was this form of temptation to the circumstances in which our Lord was placed! Bread was the one thing which above all others was wanted at the time to sustain life. But the object which Satan had in view was, if possible, to shake that filial trust in his Father by which the whole conduct of our Saviour was so conspicuously distinguished; and he tries to gain his object "by subtlety." This may be traced in the peculiar mode of address to which he resorts. He does not at once and openly say to our Lord, As you are the Son of God, why do you remain amidst the desolateness of the desert, or submit so long to unnecessary privations? As the Son of God you are surely possessed of omnipotence. Did you not miraculously feed a whole nation during forty years in the wilderness? Why, then, should you yourself suffer hunger for forty days? Speak the word, and your wants shall be supplied: "Command that these stones be made bread." From so direct an assault as this would have been, the wily serpent anticipated failure, and therefore he adopts a different plan, less direct and more insidious. His poison is ejected towards the all-important point of his sonship, "*if thou* be the Son of God;" and the suspicion which he here openly expresses, is precisely what he most anxiously desired that the Saviour himself should secretly entertain. Truly, in this "if" there is a vast deal of the subtlety of the serpent. It was designed to raise many evil and misgiving thoughts in the mind of our blessed Saviour, and we must admit that it was well fitted for the purpose. There is a great depth of meaning under the expression, "If thou be the Son of God." It is just as if he had said, Can it be that *thou* art the man on whom the Holy Ghost descended in a bodily form like a dove, and to whom there came a voice from heaven saying, "This is my beloved Son, in whom I am well pleased?" Can it be that *thou* art the eternal *Word* by whom the universe was called into being, and who was with God in the beginning, and who didst share from everlasting in all the glories of the Godhead? Can it be that God should become man? or that the God-man, the Prince of life, the Heir of all things, should be an abject on the face of this little earth,—not merely a servant, but the servant of servants,—not merely deprived of wealth, and rank, and honour, and authority, but destitute of the commonest creature comforts? Can it be that the beloved Son of God, who came from heaven to reveal the love of God to his guilty creatures, and to instruct them in the way of salvation, and even to die for their sins, should nevertheless himself be banished from the abodes of men, and doomed to wander in this wilderness among the beasts of the field, without shelter, and without food?'

Here lay the strength of the temptation; and I trust you will not charge me with an overindulgence of imagination. I have supposed nothing beyond what you must acknowledge to be naturally connected with the facts of the case. Satan tempted our Lord to contrast his real circumstances at the time with his reputed character as the Son of the Highest, and as the intended Saviour of the world. And when the wide and wondrous contrariety between his character and his circumstances was thus brought under review, the tempter might cherish some hope of success in bringing him to doubt whether he was the Son of God, since his own experience at that moment left no room for doubt as to the reality and intensity of his privations. These two things seemed to be incompatible. Thus, the insinuations and suspicions expressed in the words, "If thou be the Son of God," were not groundless. No created intelligence could account for the combination of such contrarieties; and Satan, contemplating the absolute unnaturalness and apparent unlikelihood of the Son of God being solitary in the desert, and a stranger to the barest necessaries of human existence, suggested these things to the mind of our Lord, that he himself might be tempted to doubt his sonship.

The other temptations with which our Lord was assailed, on the same occasion, might furnish additional illustrations of "the subtlety" which was employed to seduce him, if possible, from subjection as a servant to his Father's will, and from confidence as a Son in his Father's love. But I must not enlarge. I leave you, at your own leisure, to indulge your own meditations on this very interesting topic. Our Lord was proof against all the crafts and assaults of the devil. He knew his duty and his privileges as a Son, and he firmly believed his Father's love. He knew the trials and temptations that belonged to the work of man's redemption, which he had willingly undertaken, and he stood stedfast in the belief of his Father's faithfulness to uphold him. The tempter received no homage from him; nor could he prevail on him to attempt any miraculous deliverance of himself from his deserted and desolate condition, because he utterly failed in awakening within him any doubt of his actual and intimate relation to God.

Do you not think, that, as the primary object of Satan in assailing believers is to throw them into a state of doubt; so the doubt which he is chiefly solicitous to raise in their minds, is that of their adoption. He knows how their strength will dwindle into weakness, if he can only hinder them from feeling or from saying, *"Now are we the sons of God."* Indeed, it appears to me, that the temptation of Eve in Paradise may be very well explained on this principle. Satan says to her, "Hath God said, Ye shall not eat of every tree in the garden?" And was not this his meaning? "You look to God as your heavenly Father, to whom you owe obedience; but if he truly loves you as his children, for whose accommodation he has made, and enriched, and beautified the earth; how comes it that he withholds any portion of it from your use?" This cunning artifice succeeded in leading Eve to doubt her true relation to God, and then she was easily beguiled into a relinquishment of the duties and privileges which belonged to that high and honourable relation. Perhaps you will consider me fanciful in this interpretation; but surely you will not deny that most of the doubts which harass so many good people, may be all gathered up into this one point, *Am I a child of God?* and I expect you the more readily to admit that such doubts have often a satanic origin, if you reflect how generally they are associated with some peculiarity in the circumstances of each individual doubter which Satan seizes on as a fit means for exciting doubt. Thus, for instance, it may happen that one Christian is blessed with bodily health and much temporal prosperity, and Satan interrupts his thankful enjoyment of these good gifts, by suggesting to his mind that it is "through much tribulation" here below, the children of God pass onwards to their heavenly rest; and hence arises the anxious question, Can I, who am so prosperous and so free from troubles, have a place among the dear children of God? Or, another Christian is laid low under the accumulated pressure of severe and long-continued affliction. Satan stirs up his fears that God has forgotten or forsaken him. As faith languishes, he begins to think that chastisements such as he is doomed to endure, never can proceed from divine love. In this way he loses the comforting sense of God's gracious presence, and easily sinks into a state of doubt whether he is, or ever was, an adopted child of God. Or, let us suppose, what is by no means uncommon, that a Christian of weak faith,—it may be a Christian even of strong faith, has fallen into some act of open sin. Perhaps Satan himself has had a principal hand in causing so deplorable a catastrophe. At all events, Satan afterwards takes advantage of the unhappy man's situation, as far as possible, to hinder his recovery. He urges on his conscience the inconsistency of his sinful conduct with his holy profession, and insinuates a doubt whether his profession was sincere, or whether he ever was born again of the Holy Ghost. And so it is that, from circumstances in their experience of the most opposite character, Satan, "through his subtlety," leads Christians to suspect the lovingkindness of their loving Father in Christ Jesus, and to harbour depressing and dangerous doubts of their own covenant relation to him.

I suppose you are fully satisfied that the *temptations of the devil* are a real and prolific source of the doubts under which Christians suffer. And now, in conclusion, let us inquire how such doubts may best be prevented or removed.

On this topic which so directly concerns our spiritual safety and comfort, we have both negative and positive injunctions in the apostolic epistles. "Neither give place to the devil," says St. Paul, Eph 4:27. And St. James says, "Resist the devil, and he will flee from you," James 4:7. But still we want to know, in what way and by what means, we are to give effect to these divine injunctions?—how we shall overcome our great adversary, and compel him to flee from us? And here we cannot do better than study the example of our Lord and Saviour, who "was in all points tempted like as we are, yet without sin," Heb 4:15. I understand the "without sin" to apply, not to the general character of our Saviour, although it is true that he was altogether sinless, but to the fact that when tempted, he never sinned by yielding to the temptation. In him, whom we are privileged to claim as our elder brother, we have an illustrious example of a tempted man not giving place to the devil; but showing a determined and successful resistance. And in this, as well as in many other respects, Christ is held up to us as the perfect pattern which we are required not only to admire, but to imitate. If, then, you take another look at the passages in the gospel history, already referred to, which narrate the temptation in the wilderness, you will find that our blessed Lord repelled every assault of the enemy by a quotation from Scripture. "It is written;" "It is written;" "It is written;" and with these weapons, furnished from the heavenly armory, he defended himself from injury, and made the devil flee from him. Here is instruction,—here is encouragement to us. The same armory is open to all who choose to apply. The same weapons are ready for our own use. But in using them we must have an unflinching confidence in their divine origin, and in their all-conquering power. For it is only when these heavenly weapons are wielded by the arm of a heaven-wrought faith, that the tempted Christian can withstand the tempter, and triumph over him. In plain language, my friend, two things are indispensably requisite in order to our resisting the devil, when he makes us the objects of his malicious attacks. First of all, we must have an accurate and extensive *knowledge* of revealed truth: and in the next place, we must *believe* that what God has spoken he will assuredly perform. Nothing short of this combination of knowledge and of faith in the infallible word of Jehovah, will make us invincible in the day of temptation, and hinder our being beguiled by Satan from the simplicity that is in Christ.

But if the example of our tempted Lord and Master deserves the careful study of his tempted servants and followers, so likewise do the warnings and exhortations of his deeply experienced and divinely inspired apostles. Because of our having to "wrestle against spiritual wickedness in high places," St. Paul urges us not to content ourselves with the sword of the Spirit, which is the word of God, but to put on the whole provided armour. And "above all," or, rather, "over all, taking the shield of faith, wherewith ye shall be able to quench all the fiery darts of the devil." It is when thus accoutred with "the helmet of salvation," and "the breastplate of righteousness," and having our "loins girt about with truth," and our "feet shod with the preparation of the gospel of peace;"—attempting nought in our own strength, but implicitly relying on the all-sufficiency of promised grace,—that we shall withstand the onsets of the tempter, and stand fast in the faith of Christ Jesus.

We cannot escape from the tempter. We cannot secure ourselves from the continual repetition of his temptations. This is part of the moral discipline to which we are here appointed, and which is needful to keep us mindful of the evil nature of sin, and the greatness of the gospel salvation. But lest we should at any time give "our adversary the devil," the undue advantage of assailing us, defenceless and off our guard, St. Peter exhorts us to be "sober and vigilant," to be "sober and watch unto prayer," continuing "stedfast in the faith." This is our security against falling: this is the way in which we may hope to baffle all his stratagems for our destruction. Yes, my friend, if we desire to escape like a bird out of the snare of the fowler, we must exercise a watchful circumspection. If we would avoid the pit into which Eve fell, we must enter into no parley with the enemy. If we would quit us like men, we must shut our eyes when Satan transforms himself into an angel of light. We must close our ears when *he* addresses us with the beguiling words of pretended friendship. We must at once decline acceptance when *he* proposes to enlarge the sphere of our enjoyments. We must place no confidence in *his* promises of preferment. We must manfully, in the strength of the Lord, and in the power of his might, resist all "the wiles of the devil." These are our duties—these are our safeguards. But you see how essential it is to the performance of these protecting duties, that we should remain "stedfast in the faith." Nor can this be done without sobriety, and vigilance, and prayer. Oh no! Great sobriety, and unceasing watchfulness, and earnest prayer to the God of all grace, are needed to guard us against self-security, and self-indulgence, and spiritual sloth, as well as against the open or the concealed attacks of our numerous and powerful spiritual enemies. It is very observable that immediately after the injunction, "Resist the devil, and he will flee from you," the apostle adds, "Draw nigh to God, and he will draw nigh to you." Let us, therefore, be ever on our watch-tower, praying with all prayer and supplication that we may grow in grace, and in the knowledge of, and faith in, our Lord Jesus Christ. Thus shall we be delivered from the crafts and assaults of the devil, and serve God, without doubts, and without fears, and without despondency, with loving and devoted hearts all the days of our life.

Yours, etc.

LETTER 13

MORAL CAUSES OF DOUBTS, AND THEIR CURES

The causes of doubts hitherto considered have been special and subordinate.—We now come to others more general and frequent—and for which Christians are themselves responsible.—*First, Acts of sin* on the part of believers originate doubts.—No Christian perfection on earth.—Our Saviour alone was sinless.—A sense of sinfulness increases with growth in holiness.—There is safety in this state.—But believers do sometimes fall into open and scandalous sins.—Then follow spiritual distress and doubts.—Sin must never he treated lightly.—But the door of repentance stands always open.—God invites his backsliding children to return.—If sinning Christians doubt their having been *children*, still the invitations to *sinners* are free to them.—Christ died for the ungodly.—This is the gospel.—When we sin we have an advocate with the Father.—A passage in 1 John, explained.—*Second, The consciousness of shortcoming* in believers gives rise to doubts.—Remarks on the duty of *self-examination.*—Neglected by one class of Christians—Perverted by another—Misunderstood by a third.—Explanation of the apostolic precept, "Examine yourselves whether ye be in the faith."—Its object is to confirm and strengthen,—its effect is often to engender doubts and fears.—The advantages of self-examination when rightly performed.—The danger of looking too exclusively to ourselves.—The discovery of our sins and shortcomings should lead us to the Saviour.—This is the legitimate design of self-examination.

My dear Friend,

It will not be disputed by you, nor by any person of ordinary discernment, that, independent of those special and subordinate causes of doubt, which have been adverted to in the three preceding Letters, there are other causes of a moral and religious nature, of which we may safely affirm, that they operate more frequently, although not more powerfully; and for the existence and operation of which Christians are themselves more directly responsible.

At this time I shall confine myself to what may be called *moral causes of doubt*; and the illustrations I mean to submit to you shall be comprehended under two particulars. In the first place, it will be proper to notice those acts of sin on the part of believers, whether arising from ignorance, or inadvertence, or temptation, which are contrary to commanded duty and to an enlightened conscience. And, in the second place, that sensitive consciousness of shortcomings and imperfections, which leads to a perverted use of self-examination.

I know you do not countenance the vainglorious and delusive doctrine of Christian perfectibility. On the contrary, you admit that Scripture clearly reveals sinful imperfections even in the holiest of men. Of our Saviour *alone* it is written, "who did no sin, neither was guile found in his mouth," 1 Pet 2:22; and we must not forget that whilst he was truly a man, he was at the same time *more than man*. None else of human kind has ever been able, in conscious integrity of heart, to say, "Which of you convinceth me of sin?" St. John 8:46. All the most eminent saints, of whose lives mention is made in the sacred page, were chargeable with open violation of the Divine law, and were more or less removed from that perfect holiness which God requires, and the attainment of which ought to be the object of our ceaseless and prayerful desire. And if such men as Noah, and Lot, and Abraham, and David, and Jonah, and even some of the divinely-inspired apostles of our Lord, were on particular occasions guilty of great transgressions, it need not surprise us that Christians of weaker faith, and smaller attainments, should sometimes wound their own consciences by sinful conduct. But it is much to be deplored that the injury inflicted by the falls of professing Christians is not limited to the doubts and distress in which they involve themselves. They also dishonour that holy Name by which they are called, and open the mouths of the ungodly to speak reproachfully, not only of themselves as hypocrites and deceivers, but of all spiritual religion as a fanatical delusion.

Although many Christians may be sufficiently circumspect in their deportment to escape the censures of their fellow-creatures, yet I do believe there are none who do not find reason continually to mourn over the secret sins of the heart. And it is undoubtedly the case, that just as we grow in the perception of the spotless holiness of God's character and of all his requirements, we become increasingly sensible of our own great and manifold shortcomings. This indeed is very much to be desired, as a powerful means of self-abasement, and as a constant remembrancer of our obligations, from first to last, to the free and sovereign grace of God. And, on this account, our spiritual condition must be regarded as safe and wholesome when we can say with the psalmist of old, "My sins are ever before me."

There may, however, be a deep and abiding consciousness of indwelling sin, and of daily offences against God in thought, word, and deed, coexisting with a firm faith in the Lord Jesus Christ, and an abiding reliance on the cleansing virtue of his blood. When it is thus with the believer, all goes on well. His stedfast faith in Christ keeps him both from gross sin, and from doubt, or disquietude, or despondency; and he will consider it a duty to thank the God of his salvation for that sense of his sinfulness which counteracts his natural self-righteous tendencies, and continually endears the Saviour to his heart. But it is a lamentable truth that believers are not always on their guard. They forget that in themselves they have neither strength nor wisdom; and hence their liability to fall into open and even flagrant sin, either through ignorance or inadvertence, or through the weakness of faith, or the power of temptation. The first departures from the straight and narrow path of holy obedience require to be carefully watched, as they frequently lead to a downward career of the most melancholy kind. To conceal some one sin, or to prevent the disgrace which would attend its discovery, another, and perhaps a greater offence, is perpetrated; and it may be that what commenced merely with a wanton look, as in the case of David, advances from bad to worse, until it terminates in deeds of the foulest criminality.

Sins of this description, so soon as their enormity is seen and felt, must necessarily lead the fallen Christian to deep humiliation, and overwhelm him with shame and confusion of face. Whatever may have been the particular character of the offence he has committed, as a conscientious man he ought to make no attempt either to conceal or to palliate it. And, in whatever way he may have been drawn aside from his usual consistency and stedfastness, the guilt with which he stands chargeable, in his own eyes and before God, will naturally and properly occasion much inward distress. Under such circumstances, it is to be expected that doubts will spring up to augment the disquietude which is inseparable from the consciousness of having sinned against so gracious a God, rather than from the dread of deserved punishment. It would be strange could any Christian disgrace himself by open iniquity, without feeling some painful misgivings as to the reality or soundness of his principles, as well as bitter compunction of soul for the guilt he has contracted. Especially during the first ebullitions of self-reproach and remorse, it would strike us as something wonderful and unnatural if he did not look with suspicion on his previous Christian profession. He will question his former sincerity. And it may be expected that the very apprehension of his never having been a true believer, will go far to retard the renewal of his "repentance towards God, and faith in the Lord Jesus Christ."

Thus, my friend, it must be abundantly obvious, that, as all the people of God during their earthly sojourn are liable to fall into sin, not only through ignorance and sudden surprisal, but even in direct opposition to knowledge and conviction; so *the sins which they do commit cannot fail to be a fruitful cause of the doubts* with which they are oppressed.

I do not speak at present of the strong convictions of sin which sometimes drive young converts almost to the brink of despair, and exclude them from the enjoyment of that peace and consolation which the faith of the gospel imparts to the awakened sinner. It often happens at the commencement of a work of grace in the soul, that the measure of heavenly light which reveals the guilt and danger of sin, is insufficient to exhibit the glorious all-sufficiency of Jesus the anointed Saviour. And before any partially enlightened person is brought to the comfortable knowledge that his sins are forgiven him for Christ's sake, he is likely to suffer much discouragement from the recollection of his past life as a continued course of rebellion against God, and to entertain many doubts whether it is possible that so great a sinner can be forgiven at all. But where the Spirit of God begins a good work, he carries it on. Increasing supplies of light from above by degrees dispel the remaining darkness; and doubt and dejection give place to the assurance of God's love, and to the joys of his salvation. In some such way as this a man attains the stability of a Christian character. He feels himself to be a new creature in Christ Jesus. The sinner is transformed into a saint. He now hates the sins which used to yield him pleasure; and he loves that holiness which he formerly shunned as a grievous and irksome restraint. But whilst this converted man experiences, a real blessedness in serving God, and walking in the way of holy obedience, his sanctification is not complete. And it is his sins *after*, and not *before*, conversion, to which I now allude as causing him to doubt whether, in deed and in truth, he has ever had a name among the redeemed and adopted children of God. These sins are stamped with a peculiar aggravation, in consequence of the grace and goodness of which he had heretofore partaken;—of the light and knowledge of divine truths with which he had been favoured;—of the gracious pardon already bestowed;—of the progress he had made in the life of faith; and of the place which he held in society as a man of piety and of Christian principle. And, from all the circumstances of the case combined, when the unhappy transgressor contemplates the condition into which he has brought himself, he may even doubt whether guilt of such crimson dye as his can be washed away, and whether God can ever again restore him to the blissful privileges of his sons and daughters.

No sin, in any person, or under any circumstances, is to be treated lightly. But when true Christians fall into heinous sins, there is need of great caution to avoid the danger, on the one hand, of appearing to give any encouragement to sin in them, and on the other hand, of withholding from them the hope of pardon and recovery. The door of repentance stands as open to them as to other sinners; and the blood of Jesus Christ the Son of God is at all times effectual to cleanse from all sin, of whatever kind, and by whomsoever committed. These are truths never to be forgotten; never to be denied. And although we must beware of detracting aught from the evil nature of sin, which is the abominable thing that God hates, and which crucified his sinless Son; we must equally beware, either of daring to diminish by one iota "the exceeding riches" of the grace of God to the very guiltiest of his creatures, or of presuming to set a limit to its sovereign freeness. Our duty is plainly prescribed in the Scriptures. One apostle says, that instead of exposing and magnifying the faults and offences of our brethren, we must "above all things have fervent charity among ourselves; for charity shall cover the multitude of sins," 1 Pet 4:8. Another tells us, that, when a Christian brother is overtaken in a fault, we are not to cast him off as a reprobate, unless he refuses our admonitions; but we are to use our best endeavours to "restore him in the spirit of meekness," Gal 6:1. And as it concerns ourselves we must study to profit by the warning, "Let him that thinketh he standeth take heed lest he fall," 1 Cor 10:12.

Persons afflicted with doubts arising from the various causes specified in former Letters are objects of much pity; but in the cases of doubt we are now considering, the individual doubters are much to be blamed, as well as pitied. Still we should take pleasure in reminding them of the invitation and the promise which God himself gives to backsliders: "Return, ye backsliding children, and I will heal your backslidings." And should their doubts of being children, even backsliding children, hinder them from responding in the language which God himself has indited, "Behold we come unto thee; for thou art the Lord our God," Jer 3:22; we must not regard their condition as hopeless. For, although from the depth of their penitential abasement, they are ashamed so much as to look up to heaven, or afraid to call on God by the endearing and encouraging title of "our Father," they need not and should not be left as a prey to "overmuch sorrow." If they persist in doubting their adoption; if their fears continue unabated, that all their former professions were false, we can resort to a different line of argument and address. We can admit the propriety of their doubts and fears, and request them to take their place among the enemies of God, and the rejectors of his Son. Let them look upon their conduct in the worst possible light; still it is within our power to encourage their downcast spirits with "the gospel of the grace of God." We can remind them of the mercy revealed even to the wicked and the unrighteous: "Let the wicked forsake his way, and the unrighteous man his thoughts; and let him return unto the Lord, and he will have mercy upon him; and to our God, for he will abundantly pardon," Isa 55:7. We can remind them of "the faithful saying, which is worthy of all acceptation, that Christ Jesus came into the world to save sinners," 1 Tim 1:15. And in order to make this faithful saying the more acceptable, they may be exhorted to follow the example of St. Paul, and confess that they themselves are "the chief of sinners." This humbling confession, so far from engendering despair, is the best preparation for understanding and welcoming the joyful declaration of the same apostle: "For when we were yet without strength, in due time *Christ died for the ungodly*." And it is in this amazing and cheering fact that the love of God shines forth so conspicuously. "*God commendeth his love towards us, in that, while we were yet sinners, Christ died for us*," Rom 5:6,8. Nothing beyond this can be asked or expected. The one sacrifice of Christ for all sin, is the one refuge to which all sinners are invited to fly. And the warrant to avail themselves of this sure and peaceful refuge lies in the revealed love of God to "the ungodly" and to "sinners." *This is the Gospel*. And every conscience-stricken Christian, as well as every convinced sinner, who believes the glad tidings, will himself participate in the joys of salvation.

I fondly cling to the persuasion that a man who has truly tasted of the grace of God, and to whom the spirit of adoption has once been imparted, however grievously he may sin, will never finally fall away; and moreover, that, however much his sins against divine light and love may raise doubts in his mind, and envelop him in spiritual darkness for a time, perhaps for a long time, be never can wholly forget his former assurance of the sufficiency of Christ's atonement and righteousness, and of his own interest therein. Of such a man there is good hope that when he falls he will rise again. But oh! my dear friend, it is truly a painful spectacle to see a man, in whose Christian professions we had confidence, and with whom perhaps we have many times walked to the house of

God and taken sweet counsel together, fall from his stedfastness, and incur the guilt and the infamy of some glaring immorality. With what compassionate tenderness we should mourn over his fall! And if, when oppressed with the sense of his "great transgression," he appears vainly to seek for a rest which he cannot find, and to labour without success for that relief which his conscience tells him he does not deserve; oh! how should we yearn over him with affectionate and earnest prayer, that his heart may again repose in the freeness of "the great salvation." Certainly many portions of the word of God are particularly calculated to revive the drooping faith of such a fallen Christian, and to restore to him the peace and the holiness he has lost. I shall only quote the following verses from the first epistle of St. John, who addresses himself to true Christians, and who writes at an advanced age, after much experience and long observation of the workings of divine grace in human character. "God is light, and in him is no darkness at all. If we say that we have fellowship with him, and walk in darkness, we lie, and do not the truth. But if we walk in the light, as he is in the light, we have fellowship one with another, and the blood of Jesus Christ his Son cleanseth us from all sin. If we say that we have no sin, we deceive ourselves, and the truth is not in us. If we confess our sins, he is faithful and just to forgive us our sins, and to cleanse us from all unrighteousness. If we say that we have not sinned, we make him a liar, and his word is not in us. My little children, these things I write unto you, that ye sin not. And if any man sin," (or rather, when any man may have sinned,) "we have an advocate with the Father, Jesus Christ the righteous. And he is the propitiation for our sins, and not for ours only, but for the sins of the whole world," 1 John 1:5, etc.

The oftener and the more attentively you peruse this quotation, I feel confident of your finding in it a very extraordinary and emphatic exhibition of the doctrines of grace. Most pointedly does the apostle assert the necessity of personal holiness, in order to our having fellowship with God; and so important was this practical result of gospel faith regarded by him, that he states it as the avowed reason of his writing this epistle: "These things write I unto you, *that ye sin not.*" But at the same time, he honestly declares how sadly we should deceive ourselves, were we ever to say that "we have no sin." And when we do sin, instead of leaving us in despondency to smart under the tortures of an upbraiding conscience, or of urging us to some long and arduous course of penitential reformation, he directs us to a certain and instant relief: "If any man sin, *we have an advocate with the Father, Jesus Christ the righteous.*" This is our safety; and the belief of it will give us peace. Not that our humblest confessions, and the truest repentance, and the most earnest prayers, are to be undervalued or neglected. This must not be the case. Yea, I am sure it cannot, it will not, be the case with any sinning believer. But Christ himself is the one and only "propitiation for our sins;" and it is through him alone that we have hope towards God. He is now "with the Father," as the High Priest of our profession, as our Representative, as our Forerunner, as our Intercessor, as our Advocate; and the Father always hears him, and always loves him. This is our encouragement amidst all defections and delinquencies, for Christ and his people are one in the eye of God. Our sins, of whatever kind, and under whatever aggravations committed, and at whatever periods of our lives, have all been punished and atoned for in the death of our great Redeemer. The blood which he shed on earth for the remission of sin, he continually pleads in heaven on our behalf; and it is our blessed privilege to believe that he never pleads in vain. He is in himself "the righteous," and he is besides, "the Lord our righteousness." Nor is this all. He is *the* Christ. He has been anointed of God with the Holy Ghost and with power. Whatever office he fills, he has been consecrated thereunto; and whatever duty he performs, he has been qualified therefor. And thus it is difficult to conceive what else, or what more, any miserable offender could require for his consolation, or any unhappy doubter could devise for his deliverance, than the simple, but most precious assurance of the beloved disciple John, *"We have an advocate with the Father, Jesus Christ the Righteous."*

This passage of Scripture, to which I have called your attention, sets before us the completeness of the gospel salvation, and its adaptation to all the varieties of human character, and of Christian experience. It will be wise in us to drink deep into its spirit; for then we shall anxiously desire to avoid even the appearance of what is sinful, and at the same time remember that we cannot escape from sinning. Thus are we made to feel our true and constant dependence on the Lord Jesus Christ; and whether our actual offences are great or small, according to the estimation of men, the renewal of our faith in the Saviour will always restore to us the enjoyment of pardon and of peace. I say, the renewal of our faith; because every departure from obedience to God may be attributed to a temporary failure or suspension of faith. And I say, our offences whether great or small; because the apostle uses the word "sin" in its widest latitude—in its most comprehensive sense. Indeed I know no authority for dividing sins into great and small. But I do know that there is no way of obtaining the forgiveness of the very smallest sin, but that one which is available for the forgiveness of the greatest. The blood of Jesus Christ cleanseth from *all* sin, and nothing else cleanseth from *any* sin. And therefore we are brought to the conclusion, that the pious Christian who merely comes short of the divine requirements, without giving offence to his fellowmen, stands as much in need of that cleansing blood, in order to his acceptance with God, as does another, who, in consequence of having grievously failed in faith and in watchfulness, has sunk deep into the mire of sensuality, or, by some other scandalous immoralities, has subjected himself to the censure of the church and of the world. All must be brought in guilty before God, that the mercy which each experiences through faith in Christ Jesus, may redound to the praise of the glory of his own free grace.

I trust you clearly perceive that the statement now made is in strict consistency with our justification by the Saviour's atoning sacrifice and meritorious righteousness, in opposition to all works of our own. But this grand fundamental truth is so little understood, and so generally lost sight of, that even Christian people are shocked at the very thought of liars, and drunkards, and adulterers, and murderers, obtaining God's forgiveness as readily as the most virtuous and benevolent of men. The whole Gospel revelation levels those distinctions in which men are apt to pride themselves, and teaches us that as the fewness or the smallness of our sins does not, at any time, or in any degree, secure our pardon, so neither does their multiplicity or their magnitude debar us from this vast blessing. It may happen, and, indeed, it does continually happen, that a believer who falls into some foul transgression is denied the forgiveness of his fellowmen, and is ejected from their society. But in the faith of Christ Jesus every humble penitent is assured of the forgiveness of God, and once more tastes of that peace which the world can neither give nor take away. This prepares him for meekly enduring the harsh treatment he may experience at the hands of men, as a part of the punishment he so justly deserves.* And, believing that what I have stated must be a doctrine according to godliness, because it is what God himself reveals, I repeat with heartfelt thankful-

---

*See 2 Sam 12, from whence we learn, that although the prophet Nathan intimated to David that God had put away has sin, yet because the king had given great occasion to the enemies of the Lord to blaspheme by his conduct in the affair of Uriah the Hittite, the awful sentence against him was uttered, not only that the child born to him of Bathsheba should surely die, but that the sword should never depart from his house. Here is the declaration of pardon, accompanied with the continuance of punishment.

ness, as a scriptural and substantial comfort to those who are agitated with distressing doubts on account of sins they have committed, that when any man may have sinned, "we have an advocate with the Father, Jesus Christ the righteous."

Having noticed how the gross and scandalous offences with which Christian people are sometimes chargeable, naturally enough plunge them into doubts whether they are, or ever were, true believers in the Lord Jesus Christ; I now proceed to place before you a similar, and yet a very opposite cause of doubt,—similar to that we have already considered, inasmuch as it originates with the believer himself, but likewise of an opposite character, because of its connection with a strong abhorrence of sin, and earnest partings after constant and complete holiness. Is it not true, my friend, that whilst some of the people of God bring themselves into a state of doubt by reason of *the sins they commit*, there are very many whose doubts are solely occasioned by *the deficiencies and shortcomings of which they are conscious*? They weigh themselves in the balances of the sanctuary, and they are found wanting; they compare themselves with the standard of scriptural requirements, or, even with the holy attainments in other Christians of whom they read or hear, and they are discouraged by the sense of their own imperfections. They contrast what they see and feel themselves to be with what they ought to be, and desire to be, and thus they become distressed with gloomy and tormenting suspicions of the genuineness of their Christianity. The tendency of many pious people is to be looking inward upon themselves, rather than outward and upward upon Christ; and whenever they do engage in the important work of self-examination, they soon find themselves beset with anxieties, and perplexities, and fears, and doubts.

You will readily perceive that this additional cause of doubt opens up a fresh and very inviting subject of consideration. I must not, however, attempt to detail that variety of

Christian experience which the announcement of this new subject might lead you to expect, but the remarks I have to submit to you will all be concentrated under the one head of *self-examination*; and I have no hesitation in asserting that mistaken notions of the nature and design of this duty, very frequently bring tenderhearted and conscientious Christians into much spiritual discomfort and alarm. Indeed, there is a strong impression on my mind, that, of all the duties incumbent on Christians, scarcely any one is either so entirely neglected, or so grievously perverted, or so much misunderstood, as is that of self-examination.

We have amongst us a large class of persons who are altogether in a low and unhealthy condition in respect of spiritual things. We should not be warranted in excluding them from Christian fellowship, nor would they on any account exclude themselves; but, there is no denying the fact that they have no strength of Christian principle, and therefore their whole conduct exhibits a sad lack of Christian practice. It is not possible that these people can have any scriptural assurance of their salvation; and I fear that, in most instances, their spiritual lukewarmness is so great, that the want of an assured faith gives rise neither to complaint, nor to lamentation. The truth of the matter is, that they are trying to maintain a compromise between Christ and the world. They are unwilling to give up either the one or the other; and when conscience is allowed to speak, it tells them they are wrong. They are like men who are afraid of making unpleasant discoveries when their temporal affairs are not prospering, and therefore they shrink from an investigation. They have a secret persuasion that the state of their hearts towards God is not what it ought to be, and for this reason the duty of self-examination is sadly *neglected*. Now this neglect of an important duty is much to be regretted. It is, in itself, an evil which aggravates other evils; and yet it is true, that in many cases, a fair and full view of their actual condition, as "neither cold nor hot," would, in all probability, overwhelm them with doubts and fears in regard to their hopes for eternity. But, on the other hand, were they to examine themselves in a proper manner, and from proper motives, we might hope that, by the blessing of God, the sense of their past inconsistencies and defects would drive them to the foot of the cross with weeping and confession and supplication, and extort from their humbled hearts a more entire surrender of themselves than ever to the love and service of *him* who bled and died for their sins.

Within the pale of the Christian church, we meet also with people of a very different description. They do not neglect the duty of self-examination, but they grievously *pervert* it; and, by reason of their perversion they, too, for the most part, are seldom troubled with doubts. They are distinguished by much Christian circumspection and general decorum. They are seen to pay regular attention to all that is external in religion. They are punctiliously exact in whatever belongs to the "tithe and cummin," and to "the outside of the cup and platter." The building or beautifying of churches, the maintenance of a regular ministry, the propagation of the Gospel in foreign countries, the private and public worship of God, the reading and hearing of his word, an almost superstitious respect for the Christian sacraments, and, in short, a commendable desire to "walk in all the ordinances and commandments of the Lord blameless," afford a certain kind and amount of evidence that they have a zeal for God, although it may not always be "according to knowledge." It does not become us to condemn such conduct as formalism, nor, indeed, to sit in judgment on our brethren at all. But is there not a real and great danger of men surveying such outward deeds with too much satisfaction and complacency? I do apprehend that *the very consciousness of doing* many things whereby the glory of God may be advanced, pampers the spirit of self-righteousness, and tempts such people to make *their external acts* the exclusive sphere of their self-examination. They do not look inwards; they institute no scrutiny into the motives of their actions; they overlook "the weightier matters of the law;" they search not for that faith in Christ and love to him which alone render our obedience acceptable to God, and which are the specific objects for whose existence within us we are enjoined to examine. In this way, all that is evil and humbling is kept out of sight, and all that exalts man, and gratifies his pride or his vanity, is brought prominently into view; and thus these superficial and sanctimonious persons see in themselves so few imperfections and so many good works, that their minds are rarely agitated with doubts. They live in a dangerous security, and it is plain that by them the duty of self-examination, so far as they do attend to it, is grossly perverted.

But now I must explain by whom, and in what manner, this important duty is *misunderstood*; for I conceive it is altogether by a misunderstanding of its legitimate objects, that an interesting class of the true children of God are so frequently brought into a painful state of doubt. Those on whom self-examination produces this effect, are persons of decided piety, with tender, and, perhaps, we might add, scrupulous consciences. They earnestly desire in all things to please God; but their minds are not well enlightened in the gospel plan of salvation, and of course their faith wants stability. These people are neither indifferent to their spiritual well-being, nor are they designedly attempting to establish a righteousness of their own, in opposition to the righteousness of God, which is by the faith of Jesus Christ. They have come out from the world; and the Saviour is their only avowed hope of pardon and of peace. To him they look, and their hearts feel the constraining power of his dying love. Therefore it is that they love holiness, and mourn over every remnant of sin that manifests itself in their thoughts, or words, or actions. They read that the blood of Jesus Christ cleanses from *all* sin; and that the Holy Ghost is promised to *dwell* in believers; and that they who are called by the name of Jesus should *depart* from iniquity. Thus they read in the Bible; and their honest wish is to be "sanctified wholly in soul and body and spirit," so that they may shun the very appearance of what is evil. But the more they examine into their hearts and lives, instead of finding a gradual approach towards that state of sinless perfection which is the object of their holy ambition, they seem to be receding from it. And thus their self-examinations are continually driving them to doubt whether they ever have been either cleansed in the blood of Jesus Christ, or sanctified by the indwelling power of his Holy Spirit.

It is much to be regretted that the results of self-examination are so uniformly discouraging and distressing to many good people. But do you not think that the reason of this lies in their own misconceptions of the nature and design of the duty? They have a wrong object in view when they begin to examine themselves, and the examination is conducted under the influence of mistaken motives. They forget that in themselves, that is, in their fleshly nature, there dwelleth no good thing; and that, although "they delight in the law of God after the inward man," still their condition is not better than that of St. Paul, who tells us, "but I see another law in my members, warring against the law of my mind, and bringing me into captivity to the law of sin which is in my members," Rom 7:23. Instead of expecting to find such a powerful enemy as sin still lodging within them, and counteracting to the utmost the workings of the Spirit of Christ Jesus, through whom they are sanctified, they too exclusively look for "the fruits of the Spirit," or for what are usually called evidences of grace. In short, instead of examining whether their faith receives and rests upon the Lord Jesus Christ, and whether they are simply and stedfastly abiding in him as their only and their complete Saviour, they are induced, through some wrong bias, to diverge to the one hand or to the other from what ought to be their precise object. And they begin to examine either wherein they come short in the exercise of faith, and in the exhibition of those Christian graces which faith should beget, or whether their own sanctification is complete, or, at least, whether it is sufficiently advanced to quiet their consciences, and give them confidence towards God. And I do believe that into one or other of these errors many Christians are unwarily drawn, by means, it may be, of an imperfect knowledge of the work of Christ; or, of the wiles of the devil, who is ever ready to beguile us from a simple and entire dependence on the Saviour; or, of the secret leanings to self-righteousness which are so difficult of subjugation. They mistake the purpose for which self-examination is enjoined. They misunderstand the nature of the duty. And thus, whatever is the immediate source from whence their error originates, its existence and actual operation cannot fail to engender doubts and fears in abundance.

The apostolical command is in these words—"Examine yourselves, whether ye be in the faith: prove your own selves. Know ye not your own selves, how that Jesus Christ is in you, except ye be reprobates?" 2 Cor 13:5-6. And it deserves your notice that this duty is prescribed to believers at Corinth, among whom, as a church of Christ, great corruptions and abuses prevailed. It will not be questioned that St. Paul desired the removal of everything which brought dishonour on the cause of Christ, or did injury to the souls of Christians. So earnest was he for a thorough reformation and revival among these Corinthians, that he says to them, "And this also we wish, even your perfection." But it is very remarkable that he should have recommended self-examination as an essential means for promoting their improvement as a church, and their prosperity as individual members thereof. They were to examine whether they were *in* the faith, and not whether they were *out* of it. They were to mark the change which the grace of God *had already wrought* in them, and not merely how much of the work *was as yet left undone*. And assuredly the apostle never anticipated that the performance of this duty would fill their minds with doubts whether they were a church, or whether they were Christians at all. Such a result as this would have utterly frustrated the great object he had in view, which was to quicken their sense of obligation to redeeming love, and to lift them out of the inconsistent and unholy practices into which they had fallen. As a faithful pastor, his object was in nowise to shake, but by all means to strengthen, their faith in Christ Jesus; and, by reminding them of their Christian character, to stimulate them to greater watchfulness and diligence in appreciating their privileges, and in adorning their profession. And certainly this case of the Corinthians is very instructive to all Christians. To those who are not, or who do not think that they are, in a spiritually prosperous condition, it is not only instructive, but encouraging. For here we are plainly taught, that, if the duty of self-examination is discharged aright, so far from distressing the humble and pious with doubts and fears, or from driving the negligent and careless to despair, under the sense of their sins and shortcomings, it is designed to "strengthen the things that remain," and to bring forth into renewed exercise that principle of faith which divine grace has implanted in their hearts. And thus if feelings of shame and sorrow are awakened as they ought to be, they will be subdued and sanctified by the accompanying emotions of gratitude and hope. The effects of self-examination ought always to be beneficial.

But I must here observe that although believers of a certain class are more easily and more generally drawn into a state of doubt, whenever they engage in this duty, than many others are, yet it would be a great mistake to suppose that they are the only people who fall into this snare. On the contrary, we may safely conclude that all who examine themselves at all, are more or less liable to have their attention, for the time, so exclusively fixed on their own faults and failings, as to shut the Saviour out of sight. And this is a state of things which is sure to envelop the Christian in spiritual darkness, and to subject him to the depressing influence of doubts respecting his salvation.

It would be another mistake to confine our ideas or our definition of self-examination, to those periodical seasons when we retire to our closet for the express purpose of communing with our own hearts. On these occasions we formally, and it may be minutely, enter upon the duty. And it would be advantageous if all Christians were more regular in dedicating a set portion of their time to this important employment. But was there no self-examination excepting at these stated seasons of retirement, then I fear we should have cause to conclude that the duty is seldom performed, and performed only by a small number of Christians. In this case it could not with propriety be regarded as a frequent and influential source of doubt. To me, however, it appears certain, that with the great proportion of Christians who are humble, and conscientious, and earnest in the service of God, the process of self-examination is often secretly and undesignedly going forward while they are engaged in various kinds of religious occupations, both in private and in public. For example, when the gospel is being preached, at the time the minister is urging his hearers to self-application, they may be, and I believe they commonly are, carrying on an accompanying work of self-examination. This is the reason why a particular style of preaching rather drives believers away from Christ, than draws them towards him; and in this unfavourable position they are very ready to entertain doubts of their salvation. Again, when reading books which treat of practical and experimental religion, or memoirs and biographies of eminent Christians, the same sort of process spontaneously commences, and leads to a similar issue. Even the conversational intercourse which believers hold with each other, whenever it becomes deeply spiritual, and especially should it turn to points of inward experience, not unfrequently terminates in compunction and dejection, in consequence of the painful discoveries of the state of their hearts towards divine things, which result from a silent self-examination, as they talk one with another. And probably you will not object to my adding to this catalogue of examples, that when we are engaged in prayer, or, at all events, when we are preparing to prostrate ourselves before the God and Father of our Lord Jesus Christ, we are then constrained, in some measure, to examine what are the sins we have to confess, and what the blessings we require to supplicate, and what the mercies we ought to acknowledge with gratitude and praise. But so far as the tenor of their addresses to God correctly indicate the nature of their previous self-examinations, it is too true that many Christian people seem to have overlooked the grace heretofore bestowed upon them, and to have confined their attention to their manifold spiritual deficiencies. They disregard the apostle's injunction, to examine themselves whether they are "in the faith." On this account they approach the throne of grace, doubtful of the relation in which they stand to God. They pray for the forgiveness of sin, and for the renewing of the Holy Ghost, and for spiritual blessings of every description, as if they were entire strangers to these things,—as if they had never heretofore partaken of them. They pray to be adopted into the family of heaven, and to be numbered amongst the sons and daughters of the Lord Almighty, as if they knew not that without "the Spirit of adoption," which they have in Christ Jesus, they cannot cry unto God, "Abba, Father." Indeed, the amount of their supplications often is, that they may be made true Christians,—that God may begin a good work in their hearts. They content themselves with asking blessings, that are merely initiatory of the life of faith; and year after year, they persevere in presenting the same kind of petitions. They do not advance into the condition of matured and stable believers. They never come to God with the reverential and loving confidence of children. And their prayers and requests are not sufficiently accompanied with thanksgiving and praise. They do supplicate the pardoning mercy and comforting presence of God for Christ's sake, but we never find them giving utterance to those warm and animating expressions of gratitude and joy which distinguish the Scripture saints, and which naturally flow fresh and full from the hearts and lips of men who know their obligations to redeeming love.

These observations are fitted to subserve two ends: they assist in teaching us how frequently the work of self-examination is in operation, when perhaps we are not intending it; and how frequently also it produces effects prejudicial to our spiritual welfare, and directly opposed to what St. Paul desired and expected when he said, "Examine yourselves whether ye be in the faith." And I trust that you, my dear friend, will put no wrong construction on anything I have advanced, or ever for one moment imagine that indwelling sin should cease to be a grief and a burden to the believer. Nor is this enough. The duty of self-examination is not to be abandoned, because some people abuse it to their own discomfort. But surely it is most desirable that all Christians should be stimulated to its performance from proper motives, and should rightly understand in what respects it may prove to be beneficial to them.

Permit me, then, to mention that self-examination confers a vast benefit, inasmuch as it keeps the believer in perpetual remembrance of his own emptiness and poverty, that his faith may look to "the unsearchable riches of Christ" for the supply of all his spiritual necessities. Besides, it teaches him how weak and insufficient he is of himself either for duty or for trial, that he may hold fast by Christ, in whose strength alone he can do all things. It likewise reminds him of his guiltiness, that he may walk humbly with God; and withdraws the veil even from his secret sins, that he may rely on the atonement and righteousness of Christ, as his one and only hope of salvation. And in this way self-examination must be of the utmost advantage, when it makes the Saviour the more precious to us, from a deep feeling of our utter wretchedness and ruin without him.

It is possible, however, to look so exclusively to ourselves, as to look away from that all-sufficient Saviour, "who of God is made unto us wisdom, and righteousness, and sanctification, and redemption." This, as you know, is often done. Indeed, this is the grand evil from whence spring so many anxieties and doubts in connexion with self-examination. And if we wish to escape from these anxious doubtings, we must studiously guard against the evil in which they originate.

In honestly scrutinizing our hearts and lives, as in the sight of God, we should always be prepared for discovering great and numerous shortcomings. We ought also to remember that in proportion to our attainments in holiness, will be our keen perception of all that is sinful in our nature and defective in our character. As increasing light makes manifest the darkness of which we were previously insensible; so our growth in grace may be expected to make our self-examination increasingly humiliating and painful. And, therefore, it is essential to our Christian stability and progress that we stand fast in the faith of Christ Jesus. The very humiliation and sorrow which we feel, are a strong evidence in our favour; for such feelings are peculiar to the heart that has been renewed and purified by the Holy Ghost: and thus, instead of only thinking and speaking bitter things against ourselves, we should cleave with greater ardour to our loving Redeemer, in whom alone we have righteousness and strength. If we allow the eye of our faith to be diverted from *him* who is our light and life, then assuredly the sight of so much that is defective and loathing in ourselves must cause us to mourn in heaviness of spirit, and our self-examination, so far from doing us any spiritual good, will be converted into weapons for the destruction of our peace and hope and joy.

The discovery and contemplation of his remaining sins and imperfections *ought* to be of the greatest use to the true Christian; but they *never will*, unless he is thereby taught to look away from himself. It is not by thinking of a disease that it ever will be removed. Nor is it by looking at a wound that it can be healed. By looking at his wound, and brooding over his disease, a man only sickens the more, until he fancies himself to be worse than he actually is. If he wishes to be cured, he must apply to the physician,—he must use the needful medicine. And, in like manner, I would say that the believer is not employing the examination of himself to its legitimate object, unless the discovery of his spiritual wounds and maladies sends him to the great Physician of souls, who never dismisses an applicant without effecting his recovery; and unless it leads him to "the glorious gospel of the blessed God," in which he will always experience a precious and a healing balm.

We are surrounded with dangers whenever we begin to seek for rest and satisfaction in ourselves, and were we to find what we thus seek for, our condition would be still more dangerous. Although by the grace of God we are "new creatures in Christ Jesus," we must not forget that regeneration does not wholly eradicate inherent corruption, and that the life which we live in this world must continue to be a life of faith in the Son of God, who loved us, and gave himself for us. Each day and hour it behoves us to betake ourselves to that ever-flowing and inexhaustible fountain, where at first we were cleansed from our sins, and where at first we drank with joy of the water of life freely. And we may rest assured that the exhortation of St. Paul to the Colossians is needful at all times, and suitable to all Christians: "As ye have therefore received Christ Jesus the Lord, so walk ye in him; rooted and built up in him, and stablished in the faith, as ye have been taught, abounding therein with thanksgiving."

When, as convinced sinners, we feel for the first time our need of pardon and of holiness and of acceptance with God, we gladly receive the provided Saviour as all our salvation and all our hope. In ourselves we see nothing but the defilements of sin. In him we see everything that the helplessness of our situation demands. And it is not until our sanctification has been somewhat advanced that we begin to be less occupied with the Saviour, and more occupied with ourselves. This is the snare into which Satan tries to seduce us: and then, because we never attain to a state of *complete sanctification*, disappointment accompanies our self-examination, and drives us to despondency or to doubts. But this is wrong. We are to *walk* in Christ, as we *received* him at first. We are *to be built up* in him, as well as *to be rooted* in him. We must *be stablished* in the faith, abounding therein *with thanksgiving*. And this can only be accomplished by continually "looking unto Jesus, the author and finisher of our faith," O yes, my friend, this is our privilege, and this is our safety. "Looking unto Jesus" is the prescribed antidote to our besetting sin. A sight of Jesus, "full of grace and truth," will always revive our faint heart, and cheer our drooping spirit. A constant trust in Jesus as the great propitiation, "the Lord our righteousness," is the true source of spiritual comfort, and the certain means of spiritual prosperity. "Look unto me," is the gracious admonition of our Lord himself; "and be ye saved," is the happy end to be gained by a faithful compliance with the admonition. Looking to the Lamb of God who was slain for us, and in whose sacrifice God smelled a sweet savour, will keep our faith in healthful exercise. And even when our sins and shortcomings rise up in fearful array, a believing glance towards our divine Surety, "who bore our sins in his own body on the tree," will calm our fears, and scare away our doubts.

I remain, ever yours, etc.

LETTER 14

RELIGIOUS CAUSES OF DOUBTS, AND THEIR CURES

I. IMPERFECT AND INACCURATE VIEWS OF THE PERSON OF CHRIST

The Physical, Spiritual, and Moral causes of doubt explained in former Letters are generic, not specific.—The operation of *religious causes*, as a genus, is the most extensive.—Especially powerful in conjunction with other causes.—Imperfect and inaccurate views of the Gospel.—The Gospel, in one sense, is comprehensive of all revealed truth.—For present purposes, limited to *the incarnation* of the Son of God.—Highly important to know *who* the Saviour is.—Confused ideas of his *person* lead to doubts.—His humanity often overlooked in contemplating his divinity.—The Christ is as truly the Son of Mary, as he is the Son of God.—Scripture illustrations.—The charm of the name Emmanuel, "*God with us.*"—The union of Godhead and manhood in the Christ gives assurance of his ability and fitness to save sinners.—When the two natures in his one person are separated, even in thought, doubts and fears supplant the peaceful assurance of salvation.—Mistakes on this subject are commonly practical rather than doctrinal.—Clearer views of our Saviour's mysterious *person* will remove doubts.—The knowledge and faith of "Emmanuel" forms the real groundwork of all Christian character and enjoyment.—"Jesus Christ himself" is the only foundation of a sinner's hopes towards God.

My dear Friend,

We have already seen that the causes of the doubts that are prevalent among Christian people are widely diversified in their nature, as well as very powerful in their operation. Some of the causes to which I have directed your attention are entirely of a *physical* character, arising from constitutional tendency, or, from mental disease, or, from disease of the body partially affecting the mind. Others are altogether such as may properly be designated *spiritual*. They have their origin, instrumentally at least, *First*, in trials of extraordinary severity which *God* himself is pleased either to appoint or to permit: *Second*, in the temptations of *Satan*. Others, again, are of a *moral* character. They are connected with those acts of sin or of shortcoming which are contrary to Scripture or to conscience, and with which the people of God are themselves chargeable.

These different causes, which have been illustrated in separate Letters, may be considered as generic; and under each *genus* there probably may be found as many distinct *species* of doubts, as there are individual doubters. I mean that in each separate case there may be some little peculiarity by which it is distinguished from others. To sketch the bare outline of these varieties would have imposed a long and laborious task. My object has been simply so to delineate the different genera as to assist in tracing specific doubts to their proper cause. It cannot be denied that this object is of great importance, for everyone knows that it is often half the cure to ascertain the nature of our disease. And I shall be truly happy, if any of my observations should prove useful to yourself, or to any of your Christian friends, at those painful seasons when the mind becomes clouded and oppressed with doubts.

The subject, however, is not yet exhausted. One other generic cause for the existence and continuance of doubts demands consideration; and I intentionally place it last on the list, from the conviction that its operation is more extensively felt than that of any other of all the causes already enumerated. You will guess that I allude to those *imperfect and inaccurate views of gospel truth*, which are entertained by so many Christians, and which keep some of them under the bondage of doubts and fears all their lifetime. This one cause, to which, as distinct from the others, we may give the designation of *religious*, could not fail to be a mighty engine of evil, even were it left to work out its legitimate results isolated and alone. But, acting as it often does in conjunction with some other cause of doubt, or, it may be, with a combination of several distinct causes all at once, its power becomes immense. For example, if a man has a constitutional tendency to doubt,—or if his mind is somewhat impaired by disease,—or if he is laid low under extraordinary visitations of Providence,—or if he is assailed by the fiery darts of the wicked one,—or if he has fallen into any foul and scandalous sin, then the doubts which may have been raised in his mind will assuredly receive a great additional impetus, should his views of what is emphatically called *the Gospel* be indistinct or defective. On the other hand, where one or other of the causes which have just been specified plunge a Christian into a state of temporary doubt, respecting either any portion of divine truth, or his own personal forgiveness and acceptance in Christ Jesus, you must readily perceive what a favourable and speedy counteraction is likely to be effected by clear and comprehensive views of the great purposes for which the Son of God became man, and died, and rose again. These wondrous revelations of divine grace are like a house of refuge, which is always open for the reception of the needy and distressed. They are cheering cordials in the experience of the downcast and the doubting, whensoever they realize them. And simply by falling back on these old and tried foundations, the wavering Christian finds a firm footing, and is again reestablished. The doubts that were spreading over his mind like the gloomy clouds which portend a storm, are arrested in their progress towards confirmation or continuance; and the brief night of spiritual darkness in which he was enveloped, vanishes away before the returning dawn of the Sun of righteousness.

But before attempting to detail wherein consist the indistinct and inaccurate views which are so fruitful in the production of doubts, it is necessary to define what we understand by *the Gospel*; for, in a general sense, this one word may be said to inclose within it every form of divine truth, and to present us with the concentrated essence of all Scripture. For my own part I love to contemplate scriptural terms in that largeness of meaning with which the infinite Spirit has invested them, and which no created intellect of itself could ever have conceived. Such contemplations help to lift us out of those low and contracted thoughts which belong to our sinful and selfish nature, and to infuse into our minds expanded ideas of that unity of purpose and design on the part of God, which is manifested in *the Christ*; by whom we are taught to believe that the world was at first made, as it has been subsequently redeemed; and in whom all things both in heaven and in earth are to be gathered into one, in the dispensation of the fulness of times, Col 1:16-20; Eph 1:10.

Now, my friend, were we on the present occasion to interpret the word *Gospel* according to this very sublime meaning, we should of necessity be drawn into a large discourse on the attributes of God, which are seen to harmonize in the Christ, and *in him alone*. And, then, from the consideration of the character of God himself, we should have to look at those works wherein his character is reflected. Thus Creation and Providence and Redemption, in their connection with each other and with Christ, would successively claim some notice. Our discourse, indeed, would carry us backward beyond "the beginning," when God made the heavens and the earth by the word of his power, to that more remote period to which St.

Paul refers when he speaks of our having been chosen in Christ "before the foundation of the world," Eph 1:4. So, likewise, our discourse would carry us forward to that blissful consummation, in the truth of which we believe, and for the speedy coming of which we hope and pray, when this earth and its inhabitants shall be forever delivered from the curse of sin and from the usurped dominion of Satan, and when the redemption of both soul and body which is by Christ Jesus our Lord, shall be displayed in the eyes of an admiring universe to the praise of the glory of our great Redeemer.

These large and lofty subjects, bounded only by eternity on either side, are all comprehended within "the glorious gospel of the blessed God;" and most desirable it is that even the poorest and humblest of the flock of Christ should be well instructed in the knowledge of them, and thoroughly stablished in the faith of them. Still I grant that many Christians enjoy much peace and hope and consolation, whose views in regard to the origin and the progress and the fulness of redemption fall exceedingly short of what the Bible reveals. And I believe it is consistent with fact that the doubts which cause distress to Christians, are generally connected with those truths which more directly concern their own individual state and prospects. It will therefore sufficiently answer our present purpose to consider the Gospel in a restricted sense, as referring to *the incarnation of the Son of God in the character of our Saviour*. Most people have this, and nothing else in their thoughts, when mention is made of the Gospel. And, indeed, this is "the good tidings of great joy,"—that is, the Gospel—which the angel announced to the shepherds in the plains of Bethlehem,—"Unto you is born this day, in the city of David, a Saviour, which is Christ the Lord," Luke 2:10-11. But, oh, my dear friend, is there not contained in this simple fact, much—very much that escapes the attention of many—very many Christians? Do not "the good tidings" of a Saviour's birth involve most important truths which lie below the surface, and beyond the sphere, of that measure of research or reflection that is usually given to them?—truths which may indeed be dimly discerned, so as to cherish a fluctuating hope; but which are not so clearly understood or so firmly believed, as to afford an undoubting assurance of salvation?

Jesus, the child born at Bethlehem,—Jesus, the incarnate God,—Jesus, whom God anointed with the Holy Ghost and with power, exhibits to us, *in his person, in his work, and in his qualifications for the work*, what an inspired apostle has declared to be "the great mystery of godliness." And it may be instructive to glance at these several points in order; for I am persuaded that imperfect and inaccurate views in regard to everyone of them are prevalent, and that to this cause we may trace the doubts respecting their own salvation which continue to haunt and harass the minds of pious persons, who are nevertheless looking to Christ as the one and the only Saviour. This statement may appear to you to be contradictory, and certainly it has that appearance,—*for if the Saviour is really believed in, there ought to be the enjoyment of the salvation which is by the faith of him*; just as a sight of the sun insures our possession of his cheering light and genial warmth. But, in point of fact, many Christians will testify, that, in their own unhappy experience, this connexion between the Saviour and his salvation is not realized; and it will now be my endeavour to explain, that, in these anomalous cases we see nothing more than the natural consequences of not rightly understanding *who* the Saviour is, or *what* he has done for our deliverance from the wrath to come.

First, then, I apprehend that in regard to *the person* of Christ, there is much confusion of ideas in the minds of Christians. Ask them, Who is Christ? and ninety-nine out of a hundred will answer, He is the Son of God. Now, this short and simple reply is true as far as it goes, and a most precious truth it is that our Saviour is divine; but this reply does not express the whole truth. Something else, which is also very precious, is kept back, or, at all events, implied rather than expressed. And it seems to me, that in our anxiety to fortify ourselves against the heresy of the Unitarians, who deny the *divinity* of our Lord, and who, in doing so, leave us destitute of a spotless and all-atoning sacrifice, and of a sympathising and all-prevailing High Priest, we are apt to lose sight of his *humanity*, without which he could not have suffered unto death as our surety, nor could he have pleaded with God the all-sufficient virtue of his blood, which he did shed for the remission of our sins.

In allusion to *his divine nature*, Jesus the Christ is revealed to us as *the Word*, who was in the beginning, and who was with God, and who was God; and, as the second Person of the adorable Trinity, those names and titles are given to him which exclusively belong to the Godhead; but it particularly deserves your notice that the name *Jesus*, which signifies *Saviour*, is given to him as the child born of the Virgin Mary. "The *Word* was made flesh, and dwelt among us," St. John 1:14; and it is in especial and essential connection with *our nature* that the Son of God bears the name and executes the work of a Saviour. The angel who appeared unto Joseph in a dream, said, "Fear not to take unto thee Mary thy wife, for that which is conceived in her is of the Holy Ghost. And she shall bring forth a son, and thou shalt call his name Jesus, for he shall save his people from their sins," Matt 1:20-21. Here, then, is a truth in which our salvation is so directly involved, that, unless it is ever recognised and believed, we cannot, on scriptural grounds, entertain a sure and undoubting hope of pardon and of peace with God.

Our Saviour is as truly the Son of Mary as he is the Son of God; and it strikes me as a remarkable fact, that in the gospel history our blessed Lord so very frequently speaks of himself as "the Son of man." Has this ever attracted your attention? I believe in upwards of eighty different passages of Scripture this peculiar appellation is bestowed on our Lord Jesus Christ.

Hence we read: "The Son of man is come to save that which was lost." "The Son of man came to give his life a ransom for many." "He that soweth the good seed is the Son of man;" and at the harvest time "the Son of man shall send forth his angels." "The Son of man is Lord even of the sabbath." "The Son of man hath power on earth to forgive sins." "The Son of man shall be betrayed into the hands of men." "Likewise also shall the Son of man suffer of them." "The Son of man shall be three days and three nights in the heart of the earth." "The Son of man goeth as it is written of him." "They shall see the Son of man coming in the clouds of heaven." "The Son of man shall sit on the throne of his glory."—And I pray you to observe from these quotations which I have selected, how continually the Lord sets before us his real humanity, and how he does so in reference to all the varied departments of his work as our Prophet, Priest, and King.

But there are two passages to which you must allow me to allude more particularly. When Jesus was arraigned before the Jewish council, and when all his judges were eager for his condemnation, "the high priest answered and said unto him, I adjure thee by the living God, that thou tell us whether thou be *the Christ, the Son of God.*" This question distinctly implies that the Jews expected their predicted Messiah was to be *a divine person*—"the Son of God." Whether Jesus of Nazareth, now at their bar, was that person, is the precise object of their inquiry. And the answer which was returned by our Lord is very striking. "Jesus saith unto him, Thou hast said:" and in this way he plainly acknowledges himself to be "the Christ, the Son of God," notwithstanding the meanness of his outward condition, and the unfavourable circumstances in which he stood at their tribunal. "Thou hast said; nevertheless, I say unto you, hereafter shall ye see the Son of man sitting on the right hand of power, and coming in the clouds of heaven," Matt 26:63-64. We might have expected him to say, "However much ye despise me at present, and treat me as a malefactor, the time will come, when *the Son of God* shall appear in his glory, and then you shall know him to be your promised Messiah." But whilst he does speak of Messiah's coming glory, he speaks of that glory as belonging to *the Son of man*. Surely we ought to learn from this dying testimony of our Lord, that humanity is no less necessary than divinity to the constitution of *the Christ*, and that in his one person the divine and human natures are indissolubly united.

The same mysterious and most important truth is vividly impressed on another passage of gospel history. "When Jesus came into the coasts of Caesarea Philippi, he asked his disciples, saying, Whom do men say that I, the Son of man, am? And they said, Some say that thou art John the Baptist; some, Elias; and others, Jeremias, or one of the prophets. He saith unto them, But whom say ye that I am? And Simon Peter answered and said, Thou art the Christ, the Son of the living God. And Jesus answered and said unto him, Blessed art thou, Simon Barjona; for flesh and blood hath not revealed it unto thee, but my Father which is heaven," Matt 16:13-17. Here we find our Lord declaring himself to be *the Son of man*, at the very moment when he asks what were the current opinions concerning him: and the answer which Peter makes to the question submitted to the disciples, declares him to be *the Son of God*. This answer meets with high commendation; and thus when the question and the answer are combined, we are brought to the conclusion that *the Christ* is God and man;—not God alone, nor man alone, but the *God-man*;—"God manifested in the flesh," 1 Tim 3:16. Truly this is a mystery—a great mystery—the greatest of all mysteries, that the Creator should stoop to a creature-condition,—that God should become man; and in this mystery our salvation is wrapped up.

The babe at Bethlehem over whom a multitude of the heavenly hosts sang "glory to God in the highest, and on earth peace, goodwill toward men," was announced to the shepherds as *"A Saviour, who is Christ the Lord."* And this wondrous child had been conceived of the Holy Ghost, and born of the virgin Mary, that it might be fulfilled which was spoken of the Lord, by the prophet, saying, "Behold, a virgin shall be with child, and shall bring forth a son, and his name shall be called Emmanuel; which, being interpreted, is, *God with us,*" Matt 1:22-23. Do you not feel, my dear friend, that this word Emmanuel, is invested with an irresistible and unspeakable charm? It opens up to our view, as perishing sinners, a depth of divine condescension, and a fulness of divine compassion, of which we could not otherwise have formed a conception. It presents to our believing admiration an object which is well and wisely fitted, as it is most graciously designed, to make sin odious in our eyes, and to melt our hard hearts into penitence, and to fix our affections supremely and for ever on the holy God himself. "God with us." How astonishing! It is not God visibly present *in our world*, as with Moses at the bush which burned and was not consumed; nor as in the Shekinah which filled the tabernacle and the temple of old with glory; but it is God *in our nature*;—God "in fashion as a man," and in "the form of a servant," for the very purpose of becoming "obedient unto death, even the death of the cross," Phil 2:7-8. And herein lies the charm: "God with us" inspires the satisfactory assurance, that he who suffered for our sins in virtue of his humanity, is able to save us from sin itself and from all its consequences, in virtue of his divinity. This assurance, I wish you to observe, rests not solely on the Saviour's *sufferings as man*, on account of our sins; nor on *his mercy and power as God*, to save whom he pleases. No. But it rests equally on both of these strong pillars:—it rests on *the union* of Godhead and manhood in our Emmanuel, who not only suffered in our stead, but suffered in order to work out salvation for us, consistently with the justice and faithfulness of God.

I trust it appears quite evident to you, that an intelligent and practical recognition of *the incarnation of the Son of God* has very much to do with a scriptural and peace-giving hope of salvation. To believe that the Saviour is the Son of man at the same time that we believe him to be the Son of God, gives us a confidence in the reality of his sympathies, and in the efficacy of his suretiship, which it is impossible to obtain, if we separate from his one person the two distinct natures. And the reason is very obvious. We all feel that it is man who has sinned, and we cannot get rid of the impression that it is man who must also suffer for sin. The statements of the Bible are addressed to sinful men, and they exactly meet this feeling of our nature. For instance, we read, "For there is one God, and one mediator between God and men, *the man Christ Jesus*; who gave himself a ransom for all, to be testified in due time," 1 Tim 2:5-6. In the immediately preceding verses the apostle had spoken of our Saviour as God, who will have all men to be saved, and to come unto the knowledge of the truth. Here he speaks of the sinner's way of approach to God, and of "the ransom" through which alone there is salvation to any. And therefore the loving Mediator, who interposes between a holy God and his guilty creatures, is designated, for our encouragement, "*The man* Christ Jesus;" because it was his humanity that enabled him, as our substitute, to give himself,—to shed his blood, as the ransom price of our deliverance.*

Many other passages of a similar character will occur to you; and the more you make yourself familiar with them—the more you build yourself up in the faith of the doctrine I have been explaining—the more you will be convinced that we ought to cling to *the Saviour* revealed to us in the Gospel, as

---

*If the reader has happened to meet with a small volume entitled, *Perfect Peace; or Letters-Memorial of the late J. W. Howell, Esq.*, he may recollect that the subject of which this Letter treats was blessed in opening his mind to a clear knowledge of the gospel. The sentiment which most powerfully affected him was this: "We all feel that it is man who has sinned; and we cannot get rid of the impression, that it is man who must also suffer for sin." This taught him the importance of understanding and believing the true humanity of our Saviour.

bone of our bone, and flesh of our flesh. "For verily he took not on him the nature of angels, but he took on him the seed of Abraham:" and, "forasmuch as the children are partakers of flesh and blood, he also himself likewise took part of the same," Heb 2:14,16. This is precisely what we need and what we want. For something within tells us that he who is to be our Saviour must be *man's brother*, as well as *God's fellow*; that he who is to act the part of a Redeemer must be our kinsman. None else can legally and effectually interfere to raise us from the low estate into which we have fallen. None else can procure our discharge from the debts we have incurred by transgression against God. None else has right or authority to put us in possession of our forfeited inheritance. And I cannot help thinking that indistinct and inaccurate views on this deeply interesting and most important subject, are a cause of many doubtings in the minds of many Christians. They are well satisfied that Jesus Christ is the Saviour and the only Saviour of sinners; but how he comes to be so further than by the sovereign appointment of God, or in virtue of his own proper divinity, they do not clearly see. The doctrine of his true humanity is too much and too often overlooked. The real though mysterious union of the divine and human natures in his one person is not sufficiently realized. Their faith does not embrace "Emmanuel, which, being interpreted, is, God with us." They are unconscious of the intimate and endearing relationship in which the Saviour stands to them. They perceive not his peculiar fitness as the God-man to occupy the place of their surety. They lose the consolation of knowing how closely his manhood links him to themselves. And hence, as they do not thoroughly understand how the work of salvation has been accomplished by the Son of God in human nature, so they, as human beings, hesitate to believe that he is a Saviour to them. In looking too exclusively to his essential Deity, and in thus dangerously losing sight of his real humanity, they separate in their thoughts of him the two distinct natures of

God and man, of which he was, and still is, and ever will be possessed; and by means of this oversight or misconception in regard to *the person* of the Saviour, they fall short of the joyful assurance of their salvation by him.

These doubters, however, ought not to be charged with holding *heretical opinions*; neither should we blame them for intentionally running into any *false theory* on the subject of our Lord's person. I am aware how readily they will assent to the statements in the creeds and confessions and catechisms of our protestant Churches, wherein this fundamental point of theology is explicitly and beautifully expressed; and I also feel assured that what I have doctrinally stated to you at this time will receive their hearty concurrence as altogether scriptural. The only thing, therefore, we can lay to their charge, is, *the practical oversight* of a revealed truth, which they neither deny nor dislike, but the importance of which they have not been taught to value. They are only to be blamed when they make no exertion for the removal of the misconception or mistake into which they have inadvertently been drawn, and which has so direct a tendency to keep them in a state of depressing doubt and suspense, as to their personal salvation. Clearer views of *"the Gospel"* would deliver them from the bondage under which they labour. Increased light respecting the inseparable union of divinity and humanity in the one person of the Saviour, would dispel the mist in which they find themselves so painfully enveloped. When the promised Spirit of truth becomes their teacher, and brings them clearly to understand, and habitually to believe, that "God was manifested in the flesh" for the very purpose of destroying Satan and sin and death, they will then learn how this "great mystery" contains the elemental principle which preeminently displays the wisdom and goodness of the God of infinite holiness, and out of which there springs a free and perfect and everlasting salvation to sinners of mankind. Then their own experience will testify to the blessedness of this one truth, as supplying materials for the angelic song of praise,—"Glory to God in the highest, on earth peace, and goodwill to man." Yes, my friend, it is indeed a blessed thing to know, not only in what the gospel salvation consists, but in what way it has been effected; and more blessed still it is to know, that we ourselves are partakers of it. But it is vain to expect the acquisition and enjoyment of this knowledge, which so intimately concerns our present peace and eternal felicity, unless we first of all know and believe that Jesus Christ the Saviour is at once "the Son of God" and "the Son of man."

When our Lord said to Peter, "Wherefore didst thou doubt, O thou of little faith," he taught us, in a general way, apart from the particular occasion on which this reproof was uttered, that doubts proceed from "little faith." And you will allow me to remind you, that, according to the scriptural meaning of the word "faith" is to be considered in two points of view. It is either the inward principle or the outward object. It is either something external to ourselves which we believe, or it is our own belief of the truths that are presented to us. And is it not true, that, in both of these senses,—in respect to *the degree* in which the principle of faith is exercised, and in respect likewise to *the amount* of truth to which the principle is directed—"little faith" is always productive of doubts. Thus you will perceive that although a man's faith may not be defective as to the exercise of the principle, yet it must necessarily be "little," in every case where the knowledge of divine truth is defective. And before faith can be large, as well as strong, so as to guard us against the intrusion, or, at all events, against the continuance of doubts, there must be enlarged as well as enlightened views of the gospel. Our first aim should be to have accurate and distinct views; but we ought not to stop short in our pursuit of the truth, until our views are comprehensive of all that is revealed. Knowledge is at once the foundation and the boundary of faith. We may indeed know much which we do not believe; but it is out of our power to believe what we do not know.

My remarks on this first particular have been extended beyond what you, perhaps, may deem necessary. I have judged it prudent, however, to spend the more time in a plain and scriptural exhibition of "the truth as it is in Jesus," in reference to the constitution of his *person*, because it is doubly important to have clear and correct views on a point of doctrine, which is decidedly fundamental. It is self-evident, that, if we do not rightly understand *who* the Saviour is, we shall find all the greater difficulty in rightly understanding *what* he has done for our salvation, In every enterprise in which we engage, and in any hope of success which we cherish, we are wanting in ordinary wisdom, unless we have satisfied ourselves that the foundation on which we are building is sure and solid. This ought especially to be the case in a matter so momentous as is our safety and happiness for eternity. And yet is there not too much reason to fear that *the real groundwork* of all Christian character, and Christian enjoyment, and Christian expectation, is not sufficiently attended to on the part either of ministers or hearers? St. Paul says to the Corinthians, "Other foundation can no man lay than that is laid, which is *Jesus, the Christ*," 1 Cor 3:11: and in a similar strain he addresses the Ephesians, "Ye are built upon the foundation of the apostles and prophets, *Jesus Christ himself* being the chief cornerstone," Eph 2:20. It cannot escape your observation, that in these passages, *the person* of the Saviour is what the apostle presents to us rather than *his work*. Not, however, that he wishes these two things to be disjoined. For the peculiar person of the Christ was only preparatory to the peculiar work which was given him to do; and the work, apart from his person, would resemble a house without a foundation. It is well to combine the two together in our thoughts of Christ. Nevertheless, when we carefully look into the Scriptures, we find, that if the Gospel is to be stated in a short sentence, or in a single word, the inspired penmen resort to such modes of expression as the verses just quoted contain. Here is no mention of the righteousness of Christ for justification, nor of his atonement, nor of his intercession, nor of his Holy Spirit of promise for sanctification and adoption. But the one "foundation" on which the whole church, as a vast spiritual building, rests, and on which rest also each individual believer's hopes towards God of pardon and acceptance, is "*Jesus, the Christ*:" yea, the stability of the foundation, "the chief cornerstone," is "*Jesus Christ himself.*" And, in my apprehension, we miss the mark altogether, if we do not perceive that *the person* of the Saviour was chiefly in the mind of the apostle—and we may say, in the mind of the Spirit, who guided the apostle, when these portions of Scripture were penned.

At the commencement of this Letter, I adverted to the Gospel which was proclaimed to the shepherds on the plains of Bethlehem. The joyful information imparted to them concerned *the person* of the Saviour. They were told that the virgin had brought forth a son,—that a man-child had been born: and the glad tidings, "the gospel," consisted in the fact that *this child was Christ, the Saviour*. Throughout the Letter, I have endeavoured to show you how essentially the true humanity of our Lord enters into his character as a Saviour, and how prominently it is exhibited in the Holy Scriptures. And now, at the conclusion of my Letter, I hope I do not tire you with an earnest reiteration of the same most wondrous and most glorious fact. The Saviour whom the Gospel reveals is *God and man in two distinct natures, and one person forever*. This peculiar constitution of his person forms the basis of the whole active and passive obedience of our Lord; and must therefore be the real groundwork of whatever constitutes Christian character in us who believe, or affords us Christian comfort. Ministers too seldom introduce this subject into their pulpit instructions; and the Christian people too often neglect to feed upon it in their private readings and meditations. Thus many Christians are disturbed and discouraged with doubts which would have no existence, were their views of this great fundamental truth clear, and accurate, and habitual. For my own part, I feel that unless my faith embraces Jesus Christ, *the God-man*, I am not believing *the Gospel*. Whenever I forget that the Son of God took upon him my nature, my perception of his acts as my surety becomes obscure; and I am at a loss to understand how my sins should be laid upon him, or how he should suffer unto death in my stead. I dare not lose my hold of his divinity—no, not for a moment, else my hopes of salvation entirely perish. But unless, at the same time, I cling with grateful constancy to his humanity, I cannot enjoy the assurance that he is a Saviour to me. Am I wrong in supposing that your experience corresponds with mine?

Ever yours, etc.

LETTER 15

RELIGIOUS CAUSES OF DOUBTS—Continued

II. IMPERFECT AND INACCURATE VIEWS OF THE WORK OF CHRIST, AND OF HIS QUALIFICATIONS FOR THE WORK

The *work* of Christ a subject of great magnitude and importance.—His *official qualifications* a distinct subject.—The two are necessarily connected, but may be separately treated.—When the work is not clearly understood, the belief of it must partake of the same uncertain character.—The *work* of Christ, as well as his *person*, is wonderful.—Its extent and blessedness are learnt only from isolated texts.—The sufferings of Christ were sacrificial and vicarious.—*The death of God's beloved Son is life to us.*—The word "death" is significant of sin and its deserts; and the word "life" comprehends the whole gospel salvation.—The Son of God came to *save* that which was *lost*.—He delivers from sin.—He justifies, sanctifies, glorifies, the believer.—Doubts arise from inaccurate views of salvation as a *present* blessing, and as a work in itself *complete*.—The *qualifications* of Christ for effecting the salvation of sinners.—*God anointed him with the Holy Ghost and with power.*—As the God-man he was *fitted* to be the Mediator, but he was publicly and solemnly *authorized* to act, and *qualified* for acting, only by his anointing.—This truth is much overlooked.—Confused, or obscure views of it must cause doubts.—God is glorified in providing a qualified Saviour as well as a complete salvation.—The understanding of this is necessary to the stability of our faith.

My dear Friend,

I resume the subject upon which we entered in the last Letter; and unquestionably it is a subject of extreme importance. Indeed, I am oppressed with the feeling, not only of its importance, but of its magnitude. For, of a truth, in adverting to *the work* which the incarnate Son of God has undertaken in our behalf, a volume would be requisite for its rightful elucidation, whereas I must limit my remarks to one part of a Letter, which it is intended shall likewise take some notice of the *official qualifications* of our Saviour. These two things—his work as a Saviour, and his qualifications for successfully accomplishing the work, are quite distinct, although intimately and necessarily connected. And they who have not attained clear and correct views on each of them, can scarcely be expected to escape from the cloudy atmosphere of doubts. We shall, therefore, have to treat first of the one, and afterwards of the other. But even then, another important particular will demand consideration in a separate and concluding Letter; for certainly our subject, as a whole, would be left unfinished, unless there was a special allusion to *the warrant* which every sinner has to believe in the Lord Jesus Christ as his own Saviour. Confused and unscriptural views on this last point alone involve many otherwise well-informed Christians in the meshes of perplexing and harassing doubt.

Thus you see, my friend, we have still before us a large and inviting field for investigation whilst we prosecute our researches into the causes of the doubts which are so prevalent among the people of God. I sincerely regret, however, that our researches must now be conducted on a very circumscribed scale; and that we can only attempt to gather up, from the fruitful field which lies before us, such of the precious truths it contains, as chiefly concern the personal salvation of believers.

Now, then, if it is true, that imperfect and inaccurate views in regard to *the person* of Christ are productive of much doubt among those who nevertheless look to him as the only Saviour, and consequently of much injury to the peace and prosperity of doubting Christians, it is not less true, and I may add, it is far more apparent, that doubts must abound when *the work* which Christ has accomplished for sinners is not clearly and fully discerned; for unless we distinctly understand what he has already done, and what he is still doing, in the character of a Saviour, we cannot possibly understand in what the gospel salvation consists; and in such circumstances, although there may be a sufficiency of grace to enable us—yea, to incline us to exercise faith, there is a want of that sufficient knowledge which is essential to the stability of our faith. This, I think, is indisputable. In point of fact, we find that wherever views of gospel truth are dim and shadowy, the belief of them partakes of the same uncertain and unsatisfactory character; and, on this account, a painful state of doubt respecting one's own salvation cannot be avoided, unless a thorough knowledge is possessed of that great work which the Saviour has undertaken and achieved.

"*Jesus, the Christ*," deserves the name of "*Wonderful*" in respect of his *work* just as much as of his *person*. Indeed, the one is divinely prepared for the other. They both exactly harmonize; both are mysterious, and both are indispensable. No less, and no other, a work than that which the Gospel reveals to us, would have answered the purpose of recovering a lost world, and of saving perishing sinners; and no other a person than *Emmanuel*,—"God with us"—"God manifested in the flesh"—could have performed a work actually so arduous, and apparently so hopeless. Oh, then, let us with ceaseless humility, gratitude, and praise, admire and adore the infinite wisdom, and goodness, and power, displayed in contriving and executing the salvation of guilty men in a way that preeminently redounds to the glory of the justice and holiness of God!

But the question before us at present is, what is this wonderful work? what has the incarnate Son of God done for sinners of mankind? To the Bible we turn for an answer, and there we can find no formal, or lengthened, or systematic account of it in any one place; but brief announcements, short sayings, isolated sentences,—bearing on the general subject, and descriptive of some one or other of its many aspects, and its varied departments, and its precious blessings,—meet our eye in glancing over almost every page. On different occasions we hear our Lord himself declaring, "The Son of man is delivered into the hands of men, and they shall kill him, and after that he is killed, he shall rise the third day," Mark 9:31. "Ought not the Christ to have suffered these things, and to enter into his glory?" Luke 24:26. "I am the living bread which came down from heaven: if any man eat of this bread, he shall live for ever; and the bread that I will give is my flesh, which I will give for the life of the world," John 6:51. "I am the good Shepherd: the good Shepherd giveth his life for the sheep," John 10:11. "I am the Vine, ye are the branches; he that abideth in me, and I in him, the same bringeth forth much fruit; for without me ye can do nothing," John 15:5. "I am the resurrection and the life: he that believeth in me, though he were dead, yet shall he live; and whosoever liveth and believeth in me shall never die," John 11:25-26. And these declarations of our Lord are explained, and illustrated, and enforced by prophets and apostles. John the Baptist, pointing to the Saviour, says, "Behold the Lamb of God who taketh away the sin of the world," John 1:29. Isaiah says, "The Lord hath laid on him the iniquity of us all;" and, "He was wounded for our transgressions; he was bruised for our iniquities; the chastisement of our peace was upon him; and with his stripes we are healed," Isa 53:5-6. St. Peter says, "Who his own self bare our sins in his own body on the tree, that we, being dead to sin, should live unto righteousness;" and again, "For Christ also hath once suffered for sins, the just for the unjust, that he might bring us unto God," 1 Pet 2:24; and 1 Pet 3:18. St. John says, "For this purpose the Son of God was manifested, that he might destroy the works of the devil;" "And ye know that he was manifested, to take away our sins;" and again, "The blood of Jesus Christ cleanseth us from all sin," 1 John 1:7; 1 John 3:5,8. The testimonies of St. Paul to the same effect are strong and numerous throughout his epistles. He speaks of Christ as "having loved us, and given himself for us an offering and a sacrifice to God for a sweet-smelling savour;" "in whom we have redemption through his blood, the forgiveness of sins, according to the riches of his grace," Eph 1:7; Eph 5:2. Christ "gave himself for our sins, that he might deliver us from this present evil world," Gal 1:4. "Jesus, who delivered us from the wrath to come," 1 Thess 1:10. "Christ has redeemed us from the curse of the law, being made a curse for us," Gal 3:13. "For he hath made Christ to be sin for us who knew no sin, that we might be made the righteousness of God in him," 2 Cor 5:21. "But of him are ye in Christ Jesus, who of God is made unto us wisdom, and righteousness, and sanctification, and redemption," 1 Cor 1:30. And to these important quotations I shall only add one more: "God hath saved us, and called us with an holy calling, not according to our works, but according to his own purpose and grace, which was given us in Christ Jesus before the world began; but is now made manifest by the appearing of our Saviour Jesus Christ, who hath abolished death, and brought life and immortality to light through the gospel," 2 Tim 1:9-10.

I offer no apology for introducing this long catalogue of texts. It is incumbent upon us, as believers, *to live by the faith of the Son of God*; and it is from such choice flowers as I have culled from the garden of truth, that faith extracts the very nectar of life, spiritual and eternal; and I feel assured that were Christian people more prayerfully conversant with the simple and unadulterated statements of Scripture, and less entangled with the erring commentaries of men, and with the ever-shifting experience of their own hearts, the number of doubts and of doubters would be greatly reduced.

The passages now quoted, and others of a similar character which will occur to yourself, represent the Saviour of sinners as a sufferer, and as suffering in our stead, and for our deliverance. It is quite evident that his sufferings, even unto the death of the cross, were *sacrificial and substitutionary or vicarious*. He was the spotless lamb to whom *our* sins were transferred. And the shedding of *his* blood was the expiation of *our* guilt,—the atonement for *our* trespasses,—the means of *our* reconciliation unto God,—and the price paid for *our* redemption in soul and body, from sin and Satan, and death and hell. Is not this a wonderful work? *The death of God's beloved Son is life to us.* This is, in one word, the substance of all that he did, and of all that he gives. But who can estimate the value of that gift? Who can comprehend the mystery of such doings on our behalf? The Son of God in dying for us fulfilled all righteousness, and testified the perfection of his holy obedience, and magnified the holy law of God, and endured its severest penalty; and all this he did "that God might be just, and the justifier of him which believeth in Jesus," Rom 3:26. But still more: by his own death "he abolished death," and "destroyed him that had the power of death, that is the devil," Heb 2:14. These were glorious victories over *our* enemies, and for *our* benefit they were achieved. And now "Christ being raised from the dead, dieth no more: death hath no more dominion over him. For in that he died, he died unto sin once; but in that he liveth, he liveth unto God," Rom 6:9-10. These sayings of the apostle subsequent to the death of our Lord throw light on his own sayings while he was yet alive. "For as the Father hath life in himself, so hath he given to the Son to have life in himself." "For as the Father raiseth up the dead, and quickeneth them, even so the Son quickeneth whom he will," John 5:21,26. Thus we have the blissful assurance that although "the wages of sin is death," and all of us have earned these direful wages, yet "the gift of God" to us poor dying sinners "is eternal life through Jesus Christ our Lord," Rom 6:23.

Nothing is deemed so valuable as life: "yea, all that a man

hath will he give for his life," Job 2:4. This is the reason why our Saviour so frequently sums up the whole of salvation in this one word, *life*. "He that believeth on the Son hath everlasting life: and he that believeth not the Son shall not see life; but the wrath of God abideth on him," John 3:36. As sinners we are justly exposed to *death*; and Christ would be no Saviour at all if he did not deliver us from the awfulness of this condition. Newness of life here: resurrection life hereafter: a never-ending participation in the glory of the glorified Redeemer: an eternity of existence in the presence of God, where there is fulness of joy: this is the crowning blessing of the Gospel. And this, the greatest of all, includes within it every lesser and subordinate blessing; and stamps its own high character on the whole.

It is not, however, with mere generalities that we ought to be satisfied. The absence of precise and specific knowledge respecting the work of Christ, is the very thing which impoverishes faith, whilst it cherishes continued misgivings and doubts. If then you inquire, what are those various blessings which in the aggregate constitute the gospel salvation?—what are the component parts of that complete work, which the incarnate Son of God, as our Saviour, has accomplished? I must endeavour to make my reply as distinct and as short as the subject will admit of.

The salvation which the Gospel reveals is in every respect commensurate with our necessities as guilty, and accountable, and immortal creatures. The Son of God came down from heaven "*to save that which was lost*." Naturally we are all in a "lost" condition by means of sin:—*lost*! No word could more forcibly express our utter helplessness and hopelessness. And the appropriateness of this strong expression must be acknowledged, when it is considered that, 1. We stand chargeable to God with *the guilt* of innumerable offences against him; 2. We are so enslaved by *the power of sin*, that we cannot cease sinning; and 3. We are justly liable to *the punishment* which sin deserves, and from which we have in ourselves no possible way of escape. But Jesus Christ *saves* us. This word is also very forcible. Jesus Christ does not give us directions what we ought to do for our own deliverance from our sinful state of being, nor does he help us to carry his directions into effect. But he himself acts as our *Saviour*. *He* has wrought out for us an effectual deliverance not only from punishment, but from sin itself, and therefore his salvation is a present, as well as a future and eternal blessing. He secures our discharge from guilt, and he undertakes that sin shall not have the dominion over us. Thus, from the very moment that faith in the Saviour is first exercised, there is a partial enjoyment in this world of that great salvation which will only be fully enjoyed in the world to come.

You will observe there are two features in the work of Christ, which, if clearly perceived and honestly believed, must go far to banish doubts from the mind, and to confirm us in the happy assurance that by grace we are saved. The one is the entire completeness of the work, and the other is its instant commencement. Each of these distinguishing features claims our marked and grateful attention; for in each of them it is the believer's privilege to confide and rejoice. Allow me to offer a few explanations.

We have already seen that the whole of salvation is described under the emblem of "life;" and Christ himself is said to be "our life," because he is our Saviour. Now, in beautiful contrast with this, "death" is the emblem employed to represent a state of sin. Mankind are described in Scripture as "dead in trespasses and sins:" and it is true not only that the wages of sin is death, but that sin itself is death. Sin is separation from God, who alone is self-existent. Sin has robbed us of the image of God, in which our original creation was adorned. Sin has disordered our whole understanding, will, and affections, so that we neither live in God, nor to God. God is dethroned from our hearts, and sin has acquired the mastery over us. Thus it is that we are sinners. Sin is our state of being; and on the highest authority we know that he "that liveth in sin, is dead while he liveth." There is a spiritual death which preys upon all men, unless they have been quickened by the power of the Saviour's Spirit; a death under which they *now* lie, and which will be succeeded hereafter by what the Scriptures call "the second death"—that fearful state of torment, where the gnawing worm of a self-condemning conscience never dies, and where the raging fire of divine wrath is never quenched.

But the Saviour says, "He that heareth my word, and believeth on him that sent me, *hath* everlasting life, and shall not come into condemnation; *but is passed from death unto life,*" John 5:24. The believer in Jesus is no longer dead. *He has life*: and this life is holiness. He is renewed in the image of the holy God. He is a new creature in Christ Jesus. The power of sin is subdued by the greater power of divine grace. The heart is purified from the love of sin. The love of God and of holiness is implanted. There is reunion with God; and there is also communion with him. This is the true life of the creature. This is holiness; and it is part of the work of Christ. "He is made of God unto us—*sanctification.*" Our holiness is in Christ. We are sanctified by the belief of the truth as it is in Jesus. The belief of who he is, and what he has done for us, gives activity to the emotion of love, and love impels us onward in a course of holy and cheerful obedience. Moreover, Christ dwells in our hearts by faith. He sends his Spirit to enlighten and to sanctify us, and to witness to our adoption as the sons and daughters of the Lord Almighty. In this way we are guided and strengthened in following after holiness. This is passing from death unto life. It is heaven begun upon earth. It is the commencement of that blessedness which is to endure throughout eternity.

The "sanctification" which is an essential part of the work of Christ in every believer, begins now, although it is never perfected on this side the grave. The beauty of holiness in the best of men is sadly disfigured by many shortcomings and inconsistencies. But neither present holiness, supposing it were perfect, nor future holiness, which certainly will be perfect, would be availing for our salvation, unless it were accompanied with the pardon of past sin. A free and full forgiveness is indispensable. Without this no sinner can be saved; but this is another part of the work of Christ. And it is the untiring delight of the redeemed in heaven and on earth to ascribe praise and glory "unto Him that loved them, and washed them from their sins in his blood." More than mere pardon, however, is necessary. We must be acquitted of the charge of guilt,—we must be accepted as righteous in the sight of God, before we can share the privileges of his children, or be admitted as members of his household; and how this can be achieved is the grand problem of which the gospel alone furnishes a solution. Here is an obstacle to our salvation which no created wisdom could have removed. For the holiness of God can enter into no compromise with sin; and the justice of God demands satisfaction for every offence; and the faithfulness of God stands pledged for the execution of his righteous sentence,—"the soul that sinneth it shall die." How then can sin be punished, and yet the sinner be saved? To this momentous question we have a ready answer. Jesus Christ is made of God unto us—"righteousness." He, the Holy One and the Just, who knew no sin, "was made sin for us," that we, who have no righteousness of our own, "might be made the righteousness of God in him." This is marvellous indeed; and yet every Christian must feel, that, unless the Son of God had taken upon him our nature, he could not have stood forth as our surety; and unless he had, in our stead, most righteously fulfilled the law of God, both in its precepts and in its penalties, he could not have been our Saviour. But it is a most blessed truth that "Christ is the end of the law for righteousness to every one that believeth," Rom 10:4. Hence it is that we are "*justified* freely by the grace of God through the redemption that is in Christ Jesus," Rom 3:24. And justification includes both pardon and acquittal.

And now, my dear friend, I trust these explanations, brief and imperfect as they are, clearly indicate the amount of *present blessing* which every believer in Christ enjoys. We are justified and sanctified. And I trust, also, that enough has been said to show the nature of these precious blessings, and in what way they are obtained, and wherein they differ one from the other, and how they coexist and cooperate. Then, be it remembered, that when justified and sanctified through the faith of Jesus Christ our Lord, we are "alive unto God." Spiritual life has been breathed into our souls. And this is at once the precursor of, and the preparation for, the life which is to come,—the life which is never to end: and of the glory and blessedness of which we can only say, that the eye hath not seen, nor the ear heard, neither hath it entered into the heart of man to conceive, what God hath prepared for them that love him.

It thus appears that the component parts of that work which "the Lord our righteousness" has effected for us, and of which his Father and our Father has signified his approval, are, 1. Justification, that is, pardon and righteousness; 2. Sanctification, including adoption; and 3. Eternal life, which embraces both soul and body in resurrection and heavenly glory. Or, to state the answer in conformity with the question in its other shape, the Gospel salvation consists of a free and entire and everlasting deliverance from sin, 1. in its natural and contracted guilt; 2. in its domineering and defiling influence; and 3. in its consequences both now and forever. And truly this is a "great salvation:" truly *the work* of Christ is as great a mystery as is *his person*. Nor should we forget that in all the deep humiliation to which he voluntarily stooped, as our Saviour, he proved the overflowings of his own love to us, and at the same time carried into effect the predeterminate counsel and loving purpose of God. If we really understand what "God manifested in the flesh" has done for us, and why it has been done, we must, in admiring and adoring gratitude, confess that *it is a complete work*. It admits neither of enlargement nor of diminution; it cannot be amended; it must not be altered. And the belief of its completeness in itself, and of its divine adaptation to our circumstances as lost sinners, inspires the assurance that in Christ we are saved.

But many Christians have not this assurance. They are weighed down with doubts, and among the principal causes of their doubts, we need not hesitate to place a want of correct and scriptural views of the work of Christ. They do not seem to comprehend how much there is of *present blessing* in the gospel salvation; and therefore they are deprived of its sanctifying enjoyments. They are always talking of salvation as *future*,—as a thing which is only to be realized in the next world. We seldom hear them express more than a hope that *they may be saved*; and in this way they are excluded from the consolation and the stability and the holiness, too, which there is in knowing that God *hath saved us* according to his mercy in Christ Jesus; and that he who hath the Son *hath life*; and that *now* we are the sons of God, although it doth not yet appear what we shall be.

Wherever doubts exist as to a present participation in gospel blessings, they may be ascribed, in a great measure, to inaccurate and confused ideas in regard to *the completeness* of that salvation which is by the faith of Jesus Christ our Lord. I fear it is too often the case that partially enlightened Christians look to the Saviour for the pardon of their sins, without looking to him for justifying righteousness. They do not perceive that his active obedience was as much on their account as were his sufferings unto the death; and that both were alike necessary for procuring our acceptance with God. Hence they strive and labour, in one way or another, to add something of their own to that work of his which is perfect. And this again drives them farther away from a true and simple rest in Christ. They mistake the meaning of *justification*, and they will not believe that they are justified in the sight of God "freely through the redemption that is in Christ Jesus," until they have satisfactory evidence of the reality of their *sanctification*. Now, in all this there is a positive misconception and mistrust of the Saviour's work. It may be unintentional, as we believe it is through ignorance. But such is the fact of the case, to whatever cause it may be assigned. The nature and amount of that work which Christ has accomplished in their behalf is not clearly understood by many Christians. Hence they do not, and indeed cannot firmly believe in him. They halt and hesitate. They give way to doubts and fears. And this mistrust of the Saviour acts and reacts along with an unacknowledged, and perhaps unconscious, leaning to something commendable in themselves. Professedly their dependence for salvation is on Christ alone. But practically they do not know him as a *complete Saviour*; nor are they trusting in him as *all their salvation*.

I must now hasten to another cause of prevailing doubts, —a cause which is seldom noticed, but which I am persuaded operates with no inconsiderable power, and to an extent not easily ascertained. I allude to imperfect and inaccurate views of *the official qualifications* of our Lord to act the part of a Saviour.

In regard to this particular point of Christian doctrine, I feel safe in affirming that the views entertained of it are even more defective than of the person and of the work of Christ, on which we have been animadverting. And, indeed, you may have met, as I have often done, with true believers whose attention never had been directed to this subject at all. I confess this was the case with myself for a long time. It is usually thought that the Divinity of our Lord of itself accounts for his ability to save, and invests all his work as a Saviour with the efficiency of Omnipotence. Of the design and the consequences of his being anointed with the Holy Ghost, Christians in general are ill informed, and many know nothing about it. Yet this is a subject expressly revealed. It is a subject, too, of vast importance in itself, and a believing knowledge of it tends in an eminent degree to remove doubts respecting the all-sufficiency of Christ as a Saviour, and to build us up in a stedfast and unwavering confidence in that salvation which he has wrought out.

We may suppose the questions to be asked,—on what occasion, and for what purposes, was our Lord anointed? Do you not think, my friend, that very many professedly Christian people would be at a loss for the right answers? The only anointing that would suggest itself to their recollection, would probably be that which is recorded to have taken place in the house of Simon the pharisee, Luke 7:36; or of Simon the leper, Matt 26:6; or at Bethany, where Lazarus sat at meat with him, John 12:3. The women who anointed the head or the feet of our Lord on these occasions used the most precious ointment they could procure, and their object was simply to testify for him the sincerity of their respect and esteem, and the strength of their affection and gratitude. These anointings were altogether complimentary. There was nothing official in them. They were the private acts of private individuals. They conveyed no virtue; neither did they confer any authority. But my questions refer to an anointing of a totally different description. And what that special anointing was we shall find explained in part of St. Peter's discourse to Cornelius at Caesarea. The apostle says, "The word which God sent unto the children of Israel, preaching peace by Jesus Christ; (he is Lord of all;) that word, I say, ye know, which was published throughout all Judea, and began from Galilee, after the baptism which John preached: *How God anointed Jesus of Nazareth with the Holy Ghost, and with power*; who went about doing good, and healing all who were oppressed of the devil; for God was with him," Acts 10:36-38.

Here it is asserted as an undeniable and important fact, that our Lord had been solemnly and officially anointed. His anointing was of no ordinary kind. He was anointed not with ointment, but with the Holy Ghost: not by the hands of men or women, but by God himself. And St. Peter refers to this anointing, not only as something which had been so extensively published through the country, that he supposes Cornelius and his friends could not be ignorant of it; but as a fundamental point of Christian doctrine, with which he deemed it necessary to commence his discourse to this first family of Gentile believers. He does indeed declare that "Jesus of Nazareth" is "Lord of all," leading his hearers to the conviction that the Saviour, through whom he preached peace to them, was God and man. Thus the mysterious union of the divine and human natures in the one person of *the Christ*, was plainly set before them as an article of faith, and as a ground of encouragement and hope. But the grand peculiarity in the history of Jesus, to which the apostle adverts, is this,—"*how God anointed him with the Holy Ghost, and with power.*" And from the prominence given to this fact in the narrative, we cannot evade the conclusion, that these Gentile inquirers after salvation were invited to embrace a Saviour, who, in addition to the wondrous adaptation of his person to the office of Mediator between God and man, was divinely consecrated, or set apart, and likewise thoroughly replenished with every needful qualification, for discharging the arduous duties of his office. But I apprehend that this one circumstance, to which St. Peter attached so much importance, and which obtained so prominent a place in primitive discourses, is now very commonly and unhappily overlooked. Christians now-a-days are not in the habit of considering either the reality, or the necessity, or the nature, or the objects, or the results, of that official anointing which our Lord received. And I regard this ignorance or neglect of a truth so plainly revealed, and in itself so precious, as one of the causes for the prevalence of doubts among believers.

Now then, my dear friend, let us keep in mind the recorded fact, that Jesus of Nazareth was anointed;—anointed of God,—and anointed with the Holy Ghost. But still the questions which we supposed to be asked, remain unanswered;—on what occasion, and for what purposes, did this anointing take place? At some future period I may attempt to unfold the fulness of scriptural truth which lies wrapt up within these questions. For the present you must be content with a very brief reply.

In perusing the Evangelists, it cannot have escaped your observation, what a constant work of the Spirit there was on our blessed Emmanuel, from his conception in the womb of the Virgin, even until his resurrection from the womb of the grave. But it is beyond dispute, that, however numerous and important were the operations of the Holy Ghost within him or upon him, his public and solemn and official anointing took place on the banks of the Jordan, immediately after his baptism with water by John. Then and there, in the midst of assembled multitudes, God the Spirit visibly descended on Jesus of Nazareth "in a bodily shape like a dove," whilst at the same moment the voice of God the Father was audibly heard to declare, "This is my beloved Son, in whom I am well pleased."

There is an awful and indescribable grandeur in this transaction between the several persons in the glorious and adorable Godhead. Here we have Father, Son, and Holy Ghost, most impressively exhibited to our faith; not merely in the unity of their distinct and individual existence, but as a mysterious Trinity, harmonizing in their wondrous preparations for effecting the destruction of sin and Satan, and for securing the complete and eternal salvation of guilty men. The evangelists, Matthew, Mark, and Luke, agree in their statements, that the voice of God was really heard addressing his incarnate Son, and that the Spirit of God was really seen in a visible form descending and remaining upon him, precisely at that period of his history when his great mediatorial work as Prophet, Priest, and King, was about to commence. But these very extraordinary occurrences are veiled under that peculiar simplicity of narrative which distinguishes the Bible from all other books. And I imagine it not unfrequently happens, that, in regard to the portions of Scripture which detail these occurrences, the attention is so much arrested by the condescension of our Lord in requiring to be baptized with water by the hands of John, that the far more wonderful and momentous baptism of the Holy Ghost, which he received from God on the same occasion, is almost, if not entirely, lost sight of. It was, however, at that particular time, and in that remarkable manner, that our Lord was formally installed into the office of Mediator and Redeemer. Nor was this merely a ceremonial installation. Unlike that anointing with holy oil, which had been used by divine appointment in the consecration of prophets, priests, and kings, under the law; and which was only an outward and visible emblem of those inward and spiritual endowments, which were necessary for a faithful and successful discharge of their respective duties; Jesus of Nazareth was anointed with the Holy Ghost, and with power. To him, as Mediator, all judgment was committed, and on him also the plenitude of the Spirit's gifts was bestowed, that in the faithful exercise of the authority with which he was intrusted, and in the successful execution of the work for which he was set apart, all men should honour the Son, even as they honour the Father. Thus the purposes to be subserved by his anointing were most important. For in this way alone it was that Jesus became duly authorized to act, and likewise divinely qualified for acting, as our Saviour.

Some persons object to these statements. They think it dishonours the Son of God to assert that he needed the gifts of the Spirit to qualify him for accomplishing man's salvation. But such objections arise out of those imperfect and inaccurate views of gospel truth, which are prolific of doubts, and which hinder many Christians from attaining that assurance of their own salvation, which is so essential to their spiritual comfort.

Nothing, I apprehend, is more clearly revealed, than the

subordinate position which the eternal Word occupied, when he became incarnate. In respect of his divine personality, he could truthfully affirm, "I and my Father are one;" but in reference to his mediatorship, and as "Jesus the Christ," it behoved him to acknowledge, "My Father is greater than I." The God-man was the righteous servant of Jehovah. As a servant, his character and work were delineated by the ancient prophets. And when, "in the fulness of time," he appeared on earth, he continually represented himself as having been sent from heaven to do the will of his Father. He tells us again and again that he said nothing, and did nothing, of himself. He only performed that work which was given him to do: and even the words which he spake, and the doctrine which he taught, were acknowledged to have been not his own, but his who sent him. And it seems to be impossible rightly to understand either the official character in which he is revealed, or the vicarious service he so acceptably rendered unto God, unless we look to him as a servant duly commissioned and thoroughly furnished. I do believe there is a great depth of truth in what I now state to you, respecting the Saviour; and it teaches me to recognise the anointing he received at Jordan, before he entered on his public ministry, as that one memorable and distinguishing event, which marked him out as the promised *Messias*.

I expect that you also will be confirmed in the same persuasion, by a little attention to the declaration of John the Baptist on the subject. "John bare record, saying, I saw the Spirit descending from heaven like a dove, and it abode upon him (Jesus). And I knew him not; but he that sent me to baptize with water, the same said unto me, Upon whom thou shalt see the Spirit descending, and remaining on him, the same is he which baptizeth with the Holy Ghost. And I saw and bare record that this is the Son of God," John 1:32-34. The testimony here given is plain and explicit. Although the Baptist was nearly related to Jesus, and of course well acquainted with all the circumstances of his miraculous birth, yet he informs us it was only by that descent of the Spirit upon him, which he had witnessed, that he knew him to be the Son of God. And it was not until Jesus had received this extraordinary anointing that John could point to him, and say to the surrounding crowd, "Behold the Lamb of God!"—"Behold the Lamb of God, which taketh away the sin of the world!"

I consider the conviction wrought in the mind of the Baptist, and the open avowal of it which followed, as a clear and certain proof how important it is to know, that the Saviour in whom we believe for salvation was anointed of God with the Holy Ghost. Neither can I omit to mention, what strikes me as a peculiarly interesting incident illustrative of the same truth, that Andrew, one of the two disciples of John who were present when he spake of Jesus as "the Lamb of God," on finding his brother Simon, immediately said unto him, "We have found *the Messias*, which is, being interpreted, *the Christ*," John 1:41. And thus, my dear friend, you cannot fail to perceive, that it was the knowledge of his having been anointed which led men to believe and to confess, that Jesus of Nazareth was the long-promised and long-expected Messiah;—the Son of God, and the Saviour of the world.

Now you are aware that both of these two words, Messias and Christ, signify *anointed*. The one word is derived from the Hebrew language, and the other from the Greek. But it ought on no account to be forgotten, that the wondrous person, whose coming was predicted in the character of Prophet, Priest, and King, was familiarly known by the title of Messiah, only in consequence of being revealed as the anointed servant of God, for the accomplishment of his own gracious designs towards fallen man. And in very many passages of the New Testament, the meaning would be more apparent, and more emphatic too, were the word Christ translated into English, instead of being used as an appellative. For example, turn to the speech of Martha, when our Lord conversed with her at the grave of Lazarus, John 11:27. "Yea, Lord: I believe that thou art *the anointed*, the Son of God, which should come into the world." See also Matt 16:16, and John 6:69. When Peter declares that Jesus was *"the anointed*, the Son of the living God;" of which truth, he says, "we believe and are sure;" we are naturally carried back to the time when he and his brother Andrew both became the disciples of Jesus, because in him who had been baptized with the Holy Ghost they "found the Messias, which is, being interpreted, the Christ."

Strictly speaking, *Jesus* is the only *name* by which the child miraculously born of the Virgin was distinguished from other men. That name was given to him by command of the angel, who intimated his approaching nativity; and it signifies a Saviour. We justly call him, Lord; but that is not a name. It is a title which is expressive of his divine prerogatives. And when we call him *Christ*, we should remember that is not his name. The word is official. It expresses his appointment by God, and his endowment of the Spirit, to perform the work for which he was sent into our world. The two words, *Jesus Christ*, according to their literal interpretation, signify, *the anointed Saviour*. And truly this is a name which is above every name. It is as ointment poured forth. It is fragrant with all heavenly blessings. How sweet it sounds! What confidence it inspires! This is indeed the haven of refuge, where even the vilest of sinners will be safe. This is the strong tower, into which every weak and doubting believer may run, and find peaceful and durable repose. There is no room to doubt his ability to save, when we believe that Jesus was anointed of God with the Holy Ghost, and with power.

Although it is true that I have done little more than skim the surface of this subject, yet I trust the hints thrown out will induce you to investigate with care the causes and the consequences of that anointing, which, it cannot be denied, our Lord did receive. And in the meantime, I am hopeful of your having been convinced, that many of the painful doubts from which

Christian people cannot free themselves may be ascribed to their obscure and confused ideas of *his official qualifications*. This is something entirely distinct from the doubts to which inaccurate views, either of his person, or of his work, so often give rise. There may be a clear and correct knowledge, *who* the Saviour is, and *what* he has done; and still there will be misgivings and suspicions respecting his authority to act, or the validity of his actings; because we all feel that it is against God we have offended, and that from him our salvation must come. It is therefore of the utmost importance for us to know, not only that the whole active and passive obedience of the Lord Jesus Christ was according to the will of God; but that he came from God in the capacity of his servant;—that he was expressly appointed by God to this special service;—and moreover that by God, the Spirit was given to him without measure, for the very purpose of insuring the success of his merciful, but arduous undertaking. God himself must be acknowledged as the great actor in the great work of man's salvation. And we must see how God himself is glorified, not only by means of the gratuitous and complete salvation provided in Christ Jesus for millions of perishing sinners, but also in providing a Saviour so marvellously fitted and furnished for the work whereunto he was called. The advancement of his own glory is the ultimate object of God in all his works. And unless our faith is based upon this terminating point, in regard to the qualifications, as well as the person and the work of the Lord Jesus Christ, it will never attain stability.

Yours, etc.

LETTER 16

RELIGIOUS CAUSES OF DOUBTS—*Concluded*

III. IMPERFECT AND INACCURATE VIEWS OF THE SINNER'S WARRANT TO BELIEVE IN THE SAVIOUR

Christians often mistake the ground of *a sinner's warrant* to believe in Christ.—The *fulness* of the gospel salvation may be acknowledged, when the *freeness* with which it is bestowed is not understood.—Imperfect and inaccurate views of God's abounding grace cause many doubts.—To some the doctrine of election proves a stumblingblock.—This doctrine is scriptural.—Christ himself is Jehovah's elect servant.—Christ "the firstborn of every creature."—Believers are chosen "in him" from before the foundation of the world.—Election gives sublime ideas of Jehovah and of his works.—Secret things belong to God.—His revealed will, and not his secret decrees, is the object of our faith.—The knowledge of our election is not the warrant to believe in Christ for salvation.—Neither our religious frames and feelings.—The Gospel is the proclamation of God's love in Christ to the world.—The Son of God was sent to take away the sin of the world.—He connected himself with mankind.—He invites all to come to him.—*His own invitation is the true warrant to believe in him.*—An illustrative anecdote.—No rest on earth for doubters, or sinners, or believers, but in Christ.

My dear Friend,

In the two preceding Letters, it was my object to explain to you, how imperfect and inaccurate views of *the person* of the

Saviour, and of *the work* with which he was intrusted on our behalf, and also of *His qualifications* for successfully effecting the work, are necessarily productive of doubts in the minds of many persons, who are, nevertheless, to be regarded as true believers. And now, to complete my illustrations of those generic causes of doubts to which we awarded the designation of *religious*, you will permit me to notice the sad mistakes into which Christian people often run respecting *the grounds of a sinner's warrant to believe in the Lord Jesus Christ for his own salvation.*

This last cause of doubt meets with secret encouragement from our natural self-righteousness. For this reason it lingers long about the believer, and is difficult of eradication. It continues to operate with a fearful obstinacy, and to a lamentable extent, even when other coexisting causes may have yielded to the remedies applied for their removal. Corporal and mental diseases, which, for a time, involved the Christian who suffered under them in the most painful doubtings and the deepest spiritual distress, may have passed away, and left the patient in the enjoyment of comparative peace of mind, as well as renovated health of body. The hidings of God's face,—the unaccountable severity of the trials he was pleased to appoint, and which perhaps excited, not only depressing doubts of the reality of his fatherly love, but desponding fears that his mercy was clean gone forever,—may have also passed away, and given place to the light of his countenance,—to the cheering tokens of his favour. Satan, too, may have ceased to molest the believer with his fiery darts. And clearer views may have been obtained of the adaptation of the Saviour's mysterious person to the mighty work which was given him to do, and of the adaptation of that work to the sinful condition of men. In one or all of these respects, the Christian may have experienced a great and happy deliverance. But still, if there remains a want of clearness in his views of the perfect freeness of the gospel scheme of salvation;—if he but obscurely discerns the revealed way of grace, in which alone the sinner is to enjoy the full benefit of all that the Saviour is, and of all that he has done, that doubting soul cannot enter into the rest—the sweet, and satisfying, and abiding rest, which Christ has provided for his believing people.

I believe it not unfrequently happens, that persons whose minds have been enlightened in regard to the *fulness* and completeness of the gospel salvation, are left in comparative darkness as to its absolute and unconditional *freeness*. They may have learnt by experience how much it tends to the prevention, or to the removal, of doubts, clearly to see that nothing short of the mysterious union of the divine and human natures in his person, fitted the Lord Jesus Christ for mediating between God and man; and that, by his righteous obedience to the divine law, both in its precepts and in its penalties, as our divinely appointed, and divinely anointed Surety, sin was so effectually punished, that the sinner who believes in him is saved, in glorious consistency with all the attributes of the divine character. And oh, my friend, it is of immense importance rightly to understand what those truths are which constitute the Gospel, and in which the fulness of its salvation may be said to consist! An awakened and convinced sinner has much for which to be thankful, when the eyes of his understanding have been opened to behold the infinite sufficiency which belongs to the one sacrifice of himself which the Saviour once offered up, as an atonement for all sin; and the ample provision which has been made for renewing in righteousness and true holiness, all who believe in him. Truly, it is a most blessed thing to know that the active and passive obedience of Christ, in our stead, is perfect, and admits of no addition, having been sealed by the approbation and acceptance of God; and that thus, in the salvation which the Gospel reveals, and which we are required to believe, there is already procured every blessing which any sinner can desire; yea, an amount of blessing which is commensurate with the necessities of all sinners. This is what I mean by *the fulness* of the gospel salvation. But how to become a partaker of this fulness is, with many, the *troubling question*; and I am bold to affirm that the glad tidings revealed to sinners are not understood, unless the work of "the Lord our righteousness" is acknowledged to be as *freely* bestowed upon us, as it has been *completely* finished and perfected by him.

Imperfect and inaccurate views of the abounding grace of God, towards the very chief of sinners, keep many otherwise well-informed Christians in a state of anxious and uncomfortable doubt respecting their own salvation. They perceive not, that, simply as sinners, without reference to their contrition, or repentance, or faith, or love, or any other gracious disposition in themselves, they have a free warrant to embrace Christ as their own Saviour. They find it hard to believe that all and every sinner should have access to him, with an assurance of welcome; and that all should be invited to buy and eat the wine and milk of his Gospel, without money and without price; and that none are excluded from the fulness of the proffered blessings, but those who ignorantly or wilfully exclude themselves. That the salvation of his guilty creatures originated in the sovereign and spontaneous mercy of God, according to his eternal purpose in Christ Jesus our Lord, they may not deny. And they may give to Father, Son, and Holy Ghost, the glory of contriving, and carrying on, and completing, the wondrous plan which the Gospel reveals, for the overthrow of Satan's power, and for the destruction of sin and death. But from history and from observation, they are taught that this gracious plan has never yet been made known to all men; and from Scripture they learn that the eternal purpose of the Godhead has respect only to those who have been given to Christ by the Father, and who alone come to Christ because the Father draws them. For these reasons, the class of Christians to whose case I now refer bewilder themselves in their attempts to reconcile the doctrine of election with the general and unrestricted invitations of the Gospel to all sinners. These attempts are often unavailing. Their effects, however, are often far from being harmless. The minds of such people are apt to get prejudiced against some portions of God's revealed word. Perhaps they turn away with aversion from the acknowledgment of that everlasting and electing love of God, which secures the salvation of those who are its objects, and without which there would be no security for the salvation of a single soul; or, from that universality and gratuitousness with which the gospel blessings are proclaimed, and which hold out the greatest encouragement to all, without exception, to believe and enjoy them. In thus capriciously rejecting truths which equally have a place in Holy Scripture, and which are alike in their own nature most precious, the real and proper warrant which sinners have to believe in Christ for salvation is lost sight of. And in every such case, doubts, with their accompanying distraction and distress, will continue to exert their baneful influence.

Do not imagine that I am dragging you into the mazy labyrinths of theological controversy, or that I have to propound some new solution of the undoubted difficulties which encompass the divine decrees, when viewed in connection with human responsibility. But is it not surprising, my dear friend, that sensible and serious people should oppose their own ignorance to the wisdom of God, and presume to quarrel with his methods of saving the guilty and the helpless? *He* does not ask our opinion what is right or what is wrong, either in his secret purposes, or in his revealed will. Nor does *he* leave it to us to decide whether he is holy and just in choosing some of Adam's fallen race to become the heirs of "glory, honour, and immortality," whilst others are left to perish in their sins: or, whether he is consistent and sincere in declaring that he willeth not the death of a sinner, and that he so loved the world, the whole world, as to give his only begotten Son, that whosoever believeth on him, might not perish. But this he does ask us, yea, beseech and command us to do,—he asks us to believe every part and portion of the revelation of his will, with which he has favoured us. He asks us, as hell-deserving sinners, to rely with peaceful confidence on the Almighty Saviour he has sent, and, as helpless sinners, to receive with all thankfulness a complete and gratuitous salvation. He asks us on no account to doubt the truth, either of his promised mercy, or of his threatened wrath,—on no account to doubt his faithfulness to execute what he threatens against the impenitent and unbelieving, or to perform all his promises to them that believe with humble and contrite hearts. And as it is according to our reception or rejection of his grace in Christ Jesus that we shall be saved or condemned, so it is alone to the revelation of that grace that he requires our faith. His eternal purposes, which are secret things belonging to the Lord our God, however much they guide himself in his conduct towards us, are not designed to be the objects of our faith, or the motives to our obedience. And whenever Christians begin to consider a knowledge of their own election as necessary to warrant their faith in the Saviour, or their assurance of personal salvation, their gross perversion of a most blessed scriptural doctrine will infallibly beset them with perplexity and doubt, or hurry them on to a presumptuous and dangerous security.

I hope you are not one of those who would expunge the doctrine of election from the Bible, if they could, and who reluctantly give it a place in their own religious creed. It is no marvel that the Christians who do so, never escape from the cold and dreary regions of doubt. For my part, I love the doctrine of election. It inspires me with the sublimest ideas of *Jehovah*, and of his *Christ*, and of the whole work of *redemption*. Indeed, I might say, that it spreads a divine halo over all creation and providence too. And were I obliged to abandon my belief in this doctrine, I should feel utterly at a loss to account for the cheering predictions of a coming Deliverer, which are the glory of the Old Testament Scriptures;

and for the incarnation of the Son of God, in the promised fulness of time, which is the glory of the New Testament Scriptures:—for the separation of the seed of Abraham, under the law, from all the other nations of the earth; and for the engrafting of the Gentiles into the Christian church under the Gospel. Except upon the principle of election, I can in nowise explain the existence and the preservation of a church in this sinful world,—that is, of a congregation of faithful men, gathered out from amongst the faithless.

And as a member of that holy universal church, I frankly own, that, had not God of his own free grace called and chosen me, I never should have chosen or sought after him. Will not all who are taught of God make the same acknowledgment? The Bible most expressly traces up everything to election. Even of the Christ himself we hear Jehovah saying, "Behold my servant whom I uphold; mine elect, in whom my soul delighteth," Isa 42:1. And in beautiful harmony with this declared election of the Head of the church, the apostle Paul speaks of the election in him of all the members, Eph 1:3-12. The passage is too long for quotation. But let me entreat you prayerfully and profoundly to study it. No man could have penned such sentiments but by the guidance of inspiration. These verses contain an astonishing development of what the same apostle elsewhere calls "the mystery of God, and of the Father, and of Christ; in whom are hid all the treasures of wisdom and knowledge," Col 2:2-3. By them, we come to know that even the riches of divine grace, manifested in the redemption of sinners, are dispensed "according *to the purpose of him who worketh all things after the counsel of his own will;*" and that believers are blessed of God with all spiritual blessings in Christ, "*according as he hath chosen us in him before the foundation of the world.*" Grace and election go hand in hand; and both of them emanate through Christ, "in whom it hath pleased the Father that all fulness should dwell." This fixes our thoughts on Christ as existing from eternity in the purpose of God; and explains to us the reason why the incarnate Son of God is called "the firstborn of every creature." This expression intimates a priority in point of time, as well as a superiority in point of dignity and excellence. In the mind of God, the man Christ Jesus was the *first* of all created beings,—"the beginning of the creation of God," Rev 3:14; and he became "the image of the invisible God," in consequence of his being God in a creature-form. That form was manhood. Does this throw light on those texts of Scripture which speak of the face of the Lord, and of his eyes, and his ears, and his mouth, and his hands, etc.? At all events, it teaches us that, in his original creation, man was fashioned after a preexisting model or pattern. We read that "God created man in his own image," Gen 1:26. But how could man in a corporeal shape resemble God, who is a Spirit? The reference which is usually made to the mental and moral qualities with which man was endowed is not satisfactory. Is it not, however, delightful to think that we were at first created in the image and likeness of the God-man, the Christ, who himself is the only image of the invisible God, the firstborn of every creature; *for by him were all things created* that are in heaven, and that are in earth;— "all things were created by him, and for him; and he is before all things, and by him all things consist; and he is the Head of the body, the church," Col 1:15-18.

These are lofty themes. There is a grandeur in them to which our present limited faculties cannot reach. I dare not expatiate on them; nor is it necessary. But it does strike me as deserving of special attention, not only that the God-man who is our Redeemer was also our Creator; but that in the purpose of God he existed as the Redeemer before he acted as the Creator, and that Creation is a work subordinate to Redemption. "All things were created by him, and *for him*." And these two little words, "*for him*," plainly reveal this much neglected truth, that the glory of God in the manifestation of the Son of God in human nature, and in the manifestation of the exceeding riches of his grace in purifying unto himself a peculiar people to constitute his church, which is his body, was the grand object to be subserved by creation. Within the expansive folds of this one truth are shut up the whole history, from beginning to end, not only of the church of Christ, and of the human race, and of this earth which was made for man, but of the wide universe of mind and of matter. For the purpose of God from all eternity was ultimately to "*gather together in one all things in Christ, both which are in heaven, and which are on earth.*"

I am happy of an opportunity of making these observations, but must not allow myself to be drawn away from the subject more immediately in hand. My wish was to explain the grounds of my expressed predilection for the much repudiated, and also much perverted, doctrine of election. I expect your ready consent to my assertion that there is in it something truly sublime. Does it not nobly testify to the omniscience, and to the omnipotence of God, to whom everything is known, and by whom all is overruled? It sends us backwards to *a past eternity* when nothing existed except in the mind of Jehovah, and when everything was planned which has ever since existed or shall yet exist. And it directs us forwards to *a coming eternity*, when all that existed at first, only in type or in purpose, shall stand forth in exact similitude, and in living reality, to the praise and glory of *the divine Architect*.

Foreknowledge and predestination seem to me to be essential and indispensable properties of *deity*; and a special electing love can be offensive only to Christians whose views of gospel truth are obscure and superficial. To none else should this doctrine prove a stumblingblock, or cause of doubt. Those who entertain clear and comprehensive views see it, here and there, throughout the whole Scriptures, shining with the brightness of a sunbeam. And believers of experience and observation will, without difficulty, discover it, like a hidden undercurrent, pervading the whole history of the human race, as well as linking together, in one unbroken chain, the widely scattered members of the household of faith.

To the best of my recollection, the object of the sacred writers, in all their doctrinal statements of God's electing love, is to confirm the faith, and to comfort the hearts of believers; and surely such statements are wisely fitted to subserve such important ends. The words of St. Paul to the Romans are addressed to all Christians: "We know that all things work together for good to them that love God, to them who are called according to his purpose. For whom he did foreknow he also did predestinate to be conformed to the image of his Son, that he might be the firstborn among many brethren. Moreover whom he did predestinate, them he also called; and whom he called, them he also justified; and whom he justified, them he also glorified," Rom 8:28-30. This is indeed a golden chain, stretching from before the beginning even until after the end of time; and exhibiting the origin, the progress, and the finality of every individual believer's salvation. The work is all of God. To him all glory is ascribed; and is there not also an abundant consolation to the believing sinner? It is obvious, however, that ere we can draw comfort from this and similar portions of the word of God, we must have the consciousness of being amongst the persons of whom the apostle speaks. Our simple and stedfast faith in the Saviour must have warmed our cold hearts with the love of that God who first loved us, and given us some assurance of having received that grace of God which bringeth salvation. For it is not until we have, as sinners, been brought to believe "the good tidings" of a Saviour who is Christ the Lord, that we can "know our election of God," or find in the doctrine of election a strong confirmation of our faith. But the epistle of St. Paul is addressed to those who did know and acknowledge themselves to be believers. It was his desire to build them up in their most holy faith, and to stimulate them to constancy amidst present persecutions and impediments. He therefore alludes to their salvation as something certain and not contingent,—as something settled and sealed in the eternal purpose of God. And to the cheering words already quoted, he adds, with holy exultation, "What shall we say then to these things? If God be for us, who can be against us? He that spared not his own Son, but delivered him up for us all, how shall he not with him also freely give us all things? Who shall lay anything to the charge of God's elect? It is God that justifieth: who is he that condemneth?" Rom 8:31-34.

But to the believer who knows not whether he possesses saving faith,—to the Christian who unhappily doubts his own Christianity, these inspired and precious arguments tend rather to augment his uneasiness and distress, than to yield consolation and hope. For although he may admit that election is a scriptural doctrine, yet he doubts his own election of God. And although he is sensible of their safety who love God, and who are called according to his purpose, yet he enjoys no sense of his own safety, because he is not sure that God has called him, nor can he satisfy himself that he loves God as he ought to do. Perhaps he doubts, not merely whether he is a believer, but whether he has any right to believe in the Saviour, in consequence of his not knowing whether he belongs to the number of the elect. Thus it is with some Christians that *the purpose* of God in regard to a chosen few, and which is secret, is anxiously sought for, or mistakenly clung to, as the only proper warrant for an assured hope of salvation, instead of *the will* of God, which is revealed, and in which the whole fallen family of Adam is concerned. And in numberless other cases, where election is not the stumbling-block, Christian people vainly labour to extricate themselves from harassing doubts, because they seek their warrant for assurance in their own frames and feelings. This is a dangerous error. Whenever we erect our very variable experience of spiritual enjoyments into a kind of gauge by which the genuineness of our religion is to be decided, instead of resting firmly and at all times on the immutability of the grace which is so fully and freely revealed in Christ Jesus, we may expect to suffer for it. Our proneness to pride and self-righteousness draws us into this snare. It is a self-gratification to experience delight in the ordinances of God, or to find a pleasure from the manner in which the social and secret duties of religion have been discharged. But this is a ground of confidence on which no dependence should be placed. Alas! how continually it disappoints those who are looking to something favourable in themselves, from whence they may conclude that all is safe for eternity! And it is undeniable, that imperfect and inaccurate views of their real and scriptural warrant to believe in Christ, and through the faith of him alone to cherish the assurance of salvation, keep not a few of the humble and conscientious and timorous children of God, in a long-continued state of painful and perplexing doubts.

Allow me then, my dear friend, in concluding this Letter, which is the conclusion of the series, to state broadly and without hesitation, that the only warrant which any human being has to believe in the Saviour, and to rest upon him for his own salvation, lies in the general proclamations—in the free invitations—in the gracious promises of the Gospel. Of his mere good pleasure God has made guilty men the objects of his compassion. In the exercise of spontaneous love he has sent his only begotten Son into our world to expiate our guilt by the shedding of his own blood. To this all-sufficient atonement for sin, the attention of all sinners is directed. This is the one way of access to God with acceptance. This is the only way of escape from the wrath to come. This one and only way has been opened by God himself; and, blessed be his name, it is open to all. As a minister of the gospel I rejoice to repeat it:—the way of acceptable access to God is open to all men. Jesus Christ is that way. He himself has said, "I am the way, and the truth, and the life: no man cometh unto the Father but by me," John 14:6. Not one, however, ever went by him, and was rejected. It is also written, "God was in Christ reconciling *the world* unto himself, not imputing their trespasses unto them," 2 Cor 5:19. For this reason the gospel is a message and a ministry of reconciliation; and it is the happy privilege of ministers to beseech men of all sorts and conditions, yea, to beseech all men, to be reconciled unto God through the faith of Jesus Christ. This harmonizes with the Saviour's own invitation, which truly is as universal as was the announcement of his birth to the shepherds of Bethlehem. To them the angel of the Lord said, "Fear not, for behold I bring you good tidings of great joy, *which shall be to all people.*" And the blessed Saviour, contemplating the toil, the cares, the crosses, the disappointments, which sin entails upon all men, is pleased in mercy and in love, to address them all, "Come unto me, *all ye that labour and are heavy laden,* and I will give you rest," Matt 11:28. He also kindly says, "All that the Father giveth me shall come to me;" here is election with the certainty of salvation; but there instantly follows the freeness and the universality of gospel grace: "and him that cometh to me *I will in nowise cast out,*" John 6:37. What greater encouragement could be asked?

The freeness with which salvation is bestowed, should make the Gospel peculiarly precious to those who cannot plead with God on the ground of merit, and who are utterly destitute of power to save themselves. It is the glory of the Gospel to reveal a salvation as free as it is complete. But the Gospel is shorn of one of its most benign and attractive features, when any of the human family are excluded from its all-comprehending embrace. It would lose its distinguishing character, were the forgiving love which it reveals restricted to a few individuals: it would cease to be "good tidings of great joy to all people," unless all people were welcome to the fulness of its blessings.

Human systems of theology are all more or less defective,

and men are very often misled by them in their search after divine truth. They read their Bible with prejudiced minds, and miss many of its truths, because they either did not wish, or did not expect, to find them there. But no person who studies the word of God with childlike simplicity and candour, can fail to discover this delightful feature of universality, which is the glory of the Gospel as much as is its freeness and its completeness. Indeed, these three grand characteristics of the remedial scheme, devised by God himself for man's deliverance from sin and Satan, ought never to be separated: I mean, first, its *entire completeness*, so that the poor perishing sinner finds in Christ all that he needs and all that he can desire,—not merely a counsellor, a guide, a help, but a *Saviour*. Second, its *perfect freeness*, so that the sinner, notwithstanding the filthy rags in which he is clothed and the utter spiritual destitution under which he labours, is invited to receive as an undeserved gift what he never, no never could have purchased. And, third, its *godlike universality*, so that not one of the sinners of mankind need feel himself shut out from the love of God in Christ Jesus. But these things which God has so beautifully joined together, men too frequently presume to put asunder. In the littleness of their own notions, they lose sight and hold of the vastness which enters into the plans of infinite mercy and wisdom. Thus it is that "the Gospel of the grace of God" is, in many cases, not fully received, because it is misunderstood. And pious people are kept in a state of anxious doubt, without being able to attain that assurance which is so essential to their stability and comfort as Christians, because they look somewhere else than to the broad basis of *the revealed love of God to the world*, for their warrant to believe in Christ as a Saviour to themselves.

I must be brief, and therefore cannot touch upon the discussions which are now, and ever have been, rife among Christians, regarding the extent of the atonement. But why not just receive as true whatever we find in the Bible? I believe the doctrine of election, and the infallible salvation of the elect, because I read it in the Bible. But in the Bible I also read, that God "is longsuffering to usward, *not willing that any should perish*, but that *all* should come to repentance," 2 Pet 3:9:—that Jesus Christ is the propitiation "for the sins of *the whole world*," 1 John 2:2:—that he is "the Lamb of God, who taketh away *the sin of the world*," John 1:29:—and that "God so loved *the world*, that he gave his only begotten Son, that *whosoever* believeth in him should not perish, but have everlasting life," John 3:16. Surely, my friend, you will acknowledge that the Bible would lose some of its most brilliant gems—some of its most invaluable treasures, were such passages as these to be expunged from its pages. The belief of the blessed truths contained in these passages gives peace and joy to my heart; and I could not part with them without feeling that I had parted with the Gospel itself. Nor dare I mutilate one sentence or one word of them, else I should incur the fearful guilt of mutilating "the good tidings of great joy" which God has so graciously revealed, and which his servants are instructed to proclaim *to every creature* throughout the wide world.

Undoubtedly it is also true that Christ died only for his elect, and that redemption is particular; for the actual condition of the world corroborates these scriptural doctrines. The death of Christ does not necessarily involve or imply the salvation of all. Although controversies on points of doctrinal importance should never be adjusted here below, still it is the imperative duty of every professing Christian to believe what God has revealed, as it is his privilege to draw, from the declarations and promises of his mercy, that amount of encouragement and of consolation which they obviously warrant. Indeed it is the duty of all men to believe the Gospel, for it is addressed to all. Why should doubting Christians stand aloof? Does no obligation lie upon them to believe that love of God which is revealed to sinners? Are they excluded from encouragement to come unto that Saviour who addresses his gracious invitation unto all?

What a certain presage of deliverance from their bondage it would be, did they only acknowledge *the universality of the invitation*! I am aware that they might continue to doubt, even when they did acknowledge, not only that the Saviour invites them to come to him, but that the invitation is freely given without respect of personal qualifications, and that the rest which is promised can be found nowhere else, and that in the blessings provided there is enough and to spare. These are great and hopeful acknowledgments; but still Christian people may tell us that they doubt whether they have accepted the invitation, and whether they have yet found rest in Christ. This is commonly the last corner into which our doubting brethren creep. And oh! my dear friend, how anxious we should be to drive them out of it! how happy we should be to conduct them to that broad and open field of Gospel truth, where, amidst its exceeding great and precious promises, they might roam at large for their spiritual nourishment, and enjoy the glorious liberty of the sons of God!

I remember having been asked to spend an evening with an aged widow, who was sadly distressed with doubts, and who grieved that, as she approached to the confines of eternity, her prospects, instead of brightening, became more and more gloomy. I had long known her, and known her to be a Christian lady, although she never had moral courage enough to disentangle herself from worldly society. Her own consciousness of this probably had something to do with her doubts; and her desire was to pour out all her self-reproaches and regrets into my ear. But I judged it better to give the conversation a different turn altogether. I took the Bible, and, without the least allusion to her own case in particular, went from one passage to another, fixing her attention on those very characteristics of the Gospel, of which mention has been made in this Letter. We dwelt on the wonders of redeeming love, and on the inexhaustible grace that is in Christ Jesus, and on the perfect and absolute freeness with which his great salvation is offered to all, even to the greatest of transgressors. I said nothing about the evil of doubts, nor about the necessity of faith: that might have turned her thoughts towards herself, and fastened her more firmly in the corner out of which it was my object to bring her; but I simply spread before her, in rich profusion, those blessed truths which are the objects of saving faith. She saw *the Gospel* which the word of God reveals; she felt its divine suitableness to her own spiritual necessities; she believed it without an effort; and she was made a partaker of "joy and peace in believing." We prayed together to the God and Father of our Lord Jesus Christ, and we praised him together as the Father of mercies, and the God of all comfort. The dear old lady requested another visit whenever I had leisure, for she said at parting, "You have made me very happy." You will not mistake her meaning. She knew, and you also know, from whence her happiness proceeded. It was not from me. I had only given her a helping hand to come to Jesus. The invitation which he gives to *all* who are labouring and heavy laden, from whatever cause, was *her* warrant to comply. She thought neither of any worthiness in herself as a recommendation, nor of any unworthiness as a hindrance. She was encouraged by the exhibition of the freeness and fulness of the Saviour's grace. The discovery of that love of God in Christ which passeth knowledge, thawed the hardness, and enlightened the darkness, of her heart. Her suspicions, and doubts, and fears were dispersed. She came to the Saviour in faith; she came to him as a Saviour to herself; and, according to his promise, she found rest and peace unto her soul.

Perhaps this little anecdote may be of service to you some day when you happen to be thrown into the company of doubting Christians. There is no rest for them, nor for any sinner, nor for any believer, but *in Christ*. As the dove sent forth by Noah could find no place for the sole of her foot, except in the ark, whilst the waters of divine punishment still deluged the earth; so, whilst man continues the sinful inhabitant of a sin-cursed world, his enjoyment of present peace with God, and his hope of everlasting deliverance from sin itself, and from the wrath of a sin-hating God, entirely depend on his faith in the provided Saviour. Christ is the one divinely-appointed ark, where sinners of every grade may find shelter and safety. And, in dealing with doubters, our earnest aim should be to convince them, on the authority of Holy Scripture, first, that the invitation to enter in and partake of every promised blessing, is given *freely unto all*, so that not an individual dare say he is excluded; and then, that the true and only warrant to receive it, *is the invitation itself*, and nothing in themselves, nor in the secret decrees of God.

How tender and touching,—how sweetly simple and sincere, are the words of our blessed Lord! "Come unto me, all ye that labour and are heavy laden, and I will give you rest. Take my yoke upon you, and learn of me; for I am meek and lowly in heart: and ye shall find rest unto your souls. For my yoke is easy, and my burden is light," Matt 11:28-30. When these words of the Saviour are believingly listened unto, and acted upon, then every burden which oppressed the conscience of the heaviest-laden sinner will be removed, and the very weariest of the weary will be brought into the enjoyment of heavenly peace and refreshment.

Doubts which arise from physical causes, require the application of physical remedies for their removal. But these exceptions do not invalidate the general rule: *The grand and effectual antidote to all doubts and fears respecting our personal salvation, is a strong and steady faith in the Saviour of sinners.*

CHRIST IS OUR REST!

www.ingramcontent.com/pod-product-compliance
Lightning Source LLC
Chambersburg PA
CBHW021051080526
44587CB00010B/214